"THE PRICE AND THE PROMISE..."

The Essential Presidential Speeches of Barack Obama

EUPATOR CLASSICS

D1713197

Our challenges may be new. The instruments with which we meet them may be new. But those values upon which our success depends – hard work and honesty, courage and fair play, tolerance and curiosity, loyalty and patriotism – these things are old. These things are true. They have been the quiet force of progress throughout our history. What is demanded then is a return to these truths. What is required of us now is a new era of responsibility – a recognition, on the part of every American, that we have duties to ourselves, our nation, and the world, duties that we do not grudgingly accept but rather seize gladly, firm in the knowledge that there is nothing so satisfying to the spirit, so defining of our character, than giving our all to a difficult task.

This is the price and the promise of citizenship.

— BARACK OBAMA, FIRST INAUGURAL ADDRESS

CONTENTS

FIRST INAUGURAL ADDRESS

TUESDAY, JANUARY 20, 2009

My fellow citizens:

I stand here today humbled by the task before us, grateful for the trust you have bestowed, mindful of the sacrifices borne by our ancestors. I thank President Bush for his service to our nation, as well as the generosity and cooperation he has shown throughout this transition.

Forty-four Americans have now taken the presidential oath. The words have been spoken during rising tides of prosperity and the still waters of peace. Yet, every so often the oath is taken amidst gathering clouds and raging storms. At these moments, America has carried on not simply because of the skill or vision of those in high office, but because we the people have remained faithful to the ideals of our forebears, and true to our founding documents.

So it has been. So it must be with this generation of Americans.

That we are in the midst of crisis is now well understood. Our nation is at war, against a far-reaching network of violence and hatred. Our economy is badly weakened, a consequence of greed and irresponsibility on the part of some, but also our collective failure to make hard choices and prepare the nation for a new age. Homes have been lost; jobs shed; businesses shuttered. Our health care is too costly; our schools fail too many; and each day brings further evidence that the ways we use energy strengthen our adversaries and threaten our planet.

These are the indicators of crisis, subject to data and statistics. Less measurable but no less profound is a sapping of confidence across our land – a nagging fear that America's decline is inevitable, and that the next generation must lower its sights.

Today I say to you that the challenges we face are real. They are serious and they are many. They will not be met easily or in a short span of time. But know this, America – they will be met.

On this day, we gather because we have chosen hope over fear, unity of purpose over conflict and discord.

On this day, we come to proclaim an end to the petty grievances and false promises, the recriminations and worn out dogmas, that for far too long have strangled our politics.

We remain a young nation, but in the words of scripture, the time has come to set aside childish things. The time has come to reaffirm our enduring spirit; to choose our better history; to carry forward that precious gift, that noble idea, passed on from generation to generation: the God-given promise that all are equal, all are free and all deserve a chance to pursue their full measure of happiness.

In reaffirming the greatness of our nation, we understand that greatness is never a given. It must be earned. Our journey has never been one of shortcuts or settling for less. It has not been the path for the faint-hearted – for those who prefer leisure over work, or seek only the pleasures of riches and fame. Rather, it has been the risk-takers, the doers, the makers of things – some celebrated but more often men and women obscure in their labor, who have carried us up the long, rugged path towards prosperity and freedom.

For us, they packed up their few worldly possessions and traveled across oceans in search of a new life.

For us, they toiled in sweatshops and settled the West; endured the lash of the whip and plowed the hard earth.

For us, they fought and died, in places like Concord and Gettysburg; Normandy and Khe Sahn.

Time and again these men and women struggled and sacrificed and worked till their hands were raw so that we might live a better life. They saw America as bigger than the sum of our individual ambitions; greater than all the differences of birth or wealth or faction.

This is the journey we continue today. We remain the most prosperous, powerful nation on Earth. Our workers are no less productive than when this crisis began. Our minds are no less inventive, our goods and services no less needed than they were last week or last month or last year. Our capacity remains undiminished. But our time of standing pat, of protecting narrow interests and putting off unpleasant decisions – that time has surely passed. Starting today, we must pick ourselves up, dust ourselves off, and begin again the work of remaking America.

For everywhere we look, there is work to be done. The state of the economy calls for action, bold and swift, and we will act – not only to create new jobs, but to lay a new foundation for growth. We will build the roads and bridges, the electric grids and digital lines that feed our commerce and bind us together. We will restore science to its rightful place, and wield technology's wonders to raise health care's quality and lower its cost. We will harness the sun and the winds and the soil to fuel our cars and run our factories. And we will transform our schools and colleges and universities to meet the demands of a new age. All this we can do. And all this we will do.

Now, there are some who question the scale of our ambitions – who suggest that our system cannot tolerate too many big plans. Their memories are short. For they have forgotten what this country has already done; what free men and women can achieve when imagination is joined to common purpose, and necessity to courage.

What the cynics fail to understand is that the ground has shifted beneath them –

that the stale political arguments that have consumed us for so long no longer apply. The question we ask today is not whether our government is too big or too small, but whether it works – whether it helps families find jobs at a decent wage, care they can afford, a retirement that is dignified. Where the answer is yes, we intend to move forward. Where the answer is no, programs will end. And those of us who manage the public's dollars will be held to account – to spend wisely, reform bad habits, and do our business in the light of day – because only then can we restore the vital trust between a people and their government.

Nor is the question before us whether the market is a force for good or ill. Its power to generate wealth and expand freedom is unmatched, but this crisis has reminded us that without a watchful eye, the market can spin out of control – and that a nation cannot prosper long when it favors only the prosperous. The success of our economy has always depended not just on the size of our gross domestic product, but on the reach of our prosperity; on our ability to extend opportunity to every willing heart – not out of charity, but because it is the surest route to our common good.

As for our common defense, we reject as false the choice between our safety and our ideals. Our founding fathers, faced with perils we can scarcely imagine, drafted a charter to assure the rule of law and the rights of man, a charter expanded by the blood of generations. Those ideals still light the world, and we will not give them up for expedience's sake. And so to all other peoples and governments who are watching today, from the grandest capitals to the small village where my father was born: know that America is a friend of each nation and every man, woman, and child who seeks a future of peace and dignity, and that we are ready to lead once more.

Recall that earlier generations faced down fascism and communism not just with missiles and tanks, but with sturdy alliances and enduring convictions. They understood that our power alone cannot protect us, nor does it entitle us to do as we please. Instead, they knew that our power grows through its prudent use; our security emanates from the justness of our cause, the force of our example, the tempering qualities of humility and restraint.

We are the keepers of this legacy. Guided by these principles once more, we can meet those new threats that demand even greater effort – even greater cooperation and understanding between nations. We will begin to responsibly leave Iraq to its people, and forge a hard-earned peace in Afghanistan. With old friends and former foes, we will work tirelessly to lessen the nuclear threat, and roll back the specter of a warming planet. We will not apologize for our way of life, nor will we waver in its defense, and for those who seek to advance their aims by inducing terror and slaughtering innocents, we say to you now that our spirit is stronger and cannot be broken; you cannot outlast us, and we will defeat you.

For we know that our patchwork heritage is a strength, not a weakness. We are a nation of Christians and Muslims, Jews and Hindus – and non-believers. We are shaped by every language and culture, drawn from every end of this Earth; and because we have tasted the bitter swill of civil war and segregation, and emerged from that dark chapter stronger and more united, we cannot help but believe that the old hatreds shall someday pass; that the lines of tribe shall soon dissolve; that as the world grows smaller, our common humanity shall reveal itself; and that America must play its role in ushering in a new era of peace.

To the Muslim world, we seek a new way forward, based on mutual interest and mutual respect. To those leaders around the globe who seek to sow conflict, or blame their society's ills on the West – know that your people will judge you on what you can build, not what you destroy. To those who cling to power through corruption and deceit and the silencing of dissent, know that you are on the wrong side of history; but that we will extend a hand if you are willing to unclench your fist.

To the people of poor nations, we pledge to work alongside you to make your farms flourish and let clean waters flow; to nourish starved bodies and feed hungry minds. And to those nations like ours that enjoy relative plenty, we say we can no longer afford indifference to suffering outside our borders; nor can we consume the world's resources without regard to effect. For the world has changed, and we must change with it.

As we consider the road that unfolds before us, we remember with humble gratitude those brave Americans who, at this very hour, patrol far-off deserts and distant mountains. They have something to tell us today, just as the fallen heroes who lie in Arlington whisper through the ages. We honor them not only because they are guardians of our liberty, but because they embody the spirit of service; a willingness to find meaning in something greater than themselves. And yet, at this moment – a moment that will define a generation – it is precisely this spirit that must inhabit us all.

For as much as government can do and must do, it is ultimately the faith and determination of the American people upon which this nation relies. It is the kindness to take in a stranger when the levees break, the selflessness of workers who would rather cut their hours than see a friend lose their job which sees us through our darkest hours. It is the firefighter's courage to storm a stairway filled with smoke, but also a parent's willingness to nurture a child, that finally decides our fate.

Our challenges may be new. The instruments with which we meet them may be new. But those values upon which our success depends – hard work and honesty, courage and fair play, tolerance and curiosity, loyalty and patriotism – these things are old. These things are true. They have been the quiet force of progress throughout our history. What is demanded then is a return to these truths. What is required of us now is a new era of responsibility – a recognition, on the part of every American, that we have duties to ourselves, our nation, and the world, duties that we do not grudgingly accept but rather seize gladly, firm in the knowledge that there is nothing so satisfying to the spirit, so defining of our character, than giving our all to a difficult task.

This is the price and the promise of citizenship.

This is the source of our confidence – the knowledge that God calls on us to shape an uncertain destiny.

This is the meaning of our liberty and our creed – why men and women and children of every race and every faith can join in celebration across this magnificent mall, and why a man whose father less than sixty years ago might not have been served at a local restaurant can now stand before you to take a most sacred oath.

4

So let us mark this day with remembrance, of who we are and how far we have traveled. In the year of America's birth, in the coldest of months, a small band of patriots huddled by dying campfires on the shores of an icy river. The capital was abandoned. The enemy was advancing. The snow was stained with blood. At a moment when the outcome of our revolution was most in doubt, the father of our nation ordered these words be read to the people:

"Let it be told to the future world ... that in the depth of winter, when nothing but hope and virtue could survive...that the city and the country, alarmed at one common danger, came forth to meet (it)."

America, in the face of our common dangers, in this winter of our hardship, let us remember these timeless words. With hope and virtue, let us brave once more the icy currents, and endure what storms may come. Let it be said by our children's children that when we were tested we refused to let this journey end, that we did not turn back nor did we falter; and with eyes fixed on the horizon and God's grace upon us, we carried forth that great gift of freedom and delivered it safely to future generations.

❧ 2 ❧

ADDRESS BEFORE A JOINT SESSION OF CONGRESS

FEBRUARY 24, 2009

M adam Speaker, Mr. Vice President, Members of Congress, the First Lady of the United States–she's around here somewhere: I have come here tonight not only to address the distinguished men and women in this great Chamber, but to speak frankly and directly to the men and women who sent us here.

I know that for many Americans watching right now, the state of our economy is a concern that rises above all others, and rightly so. If you haven't been personally affected by this recession, you probably know someone who has: a friend, a neighbor, a member of your family. You don't need to hear another list of statistics to know that our economy is in crisis, because you live it every day. It's the worry you wake up with and the source of sleepless nights. It's the job you thought you'd retire from but now have lost, the business you built your dreams upon that's now hanging by a thread, the college acceptance letter your child had to put back in the envelope. The impact of this recession is real, and it is everywhere.

But while our economy may be weakened and our confidence shaken, though we are living through difficult and uncertain times, tonight I want every American to know this: We will rebuild, we will recover, and the United States of America will emerge stronger than before.

The weight of this crisis will not determine the destiny of this Nation. The answers to our problems don't lie beyond our reach. They exist in our laboratories and our universities, in our fields and our factories, in the imaginations of our entrepreneurs and the pride of the hardest working people on Earth. Those qualities that have made America the greatest force of progress and prosperity in human history, we still possess in ample measure. What is required now is for this country to pull together, confront boldly the challenges we face, and take responsibility for our future once more.

Now, if we're honest with ourselves, we'll admit that for too long, we have not always met these responsibilities as a Government or as a people. I say this not to lay

6

blame or to look backwards, but because it is only by understanding how we arrived at this moment that we'll be able to lift ourselves out of this predicament.

The fact is, our economy did not fall into decline overnight, nor did all of our problems begin when the housing market collapsed or the stock market sank. We have known for decades that our survival depends on finding new sources of energy, yet we import more oil today than ever before. The cost of health care eats up more and more of our savings each year, yet we keep delaying reform. Our children will compete for jobs in a global economy that too many of our schools do not prepare them for. And though all these challenges went unsolved, we still managed to spend more money and pile up more debt, both as individuals and through our Government, than ever before.

In other words, we have lived through an era where too often short-term gains were prized over long-term prosperity, where we failed to look beyond the next payment, the next quarter, or the next election. A surplus became an excuse to transfer wealth to the wealthy instead of an opportunity to invest in our future. Regulations were gutted for the sake of a quick profit at the expense of a healthy market. People bought homes they knew they couldn't afford from banks and lenders who pushed those bad loans anyway. And all the while, critical debates and difficult decisions were put off for some other time, on some other day. Well, that day of reckoning has arrived, and the time to take charge of our future is here.

Now is the time to act boldly and wisely to not only revive this economy, but to build a new foundation for lasting prosperity. Now is the time to jump-start job creation, restart lending, and invest in areas like energy, health care, and education that will grow our economy, even as we make hard choices to bring our deficit down. That is what my economic agenda is designed to do, and that is what I'd like to talk to you about tonight. It's an agenda that begins with jobs.

As soon as I took office, I asked this Congress to send me a recovery plan by President's Day that would put people back to work and put money in their pockets, not because I believe in bigger Government–I don't–not because I'm not mindful of the massive debt we've inherited- -I am. I called for action because the failure to do so would have cost more jobs and caused more hardship. In fact, a failure to act would have worsened our long-term deficit by assuring weak economic growth for years. And that's why I pushed for quick action. And tonight I am grateful that this Congress delivered and pleased to say that the American Recovery and Reinvestment Act is now law.

Over the next 2 years, this plan will save or create 3.5 million jobs. More than 90 percent of these jobs will be in the private sector: jobs rebuilding our roads and bridges, constructing wind turbines and solar panels, laying broadband and expanding mass transit.

Because of this plan, there are teachers who can now keep their jobs and educate our kids, health care professionals can continue caring for our sick. There are 57 police officers who are still on the streets of Minneapolis tonight because this plan prevented the layoffs their department was about to make. Because of this plan, 95 percent of working households in America will receive a tax cut; a tax cut that you will see in your paychecks beginning on April 1st. Because of this plan, families who are struggling to pay tuition costs will receive a $2,500 tax credit for all 4 years of college, and Americans who have lost their jobs in this recession will be able to receive extended unemployment benefits and continued health care coverage to help them weather this storm.

Now, I know there are some in this Chamber and watching at home who are skeptical of whether this plan will work, and I understand that skepticism. Here in Washington, we've all seen how quickly good intentions can turn into broken promises and wasteful spending. And with a plan of this scale comes enormous responsibility to get it right.

And that's why I've asked Vice President Biden to lead a tough, unprecedented oversight effort; because nobody messes with Joe. I–am I right? They don't mess with him. I have told each of my Cabinet, as well as mayors and Governors across the country, that they will be held accountable by me and the American people for every dollar they spend. I've appointed a proven and aggressive Inspector General to ferret out any and all cases of waste and fraud. And we have created a new web site called recovery.gov, so that every American can find out how and where their money is being spent.

So the recovery plan we passed is the first step in getting our economy back on track. But it is just the first step. Because even if we manage this plan flawlessly, there will be no real recovery unless we clean up the credit crisis that has severely weakened our financial system.

I want to speak plainly and candidly about this issue tonight, because every American should know that it directly affects you and your family's well-being. You should also know that the money you've deposited in banks across the country is safe, your insurance is secure, you can rely on the continued operation of our financial system. That's not the source of concern. The concern is that if we do not restart lending in this country, our recovery will be choked off before it even begins.

You see, the flow of credit is the lifeblood of our economy. The ability to get a loan is how you finance the purchase of everything from a home to a car to a college education, how stores stock their shelves, farms buy equipment, and businesses make payroll.

But credit has stopped flowing the way it should. Too many bad loans from the housing crisis have made their way onto the books of too many banks. And with so much debt and so little confidence, these banks are now fearful of lending out any more money to households, to businesses, or even to each other. And when there is no lending, families can't afford to buy homes or cars, so businesses are forced to make layoffs. Our economy suffers even more, and credit dries up even further. That is why this administration is moving swiftly and aggressively to break this destructive cycle, to restore confidence, and restart lending. And we will do so in several ways.

First, we are creating a new lending fund that represents the largest effort ever to help provide auto loans, college loans, and small- business loans to the consumers and entrepreneurs who keep this economy running.

Second, we have launched a housing plan that will help responsible families facing the threat of foreclosure lower their monthly payments and refinance their mortgages. It's a plan that won't help speculators or that neighbor down the street who bought a house he could never hope to afford, but it will help millions of Americans who are struggling with declining home values; Americans who will now be able to take advantage of the lower interest rates that this plan has already helped to bring about. In fact, the average family who refinances today can save nearly $2,000 per year on their mortgage.

Third, we will act with the full force of the Federal Government to ensure that the major banks that Americans depend on have enough confidence and enough money to lend even in more difficult times. And when we learn that a major bank has serious problems, we will hold accountable those responsible, force the necessary adjustments, provide the support to clean up their balance sheets, and assure the continuity of a strong, viable institution that can serve our people and our economy.

Now, I understand that on any given day, Wall Street may be more comforted by an approach that gives bank bailouts with no strings attached and that holds nobody accountable for their reckless decisions. But such an approach won't solve the problem, and our goal is to quicken the day when we restart lending to the American people and American business and end this crisis once and for all.

And I intend to hold these banks fully accountable for the assistance they receive, and this time, they will have to clearly demonstrate how taxpayer dollars result in more lending for the American taxpayer. This time, CEOs won't be able to use taxpayer money to pad their paychecks or buy fancy drapes or disappear on a private jet. Those days are over.

Still, this plan will require significant resources from the Federal Government– and, yes, probably more than we've already set aside. But while the cost of action will be great, I can assure you that the cost of inaction will be far greater, for it could result in an economy that sputters along for not months or years, but perhaps a decade. That would be worse for our deficit, worse for business, worse for you, and worse for the next generation. And I refuse to let that happen.

Now, I understand that when the last administration asked this Congress to provide assistance for struggling banks, Democrats and Republicans alike were infuriated by the mismanagement and the results that followed. So were the American taxpayers; so was I. So I know how unpopular it is to be seen as helping banks right now, especially when everyone is suffering in part from their bad decisions. I promise you, I get it.

But I also know that in a time of crisis, we cannot afford to govern out of anger or yield to the politics of the moment. My job–our job is to solve the problem. Our job is to govern with a sense of responsibility. I will not send–I will not spend a single penny for the purpose of rewarding a single Wall Street executive, but I will do whatever it takes to help the small business that can't pay its workers or the family that has saved and still can't get a mortgage. That's what this is about. It's not about helping banks; it's about helping people. [Applause]

It's not about helping banks; it's about helping people. Because when credit is available again, that young family can finally buy a new home. And then some company will hire workers to build it. And then those workers will have money to spend. And if they can get a loan too, maybe they'll finally buy that car or open their own business. Investors will return to the market, and American families will see their retirement secured once more. Slowly but surely, confidence will return and our economy will recover.

So I ask this Congress to join me in doing whatever proves necessary, because we cannot consign our Nation to an open-ended recession. And to ensure that a crisis of this magnitude never happens again, I ask Congress to move quickly on legislation that will finally reform our outdated regulatory system. It is time to put in place tough, new, commonsense rules of the road so that our financial market rewards drive and innovation, and punishes shortcuts and abuse.

The recovery plan and the financial stability plan are the immediate steps we're taking to revive our economy in the short term. But the only way to fully restore America's economic strength is to make the long-term investments that will lead to new jobs, new industries, and a renewed ability to compete with the rest of the world. The only way this century will be another American century is if we confront at last the price of our dependence on oil and the high cost of health care, the schools that aren't preparing our children and the mountain of debt they stand to inherit. That is our responsibility.

In the next few days, I will submit a budget to Congress. So often, we've come to view these documents as simply numbers on a page or a laundry list of programs. I see this document differently. I see it as a vision for America, as a blueprint for our future.

My budget does not attempt to solve every problem or address every issue. It reflects the stark reality of what we've inherited, a trillion-dollar deficit, a financial crisis, and a costly recession. Given these realities, everyone in this Chamber, Democrats and Republicans, will have to sacrifice some worthy priorities for which there are no dollars. And that includes me. But that does not mean we can afford to ignore our long-term challenges. I reject the view that says our problems will simply take care of themselves, that says Government has no role in laying the foundation for our common prosperity.

For history tells a different story. History reminds us that at every moment of economic upheaval and transformation, this Nation has responded with bold action and big ideas. In the midst of Civil War, we laid railroad tracks from one coast to another that spurred commerce and industry. From the turmoil of the Industrial Revolution came a system of public high schools that prepared our citizens for a new age. In the wake of war and depression, the GI bill sent a generation to college and created the largest middle class in history. And a twilight struggle for freedom led to a nation of highways, an American on the Moon, and an explosion of technology that still shapes our world. In each case, Government didn't supplant private enterprise; it catalyzed private enterprise. It created the conditions for thousands of entrepreneurs and new businesses to adapt and to thrive.

We are a nation that has seen promise amid peril and claimed opportunity from ordeal. Now we must be that nation again, and that is why, even as it cuts back on programs we don't need, the budget I submit will invest in the three areas that are absolutely critical to our economic future: energy, health care, and education.

It begins with energy. We know the country that harnesses the power of clean, renewable energy will lead the 21st century. And yet, it is China that has launched the largest effort in history to make their economy energy efficient. We invented solar technology, but we've fallen behind countries like Germany and Japan in producing it. New plug-in hybrids roll off our assembly lines, but they will run on batteries made in Korea. Well, I do not accept a future where the jobs and industries of tomorrow take root beyond our borders, and I know you don't either. It is time for America to lead again.

Thanks to our recovery plan, we will double this Nation's supply of renewable energy in the next 3 years. We've also made the largest investment in basic research funding in American history, an investment that will spur not only new discoveries in energy but breakthroughs in medicine and science and technology.

We will soon lay down thousands of miles of power lines that can carry new energy to cities and towns across this country. And we will put Americans to work making our homes and buildings more efficient so that we can save billions of dollars on our energy bills.

But to truly transform our economy, to protect our security, and save our planet from the ravages of climate change, we need to ultimately make clean, renewable energy the profitable kind of energy. So I ask this Congress to send me legislation that places a market-based cap on carbon pollution and drives the production of more renewable energy in America. That's what we need. And to support that innovation, we will invest $15 billion a year to develop technologies like wind power and solar power, advanced biofuels, clean coal, and more efficient cars and trucks built right here in America.

Speaking of our auto industry, everyone recognizes that years of bad decision-making and a global recession have pushed our automakers to the brink. We should not, and will not, protect them from their own bad practices. But we are committed to the goal of a retooled, reimagined auto industry that can compete and win. Millions of jobs depend on it; scores of communities depend on it. And I believe the Nation that invented the automobile cannot walk away from it.

Now, none of this will come without cost, nor will it be easy. But this is America. We don't do what's easy. We do what's necessary to move this country forward.

And for that same reason, we must also address the crushing cost of health care. This is a cost that now causes a bankruptcy in America every 30 seconds. By the end of the year, it could cause 1.5 million Americans to lose their homes. In the last 8 years, premiums have grown four times faster than wages. And in each of these years, 1 million more Americans have lost their health insurance. It is one of the major reasons why small businesses close their doors and corporations ship jobs overseas. And it's one of the largest and fastest growing parts of our budget. Given these facts, we can no longer afford to put health care reform on hold. We can't afford to do it. It's time.

Already, we've done more to advance the cause of health care reform in the last 30 days than we've done in the last decade. When it was days old, this Congress passed a law to provide and protect health insurance for 11 million American children whose parents work full time. Our recovery plan will invest in electronic health records, a new technology that will reduce errors, bring down costs, ensure privacy, and save lives. It will launch a new effort to conquer a disease that has touched the life of nearly every American, including me, by seeking a cure for cancer in our time. And it makes the largest investment ever in preventive care, because that's one of the best ways to keep our people healthy and our costs under control.

This budget builds on these reforms. It includes a historic commitment to comprehensive health care reform, a down payment on the principle that we must have quality, affordable health care for every American. It's a commitment that's paid for in part by efficiencies in our system that are long overdue. And it's a step we must take if we hope to bring down our deficit in the years to come.

Now, there will be many different opinions and ideas about how to achieve reform, and that's why I'm bringing together businesses and workers, doctors and health care providers, Democrats and Republicans to begin work on this issue next week.

I suffer no illusions that this will be an easy process. Once again, it will be hard. But I also know that nearly a century after Teddy Roosevelt first called for reform, the cost of our health care has weighed down our economy and our conscience long enough. So let there be no doubt: Health care reform cannot wait, it must not wait, and it will not wait another year.

The third challenge we must address is the urgent need to expand the promise of education in America. In a global economy where the most valuable skill you can sell is your knowledge, a good education is no longer just a pathway to opportunity, it is a prerequisite. Right now, three-quarters of the fastest growing occupations require more than a high school diploma. And yet, just over half of our citizens have that level of education. We have one of the highest high school dropout rates of any industrialized nation, and half of the students who begin college never finish.

This is a prescription for economic decline, because we know the countries that out-teach us today will outcompete us tomorrow. That is why it will be the goal of this administration to ensure that every child has access to a complete and competitive education, from the day they are born to the day they begin a career. That is a promise we have to make to the children of America.

Already, we've made historic investment in education through the economic recovery plan. We've dramatically expanded early childhood education and will continue to improve its quality, because we know that the most formative learning comes in those first years of life. We've made college affordable for nearly 7 million more students–7 million. And we have provided the resources necessary to prevent painful cuts and teacher layoffs that would set back our children's progress.

But we know that our schools don't just need more resources, they need more reform. And that is why this budget creates new teachers–new incentives for teacher performance, pathways for advancement, and rewards for success. We'll invest in innovative programs that are already helping schools meet high standards and close achievement gaps, and we will expand our commitment to charter schools.

It is our responsibility as lawmakers and as educators to make this system work. But it is the responsibility of every citizen to participate in it. So tonight I ask every American to commit to at least 1 year or more of higher education or career training. This can be community college or a 4-year school, vocational training or an apprenticeship. But whatever the training may be, every American will need to get more than a high school diploma.

And dropping out of high school is no longer an option. It's not just quitting on yourself, it's quitting on your country, and this country needs and values the talents of every American. That's why we will support—we will provide the support necessary for all young Americans to complete college and meet a new goal. By 2020, America will once again have the highest proportion of college graduates in the world. That is a goal we can meet. That's a goal we can meet.

Now, I know that the price of tuition is higher than ever, which is why if you are willing to volunteer in your neighborhood or give back to your community or serve your country, we will make sure that you can afford a higher education. And to encourage a renewed spirit of national service for this and future generations, I ask Congress to send me the bipartisan legislation that bears the name of Senator Orrin Hatch, as well as an American who has never stopped asking what he can do for his country, Senator Edward Kennedy.

These education policies will open the doors of opportunity for our children, but it is up to us to ensure they walk through them. In the end, there is no program or policy that can substitute for a parent, for a mother or father who will attend those parent-teacher conferences or help with homework or turn off the TV, put away the video games, read to their child. I speak to you not just as a President, but as a father, when I say that responsibility for our children's education must begin at home. That is not a Democratic issue or a Republican issue; that's an American issue.

There is, of course, another responsibility we have to our children. And that's the responsibility to ensure that we do not pass on to them a debt they cannot pay. That is critical. [Applause] I agree, absolutely. See, I know we can get some consensus in here. [Laughter] With the deficit we inherited, the cost of the crisis we face, and the long-term challenges we must meet, it has never been more important to ensure that as our economy recovers, we do what it takes to bring this deficit down. That is critical.

Now, I'm proud that we passed a recovery plan free of earmarks, and I want to pass a budget next year that ensures that each dollar we spend reflects only our most important national priorities.

And yesterday I held a fiscal summit where I pledged to cut the deficit in half by the end of my first term in office. My administration has also begun to go line by line through the Federal budget in order to eliminate wasteful and ineffective programs. As you can imagine, this is a process that will take some time. But we have already identified $2 trillion in savings over the next decade.

In this budget, we will end education programs that don't work and end direct payments to large agribusiness that don't need them. We'll eliminate the no-bid contracts that have wasted billions in Iraq and reform our defense budget so that we're not paying for cold war-era weapons systems we don't use. We will root out the waste and fraud and abuse in our Medicare program that doesn't make our seniors any healthier. We will restore a sense of fairness and balance to our Tax Code by finally ending the tax breaks for corporations that ship our jobs overseas.

In order to save our children from a future of debt, we will also end the tax breaks for the wealthiest 2 percent of Americans. Now, let me be clear–let me be absolutely clear, because I know you'll end up hearing some of the same claims that rolling back these tax breaks means a massive tax increase on the American people: If your family earns less than $250,000 a year, a quarter million dollars a year, you will not see your taxes increased a single dime. I repeat: Not one single dime. In fact–not a dime–in fact, the recovery plan provides a tax cut–that's right, a tax cut–for 95 percent of working families. And by the way, these checks are on the way.

Now, to preserve our long-term fiscal health, we must also address the growing costs in Medicare and Social Security. Comprehensive health care reform is the best way to strengthen Medicare for years to come. And we must also begin a conversation on how to do the same for Social Security, while creating tax-free universal savings accounts for all Americans.

Finally, because we're also suffering from a deficit of trust, I am committed to restoring a sense of honesty and accountability to our budget. That is why this budget looks ahead 10 years and accounts for spending that was left out under the old rules. And for the first time, that includes the full cost of fighting in Iraq and Afghanistan. For 7 years, we have been a nation at war. No longer will we hide its price.

Along with our outstanding national security team, I'm now carefully reviewing our policies in both wars, and I will soon announce a way forward in Iraq that leaves Iraq to its people and responsibly ends this war.

And with our friends and allies, we will forge a new and comprehensive strategy for Afghanistan and Pakistan to defeat Al Qaida and combat extremism, because I will not allow terrorists to plot against the American people from safe havens halfway around the world. We will not allow it.

As we meet here tonight, our men and women in uniform stand watch abroad and more are readying to deploy. To each and every one of them and to the families who bear the quiet burden of their absence, Americans are united in sending one message: We honor your service; we are inspired by your sacrifice; and you have our unyielding support.

To relieve the strain on our forces, my budget increases the number of our soldiers and marines. And to keep our sacred trust with those who serve, we will raise their pay and give our veterans the expanded health care and benefits that they have earned.

To overcome extremism, we must also be vigilant in upholding the values our troops defend, because there is no force in the world more powerful than the example of America. And that is why I have ordered the closing of the detention center at Guantanamo Bay and will seek swift and certain justice for captured terrorists. Because living our values doesn't make us weaker, it makes us safer and it makes us stronger. And that is why I can stand here tonight and say without exception or equivocation that the United States of America does not torture. We can make that commitment here tonight.

In words and deeds, we are showing the world that a new era of engagement has begun. For we know that America cannot meet the threats of this century alone, but the world cannot meet them without America. We cannot shun the negotiating table, nor ignore the foes or forces that could do us harm. We are instead called to move forward with the sense of confidence and candor that serious times demand.

To seek progress towards a secure and lasting peace between Israel and her neighbors, we have appointed an envoy to sustain our effort. To meet the challenges of the 21st century–from terrorism to nuclear proliferation, from pandemic disease to cyber threats to crushing poverty–we will strengthen old alliances, forge new ones, and use all elements of our national power.

And to respond to an economic crisis that is global in scope, we are working with the nations of the G-20 to restore confidence in our financial system, avoid the possibility of escalating protectionism, and spur demand for American goods in markets across the globe. For the world depends on us having a strong economy, just as our economy depends on the strength of the world's.

As we stand at this crossroads of history, the eyes of all people in all nations are once again upon us, watching to see what we do with this moment, waiting for us to lead. Those of us gathered here tonight have been called to govern in extraordinary times. It is a tremendous burden, but also a great privilege, one that has been entrusted to few generations of Americans. For in our hands lies the ability to shape our world for good or for ill.

I know that it's easy to lose sight of this truth, to become cynical and doubtful, consumed with the petty and the trivial. But in my life, I have also learned that hope is found in unlikely places, that inspiration often comes not from those with the most power or celebrity, but from the dreams and aspirations of ordinary Americans who are anything but ordinary.

I think of Leonard Abess, a bank president from Miami who reportedly cashed out of his company, took a $60 million bonus, and gave it out to all 399 people who worked for him, plus another 72 who used to work for him. He didn't tell anyone, but when the local newspaper found out, he simply said, "I knew some of these people since I was 7 years old. It didn't feel right getting the money myself."

I think about Greensburg, Kansas, a town that was completely destroyed by a tornado, but is being rebuilt by its residents as a global example of how clean energy can power an entire community, how it can bring jobs and businesses to a place where piles of bricks and rubble once lay. "The tragedy was terrible," said one of the men who helped them rebuild. "But the folks here know that it also provided an incredible opportunity."

I think about Ty'Sheoma Bethea, the young girl from that school I visited in Dillon, South Carolina, a place where the ceilings leak, the paint peels off the walls, and they have to stop teaching six times a day because the train barrels by their classroom. She had been told that her school is hopeless, but the other day after class she went to the public library and typed up a letter to the people sitting in this Chamber. She even asked her principal for the money to buy a stamp. The letter asks us for help and says: "We are just students trying to become lawyers, doctors, Congressmen like yourself, and one day President, so we can make a change to not just the State of South Carolina, but also the world. We are not quitters." That's what she said: "We are not quitters."

These words and these stories tell us something about the spirit of the people who sent us here. They tell us that even in the most trying times, amid the most difficult circumstances, there is a generosity, a resilience, a decency, and a determination that perseveres, a willingness to take responsibility for our future and for posterity. Their resolve must be our inspiration. Their concerns must be our cause. And we must show them and all our people that we are equal to the task before us.

I know–look, I know that we haven't agreed on every issue thus far. [Laughter] There are surely times in the future where we will part ways. But I also know that every American who is sitting here tonight loves this country and wants it to succeed. I know that. That must be the starting point for every debate we have in the coming months and where we return after those debates are done. That is the foundation on which the American people expect us to build common ground.

And if we do, if we come together and lift this Nation from the depths of this crisis, if we put our people back to work and restart the engine of our prosperity, if we confront without fear the challenges of our time and summon that enduring spirit of an America that does not quit, then someday years from now our children can tell their children that this was the time when we performed, in the words that are carved into this very Chamber, "something worthy to be remembered."

Thank you. God bless you, and may God bless the United States of America. Thank you.

3

CAIRO UNIVERSITY ADDRESS

JUNE 4, 2009

T hank you very much. Good afternoon. I am honored to be in the timeless city of Cairo, and to be hosted by two remarkable institutions. For over a thousand years, Al-Azhar has stood as a beacon of Islamic learning; and for over a century, Cairo University has been a source of Egypt's advancement. And together, you represent the harmony between tradition and progress. I'm grateful for your hospitality, and the hospitality of the people of Egypt. And I'm also proud to carry with me the goodwill of the American people, and a greeting of peace from Muslim communities in my country: Assalaamu alaykum.

We meet at a time of great tension between the United States and Muslims around the world – tension rooted in historical forces that go beyond any current policy debate. The relationship between Islam and the West includes centuries of coexistence and cooperation, but also conflict and religious wars. More recently, tension has been fed by colonialism that denied rights and opportunities to many Muslims, and a Cold War in which Muslim-majority countries were too often treated as proxies without regard to their own aspirations. Moreover, the sweeping change brought by modernity and globalization led many Muslims to view the West as hostile to the traditions of Islam.

Violent extremists have exploited these tensions in a small but potent minority of Muslims. The attacks of September 11, 2001 and the continued efforts of these extremists to engage in violence against civilians has led some in my country to view Islam as inevitably hostile not only to America and Western countries, but also to human rights. All this has bred more fear and more mistrust.

So long as our relationship is defined by our differences, we will empower those who sow hatred rather than peace, those who promote conflict rather than the cooperation that can help all of our people achieve justice and prosperity. And this cycle of suspicion and discord must end.

I've come here to Cairo to seek a new beginning between the United States and

Muslims around the world, one based on mutual interest and mutual respect, and one based upon the truth that America and Islam are not exclusive and need not be in competition. Instead, they overlap, and share common principles – principles of justice and progress; tolerance and the dignity of all human beings.

I do so recognizing that change cannot happen overnight. I know there's been a lot of publicity about this speech, but no single speech can eradicate years of mistrust, nor can I answer in the time that I have this afternoon all the complex questions that brought us to this point. But I am convinced that in order to move forward, we must say openly to each other the things we hold in our hearts and that too often are said only behind closed doors. There must be a sustained effort to listen to each other; to learn from each other; to respect one another; and to seek common ground. As the Holy Koran tells us, "Be conscious of God and speak always the truth." That is what I will try to do today – to speak the truth as best I can, humbled by the task before us, and firm in my belief that the interests we share as human beings are far more powerful than the forces that drive us apart.

Now part of this conviction is rooted in my own experience. I'm a Christian, but my father came from a Kenyan family that includes generations of Muslims. As a boy, I spent several years in Indonesia and heard the call of the azaan at the break of dawn and at the fall of dusk. As a young man, I worked in Chicago communities where many found dignity and peace in their Muslim faith.

As a student of history, I also know civilization's debt to Islam. It was Islam – at places like Al-Azhar – that carried the light of learning through so many centuries, paving the way for Europe's Renaissance and Enlightenment. It was innovation in Muslim communities – it was innovation in Muslim communities that developed the order of algebra; our magnetic compass and tools of navigation; our mastery of pens and printing; our understanding of how disease spreads and how it can be healed. Islamic culture has given us majestic arches and soaring spires; timeless poetry and cherished music; elegant calligraphy and places of peaceful contemplation. And throughout history, Islam has demonstrated through words and deeds the possibilities of religious tolerance and racial equality.

I also know that Islam has always been a part of America's story. The first nation to recognize my country was Morocco. In signing the Treaty of Tripoli in 1796, our second President, John Adams, wrote, "The United States has in itself no character of enmity against the laws, religion or tranquility of Muslims." And since our founding, American Muslims have enriched the United States. They have fought in our wars, they have served in our government, they have stood for civil rights, they have started businesses, they have taught at our universities, they've excelled in our sports arenas, they've won Nobel Prizes, built our tallest building, and lit the Olympic Torch. And when the first Muslim American was recently elected to Congress, he took the oath to defend our Constitution using the same Holy Koran that one of our Founding Fathers – Thomas Jefferson – kept in his personal library.

So I have known Islam on three continents before coming to the region where it was first revealed. That experience guides my conviction that partnership between America and Islam must be based on what Islam is, not what it isn't. And I consider it part of my responsibility as President of the United States to fight against negative stereotypes of Islam wherever they appear.

But that same principle must apply to Muslim perceptions of America. Just as Muslims do not fit a crude stereotype, America is not the crude stereotype of a self-interested empire. The United States has been one of the greatest sources of progress that the world has ever known. We were born out of revolution against an empire. We were founded upon the ideal that all are created equal, and we have shed blood and struggled for centuries to give meaning to those words – within our borders, and around the world. We are shaped by every culture, drawn from every end of the Earth, and dedicated to a simple concept: E pluribus unum – "Out of many, one."

Now, much has been made of the fact that an African American with the name Barack Hussein Obama could be elected President. But my personal story is not so unique. The dream of opportunity for all people has not come true for everyone in America, but its promise exists for all who come to our shores – and that includes nearly 7 million American Muslims in our country today who, by the way, enjoy incomes and educational levels that are higher than the American average.

Moreover, freedom in America is indivisible from the freedom to practice one's religion. That is why there is a mosque in every state in our union, and over 1,200 mosques within our borders. That's why the United States government has gone to court to protect the right of women and girls to wear the hijab and to punish those who would deny it.

So let there be no doubt: Islam is a part of America. And I believe that America holds within her the truth that regardless of race, religion, or station in life, all of us share common aspirations – to live in peace and security; to get an education and to work with dignity; to love our families, our communities, and our God. These things we share. This is the hope of all humanity.

Of course, recognizing our common humanity is only the beginning of our task. Words alone cannot meet the needs of our people. These needs will be met only if we act boldly in the years ahead; and if we understand that the challenges we face are shared, and our failure to meet them will hurt us all.

For we have learned from recent experience that when a financial system weakens in one country, prosperity is hurt everywhere. When a new flu infects one human being, all are at risk. When one nation pursues a nuclear weapon, the risk of nuclear attack rises for all nations. When violent extremists operate in one stretch of mountains, people are endangered across an ocean. When innocents in Bosnia and Darfur are slaughtered, that is a stain on our collective conscience. That is what it means to share this world in the 21st century. That is the responsibility we have to one another as human beings.

And this is a difficult responsibility to embrace. For human history has often been a record of nations and tribes – and, yes, religions – subjugating one another in pursuit of their own interests. Yet in this new age, such attitudes are self-defeating. Given our interdependence, any world order that elevates one nation or group of people over another will inevitably fail. So whatever we think of the past, we must not be prisoners to it. Our problems must be dealt with through partnership; our progress must be shared.

Now, that does not mean we should ignore sources of tension. Indeed, it suggests the opposite: We must face these tensions squarely. And so in that spirit, let me speak as clearly and as plainly as I can about some specific issues that I believe we must finally confront together.

The first issue that we have to confront is violent extremism in all of its forms.

In Ankara, I made clear that America is not – and never will be – at war with Islam. We will, however, relentlessly confront violent extremists who pose a grave threat to our security – because we reject the same thing that people of all faiths reject: the killing of innocent men, women, and children. And it is my first duty as President to protect the American people.

The situation in Afghanistan demonstrates America's goals, and our need to work together. Over seven years ago, the United States pursued al Qaeda and the Taliban with broad international support. We did not go by choice; we went because of necessity. I'm aware that there's still some who would question or even justify the events of 9/11. But let us be clear: Al Qaeda killed nearly 3,000 people on that day. The victims were innocent men, women and children from America and many other nations who had done nothing to harm anybody. And yet al Qaeda chose to ruthlessly murder these people, claimed credit for the attack, and even now states their determination to kill on a massive scale. They have affiliates in many countries and are trying to expand their reach. These are not opinions to be debated; these are facts to be dealt with.

Now, make no mistake: We do not want to keep our troops in Afghanistan. We see no military – we seek no military bases there. It is agonizing for America to lose our young men and women. It is costly and politically difficult to continue this conflict. We would gladly bring every single one of our troops home if we could be confident that there were not violent extremists in Afghanistan and now Pakistan determined to kill as many Americans as they possibly can. But that is not yet the case.

And that's why we're partnering with a coalition of 46 countries. And despite the costs involved, America's commitment will not weaken. Indeed, none of us should tolerate these extremists. They have killed in many countries. They have killed people of different faiths – but more than any other, they have killed Muslims. Their actions are irreconcilable with the rights of human beings, the progress of nations, and with Islam. The Holy Koran teaches that whoever kills an innocent is as – it is as if he has killed all mankind. And the Holy Koran also says whoever saves a person, it is as if he has saved all mankind. The enduring faith of over a billion people is so much bigger than the narrow hatred of a few. Islam is not part of the problem in combating violent extremism – it is an important part of promoting peace.

Now, we also know that military power alone is not going to solve the problems in Afghanistan and Pakistan. That's why we plan to invest $1.5 billion each year over the next five years to partner with Pakistanis to build schools and hospitals, roads and businesses, and hundreds of millions to help those who've been displaced. That's why we are providing more than $2.8 billion to help Afghans develop their economy and deliver services that people depend on.

Let me also address the issue of Iraq. Unlike Afghanistan, Iraq was a war of choice that provoked strong differences in my country and around the world. Although I believe that the Iraqi people are ultimately better off without the tyranny of Saddam Hussein, I also believe that events in Iraq have reminded America of the need to use diplomacy and build international consensus to resolve our problems whenever possible. Indeed, we can recall the words of Thomas Jefferson, who said: "I hope that our wisdom will grow with our power, and teach us that the less we use our power the greater it will be."

Today, America has a dual responsibility: to help Iraq forge a better future – and to leave Iraq to Iraqis. And I have made it clear to the Iraqi people – I have made it clear to the Iraqi people that we pursue no bases, and no claim on their territory or resources. Iraq's sovereignty is its own. And that's why I ordered the removal of our combat brigades by next August. That is why we will honor our agreement with Iraq's democratically elected government to remove combat troops from Iraqi cities by July, and to remove all of our troops from Iraq by 2012. We will help Iraq train its security forces and develop its economy. But we will support a secure and united Iraq as a partner, and never as a patron.

And finally, just as America can never tolerate violence by extremists, we must never alter or forget our principles. Nine-eleven was an enormous trauma to our country. The fear and anger that it provoked was understandable, but in some cases, it led us to act contrary to our traditions and our ideals. We are taking concrete actions to change course. I have unequivocally prohibited the use of torture by the United States, and I have ordered the prison at Guantanamo Bay closed by early next year.

So America will defend itself, respectful of the sovereignty of nations and the rule of law. And we will do so in partnership with Muslim communities which are also threatened. The sooner the extremists are isolated and unwelcome in Muslim communities, the sooner we will all be safer.

The second major source of tension that we need to discuss is the situation between Israelis, Palestinians and the Arab world.

America's strong bonds with Israel are well known. This bond is unbreakable. It is based upon cultural and historical ties, and the recognition that the aspiration for a Jewish homeland is rooted in a tragic history that cannot be denied.

Around the world, the Jewish people were persecuted for centuries, and anti-Semitism in Europe culminated in an unprecedented Holocaust. Tomorrow, I will visit Buchenwald, which was part of a network of camps where Jews were enslaved, tortured, shot and gassed to death by the Third Reich. Six million Jews were killed – more than the entire Jewish population of Israel today. Denying that fact is baseless, it is ignorant, and it is hateful. Threatening Israel with destruction – or repeating vile stereotypes about Jews – is deeply wrong, and only serves to evoke in the minds of Israelis this most painful of memories while preventing the peace that the people of this region deserve.

On the other hand, it is also undeniable that the Palestinian people – Muslims and Christians – have suffered in pursuit of a homeland. For more than 60 years they've endured the pain of dislocation. Many wait in refugee camps in the West Bank, Gaza, and neighboring lands for a life of peace and security that they have never been able to lead. They endure the daily humiliations – large and small – that come with occupation. So let there be no doubt: The situation for the Palestinian people is intolerable. And America will not turn our backs on the legitimate Palestinian aspiration for dignity, opportunity, and a state of their own.

For decades then, there has been a stalemate: two peoples with legitimate aspirations, each with a painful history that makes compromise elusive. It's easy to point fingers – for Palestinians to point to the displacement brought about by Israel's founding, and for Israelis to point to the constant hostility and attacks throughout its history from within its borders as well as beyond. But if we see this conflict only from one side or the other, then we will be blind to the truth: The only resolution is for the aspirations of both sides to be met through two states, where Israelis and Palestinians each live in peace and security.

That is in Israel's interest, Palestine's interest, America's interest, and the world's interest. And that is why I intend to personally pursue this outcome with all the patience and dedication that the task requires. The obligations – the obligations that the parties have agreed to under the road map are clear. For peace to come, it is time for them – and all of us – to live up to our responsibilities.

Palestinians must abandon violence. Resistance through violence and killing is wrong and it does not succeed. For centuries, black people in America suffered the lash of the whip as slaves and the humiliation of segregation. But it was not violence that won full and equal rights. It was a peaceful and determined insistence upon the ideals at the center of America's founding. This same story can be told by people from South Africa to South Asia; from Eastern Europe to Indonesia. It's a story with a simple truth: that violence is a dead end. It is a sign neither of courage nor power to shoot rockets at sleeping children, or to blow up old women on a bus. That's not how moral authority is claimed; that's how it is surrendered.

Now is the time for Palestinians to focus on what they can build. The Palestinian Authority must develop its capacity to govern, with institutions that serve the needs of its people. Hamas does have support among some Palestinians, but they also have to recognize they have responsibilities. To play a role in fulfilling Palestinian aspirations, to unify the Palestinian people, Hamas must put an end to violence, recognize past agreements, recognize Israel's right to exist.

At the same time, Israelis must acknowledge that just as Israel's right to exist cannot be denied, neither can Palestine's. The United States does not accept the legitimacy of continued Israeli settlements. This construction violates previous agreements and undermines efforts to achieve peace. It is time for these settlements to stop.

And Israel must also live up to its obligation to ensure that Palestinians can live and work and develop their society. Just as it devastates Palestinian families, the continuing humanitarian crisis in Gaza does not serve Israel's security; neither does the continuing lack of opportunity in the West Bank. Progress in the daily lives of the Palestinian people must be a critical part of a road to peace, and Israel must take concrete steps to enable such progress.

And finally, the Arab states must recognize that the Arab Peace Initiative was an important beginning, but not the end of their responsibilities. The Arab-Israeli conflict should no longer be used to distract the people of Arab nations from other problems. Instead, it must be a cause for action to help the Palestinian people develop the institutions that will sustain their state, to recognize Israel's legitimacy, and to choose progress over a self-defeating focus on the past.

America will align our policies with those who pursue peace, and we will say in public what we say in private to Israelis and Palestinians and Arabs. We cannot impose peace. But privately, many Muslims recognize that Israel will not go away. Likewise, many Israelis recognize the need for a Palestinian state. It is time for us to act on what everyone knows to be true.

Too many tears have been shed. Too much blood has been shed. All of us have a responsibility to work for the day when the mothers of Israelis and Palestinians can see their children grow up without fear; when the Holy Land of the three great faiths is the place of peace that God intended it to be; when Jerusalem is a secure and lasting home for Jews and Christians and Muslims, and a place for all of the children of Abraham to mingle peacefully together as in the story of Isra – as in the story of Isra, when Moses, Jesus, and Mohammed, peace be upon them, joined in prayer.

The third source of tension is our shared interest in the rights and responsibilities of nations on nuclear weapons.

This issue has been a source of tension between the United States and the Islamic Republic of Iran. For many years, Iran has defined itself in part by its opposition to my country, and there is in fact a tumultuous history between us. In the middle of the Cold War, the United States played a role in the overthrow of a democratically elected Iranian government. Since the Islamic Revolution, Iran has played a role in acts of hostage-taking and violence against U.S. troops and civilians. This history is well known. Rather than remain trapped in the past, I've made it clear to Iran's leaders and people that my country is prepared to move forward. The question now is not what Iran is against, but rather what future it wants to build.

I recognize it will be hard to overcome decades of mistrust, but we will proceed with courage, rectitude, and resolve. There will be many issues to discuss between our two countries, and we are willing to move forward without preconditions on the basis of mutual respect. But it is clear to all concerned that when it comes to nuclear weapons, we have reached a decisive point. This is not simply about America's interests. It's about preventing a nuclear arms race in the Middle East that could lead this region and the world down a hugely dangerous path.

I understand those who protest that some countries have weapons that others do not. No single nation should pick and choose which nation holds nuclear weapons. And that's why I strongly reaffirmed America's commitment to seek a world in which no nations hold nuclear weapons. And any nation – including Iran – should have the right to access peaceful nuclear power if it complies with its responsibilities under the nuclear Non-Proliferation Treaty. That commitment is at the core of the treaty, and it must be kept for all who fully abide by it. And I'm hopeful that all countries in the region can share in this goal.

The fourth issue that I will address is democracy.

I know – I know there has been controversy about the promotion of democracy in recent years, and much of this controversy is connected to the war in Iraq. So let me be clear: No system of government can or should be imposed by one nation by any other.

That does not lessen my commitment, however, to governments that reflect the will of the people. Each nation gives life to this principle in its own way, grounded in the traditions of its own people. America does not presume to know what is best for everyone, just as we would not presume to pick the outcome of a peaceful election. But I do have an unyielding belief that all people yearn for certain things: the ability to speak your mind and have a say in how you are governed; confidence in the rule of law and the equal administration of justice; government that is transparent and doesn't steal from the people; the freedom to live as you choose. These are not just American ideas; they are human rights. And that is why we will support them everywhere.

Now, there is no straight line to realize this promise. But this much is clear: Governments that protect these rights are ultimately more stable, successful and secure. Suppressing ideas never succeeds in making them go away. America respects the right of all peaceful and law-abiding voices to be heard around the world, even if we disagree with them. And we will welcome all elected, peaceful governments – provided they govern with respect for all their people.

This last point is important because there are some who advocate for democracy only when they're out of power; once in power, they are ruthless in suppressing the rights of others. So no matter where it takes hold, government of the people and by the people sets a single standard for all who would hold power: You must maintain your power through consent, not coercion; you must respect the rights of minorities, and participate with a spirit of tolerance and compromise; you must place the interests of your people and the legitimate workings of the political process above your party. Without these ingredients, elections alone do not make true democracy.

AUDIENCE MEMBER: Barack Obama, we love you!

PRESIDENT OBAMA: Thank you. The fifth issue that we must address together is religious freedom.

Islam has a proud tradition of tolerance. We see it in the history of Andalusia and Cordoba during the Inquisition. I saw it firsthand as a child in Indonesia, where devout Christians worshiped freely in an overwhelmingly Muslim country. That is the spirit we need today. People in every country should be free to choose and live their faith based upon the persuasion of the mind and the heart and the soul. This tolerance is essential for religion to thrive, but it's being challenged in many different ways.

Among some Muslims, there's a disturbing tendency to measure one's own faith by the rejection of somebody else's faith. The richness of religious diversity must be upheld – whether it is for Maronites in Lebanon or the Copts in Egypt. And if we are being honest, fault lines must be closed among Muslims, as well, as the divisions between Sunni and Shia have led to tragic violence, particularly in Iraq.

Freedom of religion is central to the ability of peoples to live together. We must always examine the ways in which we protect it. For instance, in the United States, rules on charitable giving have made it harder for Muslims to fulfill their religious obligation. That's why I'm committed to working with American Muslims to ensure that they can fulfill zakat.

Likewise, it is important for Western countries to avoid impeding Muslim citizens from practicing religion as they see fit – for instance, by dictating what clothes a Muslim woman should wear. We can't disguise hostility towards any religion behind the pretence of liberalism.

In fact, faith should bring us together. And that's why we're forging service projects in America to bring together Christians, Muslims, and Jews. That's why we welcome efforts like Saudi Arabian King Abdullah's interfaith dialogue and Turkey's leadership in the Alliance of Civilizations. Around the world, we can turn dialogue into interfaith service, so bridges between peoples lead to action – whether it is combating malaria in Africa, or providing relief after a natural disaster.

The sixth issue – the sixth issue that I want to address is women's rights. I know — I know – and you can tell from this audience, that there is a healthy debate about this issue. I reject the view of some in the West that a woman who chooses to cover her hair is somehow less equal, but I do believe that a woman who is denied an education is denied equality. And it is no coincidence that countries where women are well educated are far more likely to be prosperous.

Now, let me be clear: Issues of women's equality are by no means simply an issue for Islam. In Turkey, Pakistan, Bangladesh, Indonesia, we've seen Muslim-majority countries elect a woman to lead. Meanwhile, the struggle for women's equality continues in many aspects of American life, and in countries around the world.

I am convinced that our daughters can contribute just as much to society as our sons. Our common prosperity will be advanced by allowing all humanity – men and women – to reach their full potential. I do not believe that women must make the same choices as men in order to be equal, and I respect those women who choose to live their lives in traditional roles. But it should be their choice. And that is why the United States will partner with any Muslim-majority country to support expanded literacy for girls, and to help young women pursue employment through micro-financing that helps people live their dreams.

Finally, I want to discuss economic development and opportunity.

I know that for many, the face of globalization is contradictory. The Internet and television can bring knowledge and information, but also offensive sexuality and mindless violence into the home. Trade can bring new wealth and opportunities, but also huge disruptions and change in communities. In all nations – including America – this change can bring fear. Fear that because of modernity we lose control over our economic choices, our politics, and most importantly our identities – those things we most cherish about our communities, our families, our traditions, and our faith.

But I also know that human progress cannot be denied. There need not be contradictions between development and tradition. Countries like Japan and South Korea grew their economies enormously while maintaining distinct cultures. The same is true for the astonishing progress within Muslim-majority countries from Kuala

Lumpur to Dubai. In ancient times and in our times, Muslim communities have been at the forefront of innovation and education.

And this is important because no development strategy can be based only upon what comes out of the ground, nor can it be sustained while young people are out of work. Many Gulf states have enjoyed great wealth as a consequence of oil, and some are beginning to focus it on broader development. But all of us must recognize that education and innovation will be the currency of the 21st century – and in too many Muslim communities, there remains underinvestment in these areas. I'm emphasizing such investment within my own country. And while America in the past has focused on oil and gas when it comes to this part of the world, we now seek a broader engagement.

On education, we will expand exchange programs, and increase scholarships, like the one that brought my father to America. At the same time, we will encourage more Americans to study in Muslim communities. And we will match promising Muslim students with internships in America; invest in online learning for teachers and children around the world; and create a new online network, so a young person in Kansas can communicate instantly with a young person in Cairo.

On economic development, we will create a new corps of business volunteers to partner with counterparts in Muslim-majority countries. And I will host a Summit on Entrepreneurship this year to identify how we can deepen ties between business leaders, foundations and social entrepreneurs in the United States and Muslim communities around the world.

On science and technology, we will launch a new fund to support technological development in Muslim-majority countries, and to help transfer ideas to the marketplace so they can create more jobs. We'll open centers of scientific excellence in Africa, the Middle East and Southeast Asia, and appoint new science envoys to collaborate on programs that develop new sources of energy, create green jobs, digitize records, clean water, grow new crops. Today I'm announcing a new global effort with the Organization of the Islamic Conference to eradicate polio. And we will also expand partnerships with Muslim communities to promote child and maternal health.

All these things must be done in partnership. Americans are ready to join with citizens and governments; community organizations, religious leaders, and businesses in Muslim communities around the world to help our people pursue a better life.

The issues that I have described will not be easy to address. But we have a responsibility to join together on behalf of the world that we seek – a world where extremists no longer threaten our people, and American troops have come home; a world where Israelis and Palestinians are each secure in a state of their own, and nuclear energy is used for peaceful purposes; a world where governments serve their citizens, and the rights of all God's children are respected. Those are mutual interests. That is the world we seek. But we can only achieve it together.

I know there are many – Muslim and non-Muslim – who question whether we can forge this new beginning. Some are eager to stoke the flames of division, and to stand in the way of progress. Some suggest that it isn't worth the effort – that we are fated to disagree, and civilizations are doomed to clash. Many more are simply skeptical that real change can occur. There's so much fear, so much mistrust that has built up over the years. But if we choose to be bound by the past, we will never move forward. And I want to particularly say this to young people of every faith, in every country – you, more than anyone, have the ability to reimagine the world, to remake this world.

All of us share this world for but a brief moment in time. The question is whether we spend that time focused on what pushes us apart, or whether we commit ourselves to an effort – a sustained effort – to find common ground, to focus on the future we seek for our children, and to respect the dignity of all human beings.

It's easier to start wars than to end them. It's easier to blame others than to look inward. It's easier to see what is different about someone than to find the things we share. But we should choose the right path, not just the easy path. There's one rule that lies at the heart of every religion – that we do unto others as we would have them do unto us. This truth transcends nations and peoples – a belief that isn't new; that isn't black or white or brown; that isn't Christian or Muslim or Jew. It's a belief that pulsed in the cradle of civilization, and that still beats in the hearts of billions around the world. It's a faith in other people, and it's what brought me here today.

We have the power to make the world we seek, but only if we have the courage to make a new beginning, keeping in mind what has been written.

The Holy Koran tells us: "O mankind! We have created you male and a female; and we have made you into nations and tribes so that you may know one another."

The Talmud tells us: "The whole of the Torah is for the purpose of promoting peace."

The Holy Bible tells us: "Blessed are the peacemakers, for they shall be called sons of God."

The people of the world can live together in peace. We know that is God's vision. Now that must be our work here on Earth.

Thank you. And may God's peace be upon you. Thank you very much. Thank you.

4

REMARKS TO A JOINT SESSION OF CONGRESS ON HEALTH CARE

SEPTEMBER 9, 2009

Madam Speaker, Vice President Biden, members of Congress, and the American people:

When I spoke here last winter, this nation was facing the worst economic crisis since the Great Depression. We were losing an average of 700,000 jobs per month. Credit was frozen. And our financial system was on the verge of collapse.

As any American who is still looking for work or a way to pay their bills will tell you, we are by no means out of the woods. A full and vibrant recovery is still many months away. And I will not let up until those Americans who seek jobs can find them – until those businesses that seek capital and credit can thrive; until all responsible homeowners can stay in their homes. That is our ultimate goal. But thanks to the bold and decisive action we've taken since January, I can stand here with confidence and say that we have pulled this economy back from the brink.

I want to thank the members of this body for your efforts and your support in these last several months, and especially those who've taken the difficult votes that have put us on a path to recovery. I also want to thank the American people for their patience and resolve during this trying time for our nation.

But we did not come here just to clean up crises. We came here to build a future. So tonight, I return to speak to all of you about an issue that is central to that future – and that is the issue of health care.

I am not the first President to take up this cause, but I am determined to be the last. It has now been nearly a century since Theodore Roosevelt first called for health care reform. And ever since, nearly every President and Congress, whether Democrat or Republican, has attempted to meet this challenge in some way. A bill for comprehensive health reform was first introduced by John Dingell Sr. in 1943. Sixty-five years later, his son continues to introduce that same bill at the beginning of each session.

Our collective failure to meet this challenge – year after year, decade after decade

– has led us to the breaking point. Everyone understands the extraordinary hardships that are placed on the uninsured, who live every day just one accident or illness away from bankruptcy. These are not primarily people on welfare. These are middle-class Americans. Some can't get insurance on the job. Others are self-employed, and can't afford it, since buying insurance on your own costs you three times as much as the coverage you get from your employer. Many other Americans who are willing and able to pay are still denied insurance due to previous illnesses or conditions that insurance companies decide are too risky or too expensive to cover.

We are the only democracy – the only advanced democracy on Earth – the only wealthy nation – that allows such hardship for millions of its people. There are now more than 30 million American citizens who cannot get coverage. In just a two-year period, one in every three Americans goes without health care coverage at some point. And every day, 14,000 Americans lose their coverage. In other words, it can happen to anyone.

But the problem that plagues the health care system is not just a problem for the uninsured. Those who do have insurance have never had less security and stability than they do today. More and more Americans worry that if you move, lose your job, or change your job, you'll lose your health insurance too. More and more Americans pay their premiums, only to discover that their insurance company has dropped their coverage when they get sick, or won't pay the full cost of care. It happens every day.

One man from Illinois lost his coverage in the middle of chemotherapy because his insurer found that he hadn't reported gallstones that he didn't even know about. They delayed his treatment, and he died because of it. Another woman from Texas was about to get a double mastectomy when her insurance company canceled her policy because she forgot to declare a case of acne. By the time she had her insurance reinstated, her breast cancer had more than doubled in size. That is heart-breaking, it is wrong, and no one should be treated that way in the United States of America.

Then there's the problem of rising cost. We spend one and a half times more per person on health care than any other country, but we aren't any healthier for it. This is one of the reasons that insurance premiums have gone up three times faster than wages. It's why so many employers – especially small businesses – are forcing their employees to pay more for insurance, or are dropping their coverage entirely. It's why so many aspiring entrepreneurs cannot afford to open a business in the first place, and why American businesses that compete internationally – like our automakers – are at a huge disadvantage. And it's why those of us with health insurance are also paying a hidden and growing tax for those without it – about $1,000 per year that pays for somebody else's emergency room and charitable care.

Finally, our health care system is placing an unsustainable burden on taxpayers. When health care costs grow at the rate they have, it puts greater pressure on programs like Medicare and Medicaid. If we do nothing to slow these skyrocketing costs, we will eventually be spending more on Medicare and Medicaid than every other government program combined. Put simply, our health care problem is our deficit problem. Nothing else even comes close. Nothing else.

Now, these are the facts. Nobody disputes them. We know we must reform this system. The question is how.

There are those on the left who believe that the only way to fix the system is through a single-payer system like Canada's – where we would severely restrict the private insurance market and have the government provide coverage for everybody. On the right, there are those who argue that we should end employer-based systems and leave individuals to buy health insurance on their own.

I've said – I have to say that there are arguments to be made for both these approaches. But either one would represent a radical shift that would disrupt the health care most people currently have. Since health care represents one-sixth of our economy, I believe it makes more sense to build on what works and fix what doesn't, rather than try to build an entirely new system from scratch. And that is precisely what those of you in Congress have tried to do over the past several months.

During that time, we've seen Washington at its best and at its worst.

We've seen many in this chamber work tirelessly for the better part of this year to offer thoughtful ideas about how to achieve reform. Of the five committees asked to develop bills, four have completed their work, and the Senate Finance Committee announced today that it will move forward next week. That has never happened before. Our overall efforts have been supported by an unprecedented coalition of doctors and nurses; hospitals, seniors' groups, and even drug companies – many of whom opposed reform in the past. And there is agreement in this chamber on about 80 percent of what needs to be done, putting us closer to the goal of reform than we have ever been.

But what we've also seen in these last months is the same partisan spectacle that only hardens the disdain many Americans have towards their own government. Instead of honest debate, we've seen scare tactics. Some have dug into unyielding ideological camps that offer no hope of compromise. Too many have used this as an opportunity to score short-term political points, even if it robs the country of our opportunity to solve a long-term challenge. And out of this blizzard of charges and counter-charges, confusion has reigned.

Well, the time for bickering is over. The time for games has passed. Now is the season for action. Now is when we must bring the best ideas of both parties together, and show the American people that we can still do what we were sent here to do. Now is the time to deliver on health care. Now is the time to deliver on health care.

The plan I'm announcing tonight would meet three basic goals. It will provide more security and stability to those who have health insurance. It will provide insurance for those who don't. And it will slow the growth of health care costs for our families, our businesses, and our government. It's a plan that asks everyone to take responsibility for meeting this challenge – not just government, not just insurance companies, but everybody including employers and individuals. And it's a plan that incorporates ideas from senators and congressmen, from Democrats and Republicans – and yes, from some of my opponents in both the primary and general election.

Here are the details that every American needs to know about this plan. First, if you are among the hundreds of millions of Americans who already have health insurance through your job, or Medicare, or Medicaid, or the VA, nothing in this plan will require you or your employer to change the coverage or the doctor you have. Let me repeat this: Nothing in our plan requires you to change what you have.

What this plan will do is make the insurance you have work better for you. Under this plan, it will be against the law for insurance companies to deny you coverage because of a preexisting condition. As soon as I sign this bill, it will be against the law for insurance companies to drop your coverage when you get sick or water it down when you need it the most. They will no longer be able to place some arbitrary cap on the amount of coverage you can receive in a given year or in a lifetime. We will place a limit on how much you can be charged for out-of-pocket expenses, because in the United States of America, no one should go broke because they get sick. And insurance companies will be required to cover, with no extra charge, routine checkups and preventive care, like mammograms and colonoscopies – because there's no reason we shouldn't be catching diseases like breast cancer and colon cancer before they get worse. That makes sense, it saves money, and it saves lives.

Now, that's what Americans who have health insurance can expect from this plan – more security and more stability.

Now, if you're one of the tens of millions of Americans who don't currently have health insurance, the second part of this plan will finally offer you quality, affordable choices. If you lose your job or you change your job, you'll be able to get coverage. If you strike out on your own and start a small business, you'll be able to get coverage. We'll do this by creating a new insurance exchange – a marketplace where individuals and small businesses will be able to shop for health insurance at competitive prices. Insurance companies will have an incentive to participate in this exchange because it lets them compete for millions of new customers. As one big group, these customers will have greater leverage to bargain with the insurance companies for better prices and quality coverage. This is how large companies and government employees get affordable insurance. It's how everyone in this Congress gets affordable insurance. And it's time to give every American the same opportunity that we give ourselves.

Now, for those individuals and small businesses who still can't afford the lower-priced insurance available in the exchange, we'll provide tax credits, the size of which will be based on your need. And all insurance companies that want access to this new marketplace will have to abide by the consumer protections I already mentioned. This exchange will take effect in four years, which will give us time to do it right. In the meantime, for those Americans who can't get insurance today because they have preexisting medical conditions, we will immediately offer low-cost coverage that will protect you against financial ruin if you become seriously ill. This was a good idea when Senator John McCain proposed it in the campaign, it's a good idea now, and we should all embrace it.

Now, even if we provide these affordable options, there may be those – especially the young and the healthy – who still want to take the risk and go without coverage. There may still be companies that refuse to do right by their workers by giving them coverage. The problem is, such irresponsible behavior costs all the rest of us money. If there are affordable options and people still don't sign up for health insurance, it means we pay for these people's expensive emergency room visits. If some businesses don't provide workers health care, it forces the rest of us to pick up the tab when their workers get sick, and gives those businesses an unfair advantage over their competitors. And unless everybody does their part, many of the insurance reforms we seek – especially requiring insurance companies to cover preexisting conditions – just can't be achieved.

And that's why under my plan, individuals will be required to carry basic health insurance – just as most states require you to carry auto insurance. Likewise – likewise, businesses will be required to either offer their workers health care, or chip in to help cover the cost of their workers. There will be a hardship waiver for those individuals who still can't afford coverage, and 95 percent of all small businesses, because of their size and narrow profit margin, would be exempt from these requirements. But we can't have large businesses and individuals who can afford coverage game the system by avoiding responsibility to themselves or their employees. Improving our health care system only works if everybody does their part.

And while there remain some significant details to be ironed out, I believe – I believe a broad consensus exists for the aspects of the plan I just outlined: consumer protections for those with insurance, an exchange that allows individuals and small businesses to purchase affordable coverage, and a requirement that people who can afford insurance get insurance.

And I have no doubt that these reforms would greatly benefit Americans from all walks of life, as well as the economy as a whole. Still, given all the misinformation that's been spread over the past few months, I realize – I realize that many Americans have grown nervous about reform. So tonight I want to address some of the key controversies that are still out there.

Some of people's concerns have grown out of bogus claims spread by those whose only agenda is to kill reform at any cost. The best example is the claim made not just by radio and cable talk show hosts, but by prominent politicians, that we plan to set up panels of bureaucrats with the power to kill off senior citizens. Now, such a charge would be laughable if it weren't so cynical and irresponsible. It is a lie, plain and simple.

There are also those who claim that our reform efforts would insure illegal immigrants. This, too, is false. The reforms – the reforms I'm proposing would not apply to those who are here illegally.

AUDIENCE MEMBER: You lie! (Boos.)

THE PRESIDENT: It's not true. And one more misunderstanding I want to clear up – under our plan, no federal dollars will be used to fund abortions, and federal conscience laws will remain in place.

Now, my health care proposal has also been attacked by some who oppose reform as a "government takeover" of the entire health care system. As proof, critics point to a provision in our plan that allows the uninsured and small businesses to choose a publicly sponsored insurance option, administered by the government just like Medicaid or Medicare.

So let me set the record straight here. My guiding principle is, and always has been, that consumers do better when there is choice and competition. That's how the market works. Unfortunately, in 34 states, 75 percent of the insurance market is controlled by five or fewer companies. In Alabama, almost 90 percent is controlled by just one company. And without competition, the price of insurance goes up and quality goes down. And it makes it easier for insurance companies to treat their customers badly – by cherry-picking the healthiest individuals and trying to drop the sickest, by overcharging small businesses who have no leverage, and by jacking up rates.

Insurance executives don't do this because they're bad people; they do it because it's profitable. As one former insurance executive testified before Congress, insurance companies are not only encouraged to find reasons to drop the seriously ill, they are rewarded for it. All of this is in service of meeting what this former executive called "Wall Street's relentless profit expectations."

Now, I have no interest in putting insurance companies out of business. They provide a legitimate service, and employ a lot of our friends and neighbors. I just want to hold them accountable. And the insurance reforms that I've already mentioned would do just that. But an additional step we can take to keep insurance companies honest is by making a not-for-profit public option available in the insurance exchange. Now, let me be clear. Let me be clear. It would only be an option for those who don't have insurance. No one would be forced to choose it, and it would not impact those of you who already have insurance. In fact, based on Congressional Budget Office estimates, we believe that less than 5 percent of Americans would sign up.

Despite all this, the insurance companies and their allies don't like this idea. They argue that these private companies can't fairly compete with the government. And they'd be right if taxpayers were subsidizing this public insurance option. But they won't be. I've insisted that like any private insurance company, the public insurance option would have to be self-sufficient and rely on the premiums it collects. But by avoiding some of the overhead that gets eaten up at private companies by profits and excessive administrative costs and executive salaries, it could provide a good deal for consumers, and would also keep pressure on private insurers to keep their policies affordable and treat their customers better, the same way public colleges and universities provide additional choice and competition to students without in any way inhibiting a vibrant system of private colleges and universities.

Now, it is – it's worth noting that a strong majority of Americans still favor a public insurance option of the sort I've proposed tonight. But its impact shouldn't be exaggerated – by the left or the right or the media. It is only one part of my plan, and shouldn't be used as a handy excuse for the usual Washington ideological battles. To my progressive friends, I would remind you that for decades, the driving idea behind reform has been to end insurance company abuses and make coverage available for those without it. The public option – the public option is only a means to that end – and we should remain open to other ideas that accomplish our ultimate goal. And to my Republican friends, I say that rather than making wild claims about a government takeover of health care, we should work together to address any legitimate concerns you may have.

For example – for example, some have suggested that the public option go into effect only in those markets where insurance companies are not providing affordable policies. Others have proposed a co-op or another non-profit entity to administer the plan. These are all constructive ideas worth exploring. But I will not back down on the basic principle that if Americans can't find affordable coverage, we will provide you with a choice. And I will make sure that no government bureaucrat or insurance company bureaucrat gets between you and the care that you need.

Finally, let me discuss an issue that is a great concern to me, to members of this chamber, and to the public – and that's how we pay for this plan.

And here's what you need to know. First, I will not sign a plan that adds one dime to our deficits – either now or in the future. I will not sign it if it adds one dime to the deficit, now or in the future, period. And to prove that I'm serious, there will be a provision in this plan that requires us to come forward with more spending cuts if the savings we promised don't materialize. Now, part of the reason I faced a trillion-dollar deficit when I walked in the door of the White House is because too many initiatives over the last decade were not paid for – from the Iraq war to tax breaks for the wealthy. I will not make that same mistake with health care.

Second, we've estimated that most of this plan can be paid for by finding savings within the existing health care system, a system that is currently full of waste and abuse. Right now, too much of the hard-earned savings and tax dollars we spend on health care don't make us any healthier. That's not my judgment – it's the judgment of medical professionals across this country. And this is also true when it comes to Medicare and Medicaid.

In fact, I want to speak directly to seniors for a moment, because Medicare is another issue that's been subjected to demagoguery and distortion during the course of this debate.

More than four decades ago, this nation stood up for the principle that after a life-time of hard work, our seniors should not be left to struggle with a pile of medical bills in their later years. That's how Medicare was born. And it remains a sacred trust that must be passed down from one generation to the next. And that is why not a dollar of the Medicare trust fund will be used to pay for this plan.

The only thing this plan would eliminate is the hundreds of billions of dollars in waste and fraud, as well as unwarranted subsidies in Medicare that go to insurance companies – subsidies that do everything to pad their profits but don't improve the care of seniors. And we will also create an independent commission of doctors and medical experts charged with identifying more waste in the years ahead.

Now, these steps will ensure that you – America's seniors – get the benefits you've been promised. They will ensure that Medicare is there for future generations. And we can use some of the savings to fill the gap in coverage that forces too many seniors to pay thousands of dollars a year out of their own pockets for prescription drugs. That's what this plan will do for you. So don't pay attention to those scary stories about how your benefits will be cut, especially since some of the same folks who are spreading these tall tales have fought against Medicare in the past and just this year supported a budget that would essentially have turned Medicare into a privatized voucher program. That will not happen on my watch. I will protect Medicare.

Now, because Medicare is such a big part of the health care system, making the program more efficient can help usher in changes in the way we deliver health care that can reduce costs for everybody. We have long known that some places – like the Intermountain Healthcare in Utah or the Geisinger Health System in rural Pennsylvania – offer high-quality care at costs below average. So the commission can help encourage the adoption of these common-sense best practices by doctors and medical professionals throughout the system – everything from reducing hospital infection rates to encouraging better coordination between teams of doctors.

Reducing the waste and inefficiency in Medicare and Medicaid will pay for most of this plan. Now, much of the rest would be paid for with revenues from the very same drug and insurance companies that stand to benefit from tens of millions of new customers. And this reform will charge insurance companies a fee for their most expensive policies, which will encourage them to provide greater value for the money – an idea which has the support of Democratic and Republican experts. And according to these same experts, this modest change could help hold down the cost of health care for all of us in the long run.

Now, finally, many in this chamber – particularly on the Republican side of the aisle – have long insisted that reforming our medical malpractice laws can help bring down the cost of health care. Now – there you go. There you go. Now, I don't believe malpractice reform is a silver bullet, but I've talked to enough doctors to know that defensive medicine may be contributing to unnecessary costs. So I'm proposing that we move forward on a range of ideas about how to put patient safety first and let doctors focus on practicing medicine. I know that the Bush administration considered authorizing demonstration projects in individual states to test these ideas. I think it's a good idea, and I'm directing my Secretary of Health and Human Services to move forward on this initiative today.

Now, add it all up, and the plan I'm proposing will cost around $900 billion over 10 years – less than we have spent on the Iraq and Afghanistan wars, and less than the tax cuts for the wealthiest few Americans that Congress passed at the beginning of the previous administration. Now, most of these costs will be paid for with money already being spent – but spent badly – in the existing health care system. The plan will not add to our deficit. The middle class will realize greater security, not higher taxes. And if we are able to slow the growth of health care costs by just one-tenth of 1 percent each year – one-tenth of 1 percent – it will actually reduce the deficit by $4 trillion over the long term.

Now, this is the plan I'm proposing. It's a plan that incorporates ideas from many of the people in this room tonight – Democrats and Republicans. And I will continue to seek common ground in the weeks ahead. If you come to me with a serious set of proposals, I will be there to listen. My door is always open.

But know this: I will not waste time with those who have made the calculation that it's better politics to kill this plan than to improve it. I won't stand by while the special interests use the same old tactics to keep things exactly the way they are. If you misrepresent what's in this plan, we will call you out. And I will not – and I will not accept the status quo as a solution. Not this time. Not now.

Everyone in this room knows what will happen if we do nothing. Our deficit will grow. More families will go bankrupt. More businesses will close. More Americans will lose their coverage when they are sick and need it the most. And more will die as a result. We know these things to be true.

That is why we cannot fail. Because there are too many Americans counting on us to succeed – the ones who suffer silently, and the ones who shared their stories with us at town halls, in e-mails, and in letters.

I received one of those letters a few days ago. It was from our beloved friend and colleague, Ted Kennedy. He had written it back in May, shortly after he was told that his illness was terminal. He asked that it be delivered upon his death.

In it, he spoke about what a happy time his last months were, thanks to the love and support of family and friends, his wife, Vicki, his amazing children, who are all here tonight. And he expressed confidence that this would be the year that health care reform – "that great unfinished business of our society," he called it – would finally pass. He repeated the truth that health care is decisive for our future prosperity, but he also reminded me that "it concerns more than material things." "What we face," he wrote, "is above all a moral issue; at stake are not just the details of policy, but fundamental principles of social justice and the character of our country."

I've thought about that phrase quite a bit in recent days – the character of our country. One of the unique and wonderful things about America has always been our self-reliance, our rugged individualism, our fierce defense of freedom and our healthy skepticism of government. And figuring out the appropriate size and role of government has always been a source of rigorous and, yes, sometimes angry debate. That's our history.

For some of Ted Kennedy's critics, his brand of liberalism represented an affront to American liberty. In their minds, his passion for universal health care was nothing more than a passion for big government.

But those of us who knew Teddy and worked with him here – people of both parties – know that what drove him was something more. His friend Orrin Hatch – he knows that. They worked together to provide children with health insurance. His friend John McCain knows that. They worked together on a Patient's Bill of Rights. His friend Chuck Grassley knows that. They worked together to provide health care to children with disabilities.

On issues like these, Ted Kennedy's passion was born not of some rigid ideology, but of his own experience. It was the experience of having two children stricken with cancer. He never forgot the sheer terror and helplessness that any parent feels when a child is badly sick. And he was able to imagine what it must be like for those without insurance, what it would be like to have to say to a wife or a child or an aging parent, there is something that could make you better, but I just can't afford it.

That large-heartedness – that concern and regard for the plight of others – is not a partisan feeling. It's not a Republican or a Democratic feeling. It, too, is part of the American character – our ability to stand in other people's shoes; a recognition that we are all in this together, and when fortune turns against one of us, others are there to lend a helping hand; a belief that in this country, hard work and responsibility should be rewarded by some measure of security and fair play; and an acknowledgment that sometimes government has to step in to help deliver on that promise.

This has always been the history of our progress. In 1935, when over half of our seniors could not support themselves and millions had seen their savings wiped away, there were those who argued that Social Security would lead to socialism, but the men and women of Congress stood fast, and we are all the better for it. In 1965, when some argued that Medicare represented a government takeover of health care, members of Congress – Democrats and Republicans – did not back down. They joined together so that all of us could enter our golden years with some basic peace of mind.

You see, our predecessors understood that government could not, and should not, solve every problem. They understood that there are instances when the gains in security from government action are not worth the added constraints on our freedom. But they also understood that the danger of too much government is matched by the perils of too little; that without the leavening hand of wise policy, markets can crash, monopolies can stifle competition, the vulnerable can be exploited. And they knew that when any government measure, no matter how carefully crafted or beneficial, is subject to scorn; when any efforts to help people in need are attacked as un-American; when facts and reason are thrown overboard and only timidity passes for wisdom, and we can no longer even engage in a civil conversation with each other over the things that truly matter – that at that point we don't merely lose our capacity to solve big challenges. We lose something essential about ourselves.

That was true then. It remains true today. I understand how difficult this health care debate has been. I know that many in this country are deeply skeptical that government is looking out for them. I understand that the politically safe move would be to kick the can further down the road – to defer reform one more year, or one more election, or one more term.

But that is not what the moment calls for. That's not what we came here to do. We did not come to fear the future. We came here to shape it. I still believe we can act even when it's hard. I still believe – I still believe that we can act when it's hard. I still believe we can replace acrimony with civility, and gridlock with progress. I still believe we can do great things, and that here and now we will meet history's test.

Because that's who we are. That is our calling. That is our character. Thank you, God bless you, and may God bless the United States of America.

❧ 5 ❧

2010 STATE OF THE UNION ADDRESS
JANUARY 27, 2010

Madam Speaker, Vice President Biden, Members of Congress, distinguished guests, and fellow Americans: Our Constitution declares that from time to time, the President shall give to Congress information about the state of our Union. For 220 years, our leaders have fulfilled this duty. They've done so during periods of prosperity and tranquility, and they've done so in the midst of war and depression, at moments of great strife and great struggle.

It's tempting to look back on these moments and assume that our progress was inevitable, that America was always destined to succeed. But when the Union was turned back at Bull Run and the Allies first landed at Omaha Beach, victory was very much in doubt. When the market crashed on Black Tuesday and marchers were beaten on Bloody Sunday, the future was anything but certain. These were the times that tested the courage of our convictions and the strength of our Union. And despite all our divisions and disagreements, our hesitations and our fears, America prevailed because we chose to move forward as one Nation, as one people. Again, we are tested. And again, we must answer history's call.

One year ago, I took office amid two wars, an economy rocked by a severe recession, a financial system on the verge of collapse, and a Government deeply in debt. Experts from across the political spectrum warned that if we did not act, we might face a second depression. So we acted, immediately and aggressively. And 1 year later, the worst of the storm has passed.

But the devastation remains. One in 10 Americans still cannot find work. Many businesses have shuttered. Home values have declined. Small towns and rural communities have been hit especially hard. And for those who'd already known poverty, life's become that much harder.

This recession has also compounded the burdens that America's families have been dealing with for decades: the burden of working harder and longer for less, of being unable to save enough to retire or help kids with college.

So I know the anxieties that are out there right now. They're not new. These struggles are the reason I ran for President. These struggles are what I've witnessed for years, in places like Elkhart, Indiana; Galesburg, Illinois. I hear about them in the letters that I read each night. The toughest to read are those written by children asking why they have to move from their home, asking when their mom or dad will be able to go back to work.

For these Americans and so many others, change has not come fast enough. Some are frustrated, some are angry. They don't understand why it seems like bad behavior on Wall Street is rewarded, but hard work on Main Street isn't, or why Washington has been unable or unwilling to solve any of our problems. They're tired of the partisanship and the shouting and the pettiness. They know we can't afford it. Not now.

So we face big and difficult challenges. And what the American people hope, what they deserve, is for all of us, Democrats and Republicans, to work through our differences, to overcome the numbing weight of our politics. For while the people who sent us here have different backgrounds, different stories, different beliefs, the anxieties they face are the same. The aspirations they hold are shared: a job that pays the bills, a chance to get ahead, most of all, the ability to give their children a better life.

And you know what else they share? They share a stubborn resilience in the face of adversity. After one of the most difficult years in our history, they remain busy building cars and teaching kids, starting businesses and going back to school. They're coaching Little League and helping their neighbors. One woman wrote to me and said, "We are strained but hopeful, struggling but encouraged."

It's because of this spirit, this great decency and great strength, that I have never been more hopeful about America's future than I am tonight. Despite our hardships, our Union is strong. We do not give up. We do not quit. We do not allow fear or division to break our spirit. In this new decade, it's time the American people get a Government that matches their decency, that embodies their strength. And tonight I'd like to talk about how together we can deliver on that promise.

It begins with our economy. Our most urgent task upon taking office was to shore up the same banks that helped cause this crisis. It was not easy to do. And if there's one thing that has unified Democrats and Republicans and everybody in between, it's that we all hated the bank bailout. I hated it. I hated it; you hated it. It was about as popular as a root canal. [Laughter]

But when I ran for President, I promised I wouldn't just do what was popular; I would do what was necessary. And if we had allowed the meltdown of the financial system, unemployment might be double what it is today. More businesses would certainly have closed. More homes would have surely been lost.

So I supported the last administration's efforts to create the financial rescue program. And when we took that program over, we made it more transparent and more accountable. And as a result, the markets are now stabilized, and we've recovered most of the money we spent on the banks–most but not all.

To recover the rest, I've proposed a fee on the biggest banks. Now, I know Wall Street isn't keen on this idea. But if these firms can afford to hand out big bonuses again, they can afford a modest fee to pay back the taxpayers who rescued them in their time of need.

Now, as we stabilized the financial system, we also took steps to get our economy growing again, save as many jobs as possible, and help Americans who had become unemployed. That's why we extended or increased unemployment benefits for more than 18 million Americans, made health insurance 65 percent cheaper for families who get their coverage through COBRA, and passed 25 different tax cuts.

Now, let me repeat: We cut taxes. We cut taxes for 95 percent of working families. We cut taxes for small businesses. We cut taxes for first-time home buyers. We cut taxes for parents trying to care for their children. We cut taxes for 8 million Americans paying for college. [Applause] I thought I'd get some applause on that one. [Laughter]

As a result, millions of Americans had more to spend on gas and food and other necessities, all of which helped businesses keep more workers. And we haven't raised income taxes by a single dime on a single person- -not a single dime.

Now, because of the steps we took, there are about 2 million Americans working right now who would otherwise be unemployed. Two hundred thousand work in construction and clean energy. Three hundred thousand are teachers and other education workers. Tens of thousands are cops, firefighters, correctional officers, first-responders. And we're on track to add another 1 1/2 million jobs to this total by the end of the year.

The plan that has made all of this possible, from the tax cuts to the jobs, is the Recovery Act. That's right, the Recovery Act, also known as the stimulus bill. Economists on the left and the right say this bill has helped save jobs and avert disaster. But you don't have to take their word for it. Talk to the small business in Phoenix that will triple its workforce because of the Recovery Act. Talk to the window manufacturer in Philadelphia who said he used to be skeptical about the Recovery Act, until he had to add two more work shifts just because of the business it created. Talk to the single teacher raising two kids who was told by her principal in the last week of school that because of the Recovery Act, she wouldn't be laid off after all.

There are stories like this all across America. And after 2 years of recession, the economy is growing again. Retirement funds have started to gain back some of their value. Businesses are beginning to invest again, and slowly some are starting to hire again.

But I realize that for every success story, there are other stories, of men and women who wake up with the anguish of not knowing where their next paycheck will come from, who send out resumes week after week and hear nothing in response. That is why jobs must be our number-one focus in 2010, and that's why I'm calling for a new jobs bill tonight.

Now, the true engine of job creation in this country will always be America's businesses. [Applause] I agree, absolutely. But Government can create the conditions necessary for businesses to expand and hire more workers. We should start where most new jobs do, in small businesses, companies that begin when an entrepreneur takes a chance on a dream or a worker decides it's time she became her own boss. Through sheer grit and determination, these companies have weathered the recession, and they're ready to grow. But when you talk to small- business owners in places like Allentown, Pennsylvania, or Elyria, Ohio, you find out that even though banks on Wall Street are lending again, they're mostly lending to bigger companies. Financing remains difficult for small-business owners across the country, even those that are making a profit.

So tonight I'm proposing that we take $30 billion of the money Wall Street banks have repaid and use it to help community banks give small businesses the credit they need to stay afloat. I'm also proposing a new small business tax credit, one that will go to over 1 million small businesses who hire new workers or raise wages. While we're at it, let's also eliminate all capital gains taxes on small-business investment and provide a tax incentive for all large businesses and all small businesses to invest in new plants and equipment.

Next, we can put Americans to work today building the infrastructure of tomorrow. From the first railroads to the Interstate Highway System, our Nation has always been built to compete. There's no reason Europe or China should have the fastest trains or the new factories that manufacture clean energy products. Tomorrow I'll visit Tampa, Florida, where workers will soon break ground on a new high-speed railroad funded by the Recovery Act. There are projects like that all across this country that will create jobs and help move our Nation's goods, services, and information.

We should put more Americans to work building clean energy facilities and give rebates to Americans who make their homes more energy efficient, which supports clean energy jobs. And to encourage these and other businesses to stay within our borders, it is time to finally slash the tax breaks for companies that ship our jobs overseas and give those tax breaks to companies that create jobs right here in the United States of America.

Now, the House has passed a jobs bill that includes some of these steps. As the first order of business this year, I urge the Senate to do the same, and I know they will. They will. People are out of work. They're hurting. They need our help. And I want a jobs bill on my desk without delay.

But the truth is, these steps won't make up for the 7 million jobs that we've lost over the last 2 years. The only way to move to full employment is to lay a new foundation for long-term economic growth and finally address the problems that America's families have confronted for years.

We can't afford another so-called economic expansion like the one from the last decade, what some call the "lost decade," where jobs grew more slowly than during any prior expansion, where the income of the average American household declined while the cost of health care and tuition reached record highs, where prosperity was built on a housing bubble and financial speculation.

From the day I took office, I've been told that addressing our larger challenges is too ambitious; such an effort would be too contentious. I've been told that our political system is too gridlocked and that we should just put things on hold for a while. For those who make these claims, I have one simple question: How long should we wait? How long should America put its future on hold?

You see, Washington has been telling us to wait for decades, even as the problems have grown worse. Meanwhile, China's not waiting to revamp its economy. Germany's not waiting. India's not waiting. These nations are–they're not standing still. These nations aren't playing for second place. They're putting more emphasis on math and science. They're rebuilding their infrastructure. They're making serious investments in clean energy because they want those jobs. Well, I do not accept second place for the United States of America. As hard as it may be, as uncomfortable and contentious as the debates may become, it's time to get serious about fixing the problems that are hampering our growth.

Now, one place to start is serious financial reform. Look, I am not interested in punishing banks. I'm interested in protecting our economy. A strong, healthy financial market makes it possible for businesses to access credit and create new jobs. It channels the savings of families into investments that raise incomes. But that can only happen if we guard against the same recklessness that nearly brought down our entire economy.

We need to make sure consumers and middle class families have the information they need to make financial decisions. We can't allow financial institutions, including those that take your deposits, to take risks that threaten the whole economy.

Now, the House has already passed financial reform with many of these changes, and the lobbyists are trying to kill it. But we cannot let them win this fight. And if the bill that ends up on my desk does not meet the test of real reform, I will send it back until we get it right. We've got to get it right.

Next, we need to encourage American innovation. Last year, we made the largest investment in basic research funding in history, an investment that could lead to the world's cheapest solar cells or treatment that kills cancer cells, but leaves healthy ones untouched. And no area is more ripe for such innovation than energy. You can see the results of last year's investments in clean energy in the North Carolina company that will create 1,200 jobs nationwide helping to make advanced batteries or in the California business that will put a thousand people to work making solar panels.

But to create more of these clean energy jobs, we need more production, more efficiency, more incentives. And that means building a new generation of safe, clean nuclear power plants in this country. It means making tough decisions about opening new offshore areas for oil and gas development. It means continued investment in advanced biofuels and clean coal technologies. And yes, it means passing a comprehensive energy and climate bill with incentives that will finally make clean energy the profitable kind of energy in America. Now, I am grateful to the House for passing such a bill last year. And this year, I'm eager to help advance the bipartisan effort in the Senate.

I know there have been questions about whether we can afford such changes in a tough economy. I know that there are those who disagree with the overwhelming scientific evidence on climate change. But here's the thing: Even if you doubt the evidence, providing incentives for energy efficiency and clean energy are the right thing to do for our future, because the nation that leads the clean energy economy will be the nation that leads the global economy. And America must be that nation.

Third, we need to export more of our goods, because the more products we make and sell to other countries, the more jobs we support right here in America. So tonight we set a new goal: We will double our exports over the next 5 years, an increase that will support 2 million jobs in America. To help meet this goal, we're launching a National Export Initiative that will help farmers and small businesses increase their exports and reform export controls consistent with national security.

We have to seek new markets aggressively, just as our competitors are. If America sits on the sidelines while other nations sign trade deals, we will lose the chance to create jobs on our shores. But realizing those benefits also means enforcing those agreements so our trading partners play by the rules. And that's why we'll continue to shape a Doha trade agreement that opens global markets and why we will strengthen our trade relations in Asia and with key partners like South Korea and Panama and Colombia.

Fourth, we need to invest in the skills and education of our people. Now, this year, we've broken through the stalemate between left and right by launching a national competition to improve our schools. And the idea here is simple: Instead of rewarding failure, we only reward success. Instead of funding the status quo, we only invest in reform, reform that raises student achievement, inspires students to excel in math and science, and turns around failing schools that steal the future of too many young Americans, from rural communities to the inner city. In the 21st century, the best antipoverty program around is a world-class education. And in this country, the success of our children cannot depend more on where they live than on their potential. When we renew the Elementary and Secondary Education Act, we will work with Congress to expand these reforms to all 50 States.

Still, in this economy, a high school diploma no longer guarantees a good job. That's why I urge the Senate to follow the House and pass a bill that will revitalize our community colleges, which are a career pathway to the children of so many working families.

To make college more affordable, this bill will finally end the unwarranted taxpayer subsidies that go to banks for student loans. Instead, let's take that money and give families a $10,000 tax credit for 4 years of college and increase Pell grants. And let's tell another 1 million students that when they graduate, they will be required to pay only 10 percent of their income on student loans and all of their debt will be forgiven after 20 years and forgiven after 10 years if they choose a career in public service, because in the United States of America, no one should go broke because they chose to go to college. And by the way, it's time for colleges and universities to get serious about cutting their own costs, because they too have a responsibility to help solve this problem.

Now, the price of college tuition is just one of the burdens facing the middle class. That's why last year, I asked Vice President Biden to chair a task force on middle class families. That's why we're nearly doubling the childcare tax credit and making it easier to save for retirement by giving access to every worker a retirement account and expanding the tax credit for those who start a nest egg. That's why we're working to lift the value of a family's single largest investment, their home. The steps we took last year to shore up the housing market have allowed millions of Americans to take out new loans and save an average of $1,500 on mortgage payments. This year, we will step up refinancing so that homeowners can move into more affordable mortgages.

And it is precisely to relieve the burden on middle class families that we still need health insurance reform. Yes, we do.

Now, let's clear a few things up. I didn't choose to tackle this issue to get some legislative victory under my belt. And by now it should be fairly obvious that I didn't take on health care because it was good politics. [Laughter] I took on health care because of the stories I've heard from Americans with preexisting conditions whose lives depend on getting coverage, patients who've been denied coverage, families, even those with insurance, who are just one illness away from financial ruin.

After nearly a century of trying–Democratic administrations, Republican administrations–we are closer than ever to bringing more security to the lives of so many Americans. The approach we've taken would protect every American from the worst practices of the insurance industry. It would give small businesses and uninsured Americans a chance to choose an affordable health care plan in a competitive market. It would require every insurance plan to cover preventive care.

And by the way, I want to acknowledge our First Lady, Michelle Obama, who this year is creating a national movement to tackle the epidemic of childhood obesity and make kids healthier. [Applause] Thank you, honey. She gets embarrassed. [Laughter]

Our approach would preserve the right of Americans who have insurance to keep their doctor and their plan. It would reduce costs and premiums for millions of families and businesses. And according to the Congressional Budget Office, the independent organization that both parties have cited as the official scorekeeper for Congress, our approach would bring down the deficit by as much as $1 trillion over the next two decades.

Still, this is a complex issue, and the longer it was debated, the more skeptical people became. I take my share of the blame for not explaining it more clearly to the American people. And I know that with all the lobbying and horse-trading, the process left most Americans wondering, "What's in it for me?"

But I also know this problem is not going away. By the time I'm finished speaking tonight, more Americans will have lost their health insurance. Millions will lose it this year. Our deficit will grow. Premiums will go up. Patients will be denied the care they need. Small- business owners will continue to drop coverage altogether. I will not walk away from these Americans, and neither should the people in this Chamber.

So as temperatures cool, I want everyone to take another look at the plan we've proposed. There's a reason why many doctors, nurses, and health care experts who know our system best consider this approach a vast improvement over the status quo. But if anyone from either party has a better approach that will bring down premiums, bring down the deficit, cover the uninsured, strengthen Medicare for seniors, and stop insurance company abuses, let me know. Let me know. Let me know. I'm eager to see it.

Here's what I ask Congress, though: Don't walk away from reform. Not now. Not when we are so close. Let us find a way to come together and finish the job for the American people. Let's get it done. Let's get it done.

Now, even as health care reform would reduce our deficit, it's not enough to dig us out of a massive fiscal hole in which we find ourselves. It's a challenge that makes all others that much harder to solve and one that's been subject to a lot of political posturing. So let me start the discussion of Government spending by setting the record straight.

At the beginning of the last decade, the year 2000, America had a budget surplus of over $200 billion. By the time I took office, we had a 1-year deficit of over $1 trillion and projected deficits of $8 trillion over the next decade. Most of this was the result of not paying for two wars, two tax cuts, and an expensive prescription drug program. On top of that, the effects of the recession put a $3 trillion hole in our budget. All this was before I walked in the door. [Laughter]

Now–[applause]–just stating the facts. Now, if we had taken office in ordinary times, I would have liked nothing more than to start bringing down the deficit. But we took office amid a crisis. And our efforts to prevent a second depression have added another $1 trillion to our national debt. That too is a fact.

I'm absolutely convinced that was the right thing to do. But families across the country are tightening their belts and making tough decisions. The Federal Government should do the same. So tonight I'm proposing specific steps to pay for the trillion dollars that it took to rescue the economy last year.

Starting in 2011, we are prepared to freeze Government spending for 3 years. Spending related to our national security, Medicare, Medicaid, and Social Security will not be affected. But all other discretionary Government programs will. Like any cash-strapped family, we will work within a budget to invest in what we need and sacrifice what we don't. And if I have to enforce this discipline by veto, I will.

We will continue to go through the budget, line by line, page by page, to eliminate programs that we can't afford and don't work. We've already identified $20 billion in savings for next year. To help working families, we'll extend our middle class tax cuts. But at a time of record deficits, we will not continue tax cuts for oil companies, for investment fund managers, and for those making over $250,000 a year. We just can't afford it.

Now, even after paying for what we spent on my watch, we'll still face the massive deficit we had when I took office. More importantly, the cost of Medicare, Medicaid, and Social Security will continue to skyrocket. That's why I've called for a bipartisan fiscal commission, modeled on a proposal by Republican Judd Gregg and Democrat Kent Conrad. This can't be one of those Washington gimmicks that lets us pretend we solve a problem. The commission will have to provide a specific set of solutions by a certain deadline.

Now, yesterday the Senate blocked a bill that would have created this commission, so I'll issue an Executive order that will allow us to go forward, because I refuse to pass this problem on to another generation of Americans. And when the vote comes tomorrow, the Senate should restore the pay-as-you-go law that was a big reason for why we had record surpluses in the 1990s.

Now, I know that some in my own party will argue that we can't address the deficit or freeze Government spending when so many are still hurting. And I agree, which is why this freeze won't take effect until next year, when the economy is stronger. That's how budgeting works. [Laughter] But understand, if we don't take meaningful steps to rein in our debt, it could damage our markets, increase the cost of borrowing, and jeopardize our recovery, all of which would have an even worse effect on our job growth and family incomes.

From some on the right, I expect we'll hear a different argument, that if we just make fewer investments in our people, extend tax cuts, including those for the wealthier Americans, eliminate more regulations, maintain the status quo on health care, our deficits will go away. The problem is, that's what we did for 8 years. That's what helped us into this crisis. It's what helped lead to these deficits. We can't do it again.

Rather than fight the same tired battles that have dominated Washington for decades, it's time to try something new. Let's invest in our people without leaving them a mountain of debt. Let's meet our responsibility to the citizens who sent us here. Let's try common sense–[Laughter]–a novel concept.

Now, to do that, we have to recognize that we face more than a deficit of dollars right now. We face a deficit of trust, deep and corrosive doubts about how Washington works that have been growing for years. To close that credibility gap, we have to take action on both ends of Pennsylvania Avenue to end the outsized influence of lobbyists, to do our work openly, to give our people the Government they deserve.

Now, that's what I came to Washington to do. That's why, for the first time in history, my administration posts on–our White House visitors online. That's why we've excluded lobbyists from policymaking jobs or seats on Federal boards and commissions. But we can't stop there. It's time to require lobbyists to disclose each contact they make on behalf of a client, with my administration or with Congress. It's time to put strict limits on the contributions that lobbyists give to candidates for Federal office.

With all due deference to separation of powers, last week, the Supreme Court reversed a century of law that I believe will open the floodgates for special interests, including foreign corporations, to spend without limit in our elections. I don't think American elections should be bankrolled by America's most powerful interests, or worse, by foreign entities. They should be decided by the American people. And I'd urge Democrats and Republicans to pass a bill that helps correct some of these problems.

I'm also calling on Congress to continue down the path of earmark reform, Democrats and Republicans–Democrats and Republicans. Look, you've trimmed some of this spending, you've embraced some meaningful change, but restoring the public trust demands more. For example, some Members of Congress post some earmark requests online. Tonight I'm calling on Congress to publish all earmark requests on a single web site before there's a vote so that the American people can see how their money is being spent.

Of course, none of these reforms will even happen if we don't also reform how we work with one another. Now, I'm not naive. I never thought that the mere fact of my election would usher in peace and harmony and–[Laughter]–some postpartisan era. I knew that both parties have fed divisions that are deeply entrenched. And on some issues, there are simply philosophical differences that will always cause us to part ways. These disagreements, about the role of government in our lives, about our national priorities and our national security, they've been taking place for over 200 years. They're the very essence of our democracy.

But what frustrates the American people is a Washington where every day is election day. We can't wage a perpetual campaign where the only goal is to see who can get the most embarrassing headlines about the other side, a belief that if you lose, I win. Neither party should delay or obstruct every single bill just because they can. The confirmation of– I'm speaking to both parties now–the confirmation of well-qualified public servants shouldn't be held hostage to the pet projects or grudges of a few individual Senators.

Washington may think that saying anything about the other side, no matter how false, no matter how malicious, is just part of the game. But it's precisely such politics that has stopped either party from helping the American people. Worse yet, it's sowing further division among our citizens, further distrust in our Government. So no, I will not give up on trying to change the tone of our politics. I know it's an election year. And after last week, it's clear that campaign fever has come even earlier than usual. But we still need to govern.

To Democrats, I would remind you that we still have the largest majority in decades and the people expect us to solve problems, not run for the hills. And if the Republican leadership is going to insist that 60 votes in the Senate are required to do any business at all in this town–a supermajority–then the responsibility to govern is now yours as well. Just saying no to everything may be good short-term politics, but it's not leadership. We were sent here to serve our citizens, not our ambitions. So let's show the American people that we can do it together.

This week, I'll be addressing a meeting of the House Republicans. I'd like to begin monthly meetings with both Democratic and Republican leadership. I know you can't wait. [Laughter]

Now, throughout our history, no issue has united this country more than our security. Sadly, some of the unity we felt after 9/11 has dissipated. And we can argue all we want about who's to blame for this, but I'm not interested in relitigating the past. I know that all of us love this country. All of us are committed to its defense. So let's put aside the schoolyard taunts about who's tough. Let's reject the false choice between protecting our people and upholding our values. Let's leave behind the fear and division and do what it takes to defend our Nation and forge a more hopeful future for America and for the world.

That's the work we began last year. Since the day I took office, we've renewed our focus on the terrorists who threaten our Nation. We've made substantial investments in our homeland security and disrupted plots that threatened to take American lives. We are filling unacceptable gaps revealed by the failed Christmas attack, with better airline security and swifter action on our intelligence. We've prohibited torture and strengthened partnerships from the Pacific to South Asia to the Arabian Peninsula. And in the last year, hundreds of Al Qaida's fighters and affiliates, including many senior leaders, have been captured or killed, far more than in 2008.

And in Afghanistan, we're increasing our troops and training Afghan security forces so they can begin to take the lead in July of 2011 and our troops can begin to come home. We will reward good governance, work to reduce corruption, and support the rights of all Afghans, men and women alike. We're joined by allies and partners who have increased their own commitments and who will come together tomorrow in London to reaffirm our common purpose. There will be difficult days ahead, but I am absolutely confident we will succeed.

As we take the fight to Al Qaida, we are responsibly leaving Iraq to its people. As a candidate, I promised that I would end this war, and that is what I am doing as President. We will have all of our combat troops out of Iraq by the end of this August. We will support the Iraqi Government as they hold elections, and we will continue to partner with the Iraqi people to promote regional peace and prosperity. But make no mistake: This war is ending, and all of our troops are coming home.

Tonight all of our men and women in uniform, in Iraq, in Afghanistan, and around the world, they have to know that we–that they have our respect, our gratitude, our full support. And just as they must have the resources they need in war, we all have a responsibility to support them when they come home. That's why we made the largest increase in investments for veterans in decades last year. That's why we're building a 21st-century VA. And that's why Michelle has joined with Jill Biden to forge a national commitment to support military families.

Now, even as we prosecute two wars, we're also confronting perhaps the greatest danger to the American people, the threat of nuclear weapons. I've embraced the vision of John F. Kennedy and Ronald Reagan through a strategy that reverses the spread of these weapons and seeks a world without them. To reduce our stockpiles and launchers, while ensuring our deterrent, the United States and Russia are completing negotiations on the farthest reaching arms control treaty in nearly two decades. And at April's Nuclear Security Summit, we will bring 44 nations together here in Washington, DC, behind a clear goal: securing all vulnerable nuclear materials around the world in 4 years so that they never fall into the hands of terrorists.

Now, these diplomatic efforts have also strengthened our hand in dealing with those nations that insist on violating international agreements in pursuit of nuclear weapons. That's why North Korea now faces increased isolation and stronger sanctions, sanctions that are being vigorously enforced. That's why the international community is more united and the Islamic Republic of Iran is more isolated. And as Iran's leaders continue to ignore their obligations, there should be no doubt: They too will face growing consequences. That is a promise.

That's the leadership we are providing: engagement that advances the common security and prosperity of all people. We're working through the G-20 to sustain a lasting global recovery. We're working with Muslim communities around the world to promote science and education and innovation. We have gone from a bystander to a leader in the fight against climate change. We're helping developing countries to feed themselves and continuing the fight against HIV/AIDS. And we are launching a new initiative that will give us the capacity to respond faster and more effectively to bioterrorism or an infectious disease, a plan that will counter threats at home and strengthen public health abroad.

As we have for over 60 years, America takes these actions because our destiny is connected to those beyond our shores. But we also do it because it is right. That's why, as we meet here tonight, over 10,000 Americans are working with many nations to help the people of Haiti recover and rebuild. That's why we stand with the girl who yearns to go to school in Afghanistan, why we support the human rights of the women marching through the streets of Iran, why we advocate for the young man denied a job by corruption in Guinea. For America must always stand on the side of freedom and human dignity–always.

Abroad, America's greatest source of strength has always been our ideals. The same is true at home. We find unity in our incredible diversity, drawing on the promise enshrined in our Constitution: The notion that we're all created equal; that no matter who you are or what you look like, if you abide by the law, you should be protected by it; if you adhere to our common values, you should be treated no different than anyone else.

We must continually renew this promise. My administration has a Division that is once again prosecuting violations and employment discrimination. We finally strengthened our laws to protect against crimes driven by hate. This year, I will work with Congress and our military to finally repeal the law that denies gay Americans the right to serve the country they love because of who they are. It's the right thing to do.

We're going to crack down on violations of equal pay laws so that women get equal pay for an equal day's work. And we should continue the work of fixing our broken immigration system, to secure our borders and enforce our laws and ensure that everyone who plays by the rules can contribute to our economy and enrich our Nation.

In the end, it's our ideals, our values that built America, values that allowed us to forge a nation made up of immigrants from every corner of the globe, values that drive our citizens still. Every day, Americans meet their responsibilities to their families and their employers. Time and again, they lend a hand to their neighbors and give back to their country. They take pride in their labor and are generous in spirit. These aren't Republican values or Democratic values that they're living by, business values or labor values, they're American values.

Unfortunately, too many of our citizens have lost faith that our biggest institutions–our corporations, our media, and, yes, our Government–still reflect these same values. Each of these institutions are full of honorable men and women doing important work that helps our country prosper. But each time a CEO rewards himself for failure or a banker puts the rest of us at risk for his own selfish gain, people's doubts grow. Each time lobbyists game the system or politicians tear each other down instead of lifting this country up, we lose faith. The more that TV pundits reduce serious debates to silly arguments, big issues into sound bites, our citizens turn away. No wonder there's so much cynicism out there. No wonder there's so much disappointment.

I campaigned on the promise of change. Change we can believe in, the slogan went. And right now I know there are many Americans who aren't sure if they still believe we can change or that I can deliver it.

But remember this: I never suggested that change would be easy or that I could do it alone. Democracy in a nation of 300 million people can be noisy and messy and complicated. And when you try to do big things and make big changes, it stirs passions and controversy. That's just how it is.

Those of us in public office can respond to this reality by playing it safe and avoid telling hard truths and pointing fingers. We can do what's necessary to keep our poll numbers high and get through the next election, instead of doing what's best for the next generation.

But I also know this: If people had made that decision 50 years ago or 100 years ago or 200 years ago, we wouldn't be here tonight. The only reason we are here is because generations of Americans were unafraid to do what was hard, to do what was needed even when success was uncertain, to do what it took to keep the dream of this Nation alive for their children and their grandchildren.

Now, our administration has had some political setbacks this year, and some of them were deserved. But I wake up every day knowing that they are nothing compared to the setbacks that families all across this country have faced this year. And what keeps me going, what keeps me fighting, is that despite all these setbacks, that spirit of determination and optimism, that fundamental decency that has always been at the core of the American people, that lives on.

It lives on in the struggling small-business owner who wrote to me of his company, "None of us," he said, ". . . are willing to consider, even slightly, that we might fail." It lives on in the woman who said that even though she and her neighbors have felt the pain of recession, "We are strong. We are resilient. We are American." It lives on in the 8-year-old boy in Louisiana who just sent me his allowance and asked if I would give it to the people of Haiti. And it lives on in all the Americans who've dropped everything to go someplace they've never been and pull people they've never known from the rubble, prompting chants of "U.S.A.! U.S.A.! U.S.A.!" when another life was saved.

The spirit that has sustained this Nation for more than two centuries lives on in you, its people. We have finished a difficult year. We have come through a difficult decade. But a new year has come. A new decade stretches before us. We don't quit. I don't quit. Let's seize this moment to start anew, to carry the dream forward, and to strengthen our Union once more.

Thank you. God bless you, and God bless the United States of America.

6

SPEECH AT THE JOHN F. KENNEDY SPACE CENTER

APRIL 15, 2010

Thank you, everybody. Thank you. Thank you so much. Thank you, everybody. Please have a seat. Thank you.

I want to thank Senator Bill Nelson and NASA Administrator Charlie Bolden for their extraordinary leadership. I want to recognize Dr. Buzz Aldrin as well, who's in the house. Four decades ago, Buzz became a legend. But in the four decades since he's also been one of America's leading visionaries and authorities on human space flight.

Few people – present company excluded – can claim the expertise of Buzz and Bill and Charlie when it comes to space exploration. I have to say that few people are as singularly unimpressed by Air Force One as those three. Sure, it's comfortable, but it can't even reach low Earth orbit. And that obviously is in striking contrast to the Falcon 9 rocket we just saw on the launch pad, which will be tested for the very first time in the coming weeks.

A couple of other acknowledgments I want to make. We've got Congresswoman Sheila Jackson Lee from Texas visiting us, a big supporter of the space program. My director, Office of Science and Technology Policy – in other words my chief science advisor – John Holdren is here. And most of all I want to acknowledge your congresswoman Suzanne Kosmas, because every time I meet with her, including the flight down here, she reminds me of how important our NASA programs are and how important this facility is. And she is fighting for every single one of you and for her district and for the jobs in her district. And you should know that you've got a great champion in Congresswoman Kosmas. Please give her a big round of applause.

I also want to thank everybody for participating in today's conference. And gathered here are scientists, engineers, business leaders, public servants, and a few more astronauts as well. Last but not least, I want to thank the men and women of NASA for welcoming me to the Kennedy Space Center, and for your contributions not only to America, but to the world.

Here at the Kennedy Space Center we are surrounded by monuments and milestones of those contributions. It was from here that NASA launched the missions of Mercury and Gemini and Apollo. It was from here that Space Shuttle Discovery, piloted by Charlie Bolden, carried the Hubble Telescope into orbit, allowing us to plumb the deepest recesses of our galaxy. And I should point out, by the way, that in my private office just off the Oval, I've got the picture of Jupiter from the Hubble. So thank you, Charlie, for helping to decorate my office. It was from here that men and women, propelled by sheer nerve and talent, set about pushing the boundaries of humanity's reach.

That's the story of NASA. And it's a story that started a little more than half a century ago, far from the Space Coast, in a remote and desolate region of what is now called Kazakhstan. Because it was from there that the Soviet Union launched Sputnik, the first artificial satellite to orbit the Earth, which was little more than a few pieces of metal with a transmitter and a battery strapped to the top of a missile. But the world was stunned. Americans were dumbfounded. The Soviets, it was perceived, had taken the lead in a race for which we were not yet fully prepared.

But we caught up very quick. President Eisenhower signed legislation to create NASA and to invest in science and math education, from grade school to graduate school. In 1961, President Kennedy boldly declared before a joint session of Congress that the United States would send a man to the Moon and return him safely to the Earth within the decade. And as a nation, we set about meeting that goal, reaping rewards that have in the decades since touched every facet of our lives. NASA was at the forefront. Many gave their careers to the effort. And some have given far more.

In the years that have followed, the space race inspired a generation of scientists and innovators, including, I'm sure, many of you. It's contributed to immeasurable technological advances that have improved our health and well-being, from satellite navigation to water purification, from aerospace manufacturing to medical imaging. Although, I have to say, during a meeting right before I came out on stage somebody said, you know, it's more than just Tang – and I had to point out I actually really like Tang. (Laughter.) I thought that was very cool.

And leading the world to space helped America achieve new heights of prosperity here on Earth, while demonstrating the power of a free and open society to harness the ingenuity of its people.

And on a personal note, I have been part of that generation so inspired by the space program. 1961 was the year of my birth – the year that Kennedy made his announcement. And one of my earliest memories is sitting on my grandfather's shoulders, waving a flag as astronauts arrived in Hawaii. For me, the space program has always captured an essential part of what it means to be an American – reaching for new heights, stretching beyond what previously did not seem possible. And so, as President, I believe that space exploration is not a luxury, it's not an afterthought in America's quest for a brighter future – it is an essential part of that quest.

So today, I'd like to talk about the next chapter in this story. The challenges facing our space program are different, and our imperatives for this program are different, than in decades past. We're no longer racing against an adversary. We're no longer competing to achieve a singular goal like reaching the Moon. In fact, what was once a global competition has long since become a global collaboration. But while the measure of our achievements has changed a great deal over the past 50 years, what we do – or fail to do – in seeking new frontiers is no less consequential for our future in space and here on Earth.

So let me start by being extremely clear: I am 100 percent committed to the mission of NASA and its future. Because broadening our capabilities in space will continue to serve our society in ways that we can scarcely imagine. Because exploration will once more inspire wonder in a new generation – sparking passions and launching careers. And because, ultimately, if we fail to press forward in the pursuit of discovery, we are ceding our future and we are ceding that essential element of the American character.

I know there have been a number of questions raised about my administration's plan for space exploration, especially in this part of Florida where so many rely on NASA as a source of income as well as a source of pride and community. And these questions come at a time of transition, as the space shuttle nears its scheduled retirement after almost 30 years of service. And understandably, this adds to the worries of folks concerned not only about their own futures but about the future of the space program to which they've devoted their lives.

But I also know that underlying these concerns is a deeper worry, one that precedes not only this plan but this administration. It stems from the sense that people in Washington – driven sometimes less by vision than by politics – have for years neglected NASA's mission and undermined the work of the professionals who fulfill it. We've seen that in the NASA budget, which has risen and fallen with the political winds.

But we can also see it in other ways: in the reluctance of those who hold office to set clear, achievable objectives; to provide the resources to meet those objectives; and to justify not just these plans but the larger purpose of space exploration in the 21st century.

All that has to change. And with the strategy I'm outlining today, it will. We start by increasing NASA's budget by $6 billion over the next five years, even – I want people to understand the context of this. This is happening even as we have instituted a freeze on discretionary spending and sought to make cuts elsewhere in the budget.

So NASA, from the start, several months ago when I issued my budget, was one of the areas where we didn't just maintain a freeze but we actually increased funding by $6 billion. By doing that we will ramp up robotic exploration of the solar system, including a probe of the Sun's atmosphere; new scouting missions to Mars and other destinations; and an advanced telescope to follow Hubble, allowing us to peer deeper into the universe than ever before.

We will increase Earth-based observation to improve our understanding of our climate and our world – science that will garner tangible benefits, helping us to protect our environment for future generations.

And we will extend the life of the International Space Station likely by more than five years, while actually using it for its intended purpose: conducting advanced research that can help improve the daily lives of people here on Earth, as well as testing and improving upon our capabilities in space. This includes technologies like more efficient life support systems that will help reduce the cost of future missions. And in order to reach the space station, we will work with a growing array of private companies competing to make getting to space easier and more affordable.

Now, I recognize that some have said it is unfeasible or unwise to work with the private sector in this way. I disagree. The truth is, NASA has always relied on private industry to help design and build the vehicles that carry astronauts to space, from the Mercury capsule that carried John Glenn into orbit nearly 50 years ago, to the space shuttle Discovery currently orbiting overhead. By buying the services of space transportation – rather than the vehicles themselves – we can continue to ensure rigorous safety standards are met. But we will also accelerate the pace of innovations as companies – from young startups to established leaders – compete to design and build and launch new means of carrying people and materials out of our atmosphere.

In addition, as part of this effort, we will build on the good work already done on the Orion crew capsule. I've directed Charlie Bolden to immediately begin developing a rescue vehicle using this technology, so we are not forced to rely on foreign providers if it becomes necessary to quickly bring our people home from the International Space Station. And this Orion effort will be part of the technological foundation for advanced spacecraft to be used in future deep space missions. In fact, Orion will be readied for flight right here in this room.

Next, we will invest more than $3 billion to conduct research on an advanced "heavy lift rocket" – a vehicle to efficiently send into orbit the crew capsules, propulsion systems, and large quantities of supplies needed to reach deep space. In developing this new vehicle, we will not only look at revising or modifying older models; we want to look at new designs, new materials, new technologies that will transform not just where we can go but what we can do when we get there. And we will finalize a rocket design no later than 2015 and then begin to build it. And I want everybody to understand: That's at least two years earlier than previously planned – and that's conservative, given that the previous program was behind schedule and over budget.

At the same time, after decades of neglect, we will increase investment – right away – in other groundbreaking technologies that will allow astronauts to reach space sooner and more often, to travel farther and faster for less cost, and to live and work in space for longer periods of time more safely. That means tackling major scientific and technological challenges. How do we shield astronauts from radiation on longer missions? How do we harness resources on distant worlds? How do we supply spacecraft with energy needed for these far-reaching journeys? These are questions that we can answer and will answer. And these are the questions whose answers no doubt will reap untold benefits right here on Earth.

So the point is what we're looking for is not just to continue on the same path – we want to leap into the future; we want major breakthroughs; a transformative agenda for NASA.

Now, yes, pursuing this new strategy will require that we revise the old strategy. In part, this is because the old strategy – including the Constellation program – was not fulfilling its promise in many ways. That's not just my assessment; that's also the assessment of a panel of respected non-partisan experts charged with looking at these issues closely. Now, despite this, some have had harsh words for the decisions we've made, including some individuals who I've got enormous respect and admiration for.

But what I hope is, is that everybody will take a look at what we are planning, consider the details of what we've laid out, and see the merits as I've described them. The bottom line is nobody is more committed to manned space flight, to human exploration of space than I am. But we've got to do it in a smart way, and we can't just keep on doing the same old things that we've been doing and thinking that somehow is going to get us to where we want to go.

Some have said, for instance, that this plan gives up our leadership in space by failing to produce plans within NASA to reach low Earth orbit, instead of relying on companies and other countries. But we will actually reach space faster and more often under this new plan, in ways that will help us improve our technological capacity and lower our costs, which are both essential for the long-term sustainability of space flight. In fact, through our plan, we'll be sending many more astronauts to space over the next decade.

There are also those who criticized our decision to end parts of Constellation as one that will hinder space exploration below [sic] low Earth orbit. But it's precisely by investing in groundbreaking research and innovative companies that we will have the potential to rapidly transform our capabilities – even as we build on the important work already completed, through projects like Orion, for future missions. And unlike the previous program, we are setting a course with specific and achievable milestones.

Early in the next decade, a set of crewed flights will test and prove the systems required for exploration beyond low Earth orbit. And by 2025, we expect new space-craft designed for long journeys to allow us to begin the first-ever crewed missions beyond the Moon into deep space. So we'll start – we'll start by sending astronauts to an asteroid for the first time in history. By the mid-2030s, I believe we can send humans to orbit Mars and return them safely to Earth. And a landing on Mars will follow. And I expect to be around to see it.

But I want to repeat – I want to repeat this: Critical to deep space exploration will be the development of breakthrough propulsion systems and other advanced tech-nologies. So I'm challenging NASA to break through these barriers. And we'll give you the resources to break through these barriers. And I know you will, with inge-nuity and intensity, because that's what you've always done.

Now, I understand that some believe that we should attempt a return to the surface of the Moon first, as previously planned. But I just have to say pretty bluntly here: We've been there before. Buzz has been there. There's a lot more of space to explore, and a lot more to learn when we do. So I believe it's more important to ramp up our capabilities to reach – and operate at – a series of increasingly demanding targets, while advancing our technological capabilities with each step forward. And that's what this strategy does. And that's how we will ensure that our leadership in space is even stronger in this new century than it was in the last.

Finally, I want to say a few words about jobs. Suzanne pointed out to me that the last time I was here, I made a very clear promise that I would help in the transition into a new program to make sure that people who are already going through a tough time here in this region were helped. And despite some reports to the contrary, my plan will add more than 2,500 jobs along the Space Coast in the next two years compared to the plan under the previous administration. So I want to make that point.

We're going to modernize the Kennedy Space Center, creating jobs as we upgrade launch facilities. And there's potential for even more jobs as companies in Florida and across America compete to be part of a new space transportation industry. And some of those industry leaders are here today. This holds the promise of generating more than 10,000 jobs nationwide over the next few years. And many of these jobs will be created right here in Florida because this is an area primed to lead in this competition.

Now, it's true – there are Floridians who will see their work on the shuttle end as the program winds down. This is based on a decision that was made six years ago, not six months ago, but that doesn't make it any less painful for families and communities affected as this decision becomes reality.

So I'm proposing – in part because of strong lobbying by Bill and by Suzanne, as well as Charlie – I'm proposing a $40 million initiative led by a high-level team from the White House, NASA, and other agencies to develop a plan for regional economic growth and job creation. And I expect this plan to reach my desk by August 15th. It's an effort that will help prepare this already skilled workforce for new opportunities in the space industry and beyond.

So this is the next chapter that we can write together here at NASA. We will partner with industry. We will invest in cutting-edge research and technology. We will set far-reaching milestones and provide the resources to reach those milestones. And step by step, we will push the boundaries not only of where we can go but what we can do.

Fifty years after the creation of NASA, our goal is no longer just a destination to reach. Our goal is the capacity for people to work and learn and operate and live safely beyond the Earth for extended periods of time, ultimately in ways that are more sustainable and even indefinite. And in fulfilling this task, we will not only extend humanity's reach in space – we will strengthen America's leadership here on Earth.

Now, I'll close by saying this. I know that some Americans have asked a question that's particularly apt on Tax Day: Why spend money on NASA at all? Why spend money solving problems in space when we don't lack for problems to solve here on the ground? And obviously our country is still reeling from the worst economic turmoil we've known in generations. We have massive structural deficits that have to be closed in the coming years.

But you and I know this is a false choice. We have to fix our economy. We need to close our deficits. But for pennies on the dollar, the space program has fueled jobs and entire industries. For pennies on the dollar, the space program has improved our lives, advanced our society, strengthened our economy, and inspired generations of

Americans. And I have no doubt that NASA can continue to fulfill this role. But that is why – but I want to say clearly to those of you who work for NASA, but to the entire community that has been so supportive of the space program in this area: That is exactly why it's so essential that we pursue a new course and that we revitalize NASA and its mission – not just with dollars, but with clear aims and a larger purpose.

Now, little more than 40 years ago, astronauts descended the nine-rung ladder of the lunar module called Eagle, and allowed their feet to touch the dusty surface of the Earth's only Moon. This was the culmination of a daring and perilous gambit – of an endeavor that pushed the boundaries of our knowledge, of our technological prowess, of our very capacity as human beings to solve problems. It wasn't just the greatest achievement in NASA's history – it was one of the greatest achievements in human history.

And the question for us now is whether that was the beginning of something or the end of something. I choose to believe it was only the beginning.

So thank you. God bless you. And may God bless the United States of America. Thank you.

7

2011 STATE OF THE UNION ADDRESS
JANUARY 25, 2011

M r. Speaker, Mr. Vice President, Members of Congress, distinguished guests, and fellow Americans: Tonight I want to begin by congratulating the men and women of the 112th Congress, as well as your new Speaker, John Boehner. And as we mark this occasion, we're also mindful of the empty chair in this Chamber, and we pray for the health of our colleague and our friend Gabby Giffords.

It's no secret that those of us here tonight have had our differences over the last 2 years. The debates have been contentious; we have fought fiercely for our beliefs. And that's a good thing. That's what a robust democracy demands. That's what helps set us apart as a nation.

But there's a reason the tragedy in Tucson gave us pause. Amid all the noise and passion and rancor of our public debate, Tucson reminded us that no matter who we are or where we come from, each of us is a part of something greater, something more consequential than party or political preference.

We are part of the American family. We believe that in a country where every race and faith and point of view can be found, we are still bound together as one people, that we share common hopes and a common creed, that the dreams of a little girl in Tucson are not so different than those of our own children, that they all deserve the chance to be fulfilled. That too is what sets us apart as a nation.

Now, by itself, this simple recognition won't usher in a new era of cooperation. What comes of this moment is up to us. What comes of this moment will be determined not by whether we can sit together tonight, but whether we can work together tomorrow.

I believe we can, and I believe we must. That's what the people who sent us here expect of us. With their votes, they've determined that governing will now be a shared responsibility between parties. New laws will only pass with support from

Democrats and Republicans. We will move forward together or not at all, for the challenges we face are bigger than party and bigger than politics.

At stake right now is not who wins the next election. After all, we just had an election. At stake is whether new jobs and industries take root in this country or somewhere else. It's whether the hard work and industry of our people is rewarded. It's whether we sustain the leadership that has made America not just a place on a map, but the light to the world.

We are poised for progress. Two years after the worst recession most of us have ever known, the stock market has come roaring back, corporate profits are up, the economy is growing again.

But we have never measured progress by these yardsticks alone. We measure progress by the success of our people, by the jobs they can find and the quality of life those jobs offer, by the prospects of a small-business owner who dreams of turning a good idea into a thriving enterprise, by the opportunities for a better life that we pass on to our children.

That's the project the American people want us to work on–together.

Now, we did that in December. Thanks to the tax cuts we passed, Americans' paychecks are a little bigger today. Every business can write off the full cost of new investments that they make this year. And these steps, taken by Democrats and Republicans, will grow the economy and add to the more than 1 million private sector jobs created last year.

But we have to do more. These steps we've taken over the last 2 years may have broken the back of this recession, but to win the future, we'll need to take on challenges that have been decades in the making.

Many people watching tonight can probably remember a time when finding a good job meant showing up at a nearby factory or a business downtown. You didn't always need a degree, and your competition was pretty much limited to your neighbors. If you worked hard, chances are you'd have a job for life, with a decent paycheck and good benefits and the occasional promotion. Maybe you'd even have the pride of seeing your kids work at the same company.

That world has changed. And for many, the change has been painful. I've seen it in the shuttered windows of once booming factories and the vacant storefronts on once busy Main Streets. I've heard it in the frustrations of Americans who've seen their paychecks dwindle or their jobs disappear, proud men and women who feel like the rules have been changed in the middle of the game.

They're right. The rules have changed. In a single generation, revolutions in technology have transformed the way we live, work, and do business. Steel mills that once needed 1,000 workers can now do the same work with 100. Today, just about any company can set up shop, hire workers, and sell their products wherever there's an Internet connection.

Meanwhile, nations like China and India realized that with some changes of their own, they could compete in this new world. And so they started educating their children earlier and longer, with greater emphasis on math and science. They're investing in research and new technologies. Just recently, China became the home to the world's largest private solar research facility and the world's fastest computer.

So yes, the world is changed. The competition for jobs is real. But this shouldn't discourage us. It should challenge us. Remember, for all the hits we've taken these last few years, for all the naysayers predicting our decline, America still has the largest, most prosperous economy in the world. No workers are more productive than ours. No country has more successful companies or grants more patents to inventors and entrepreneurs. We're the home to the world's best colleges and universities, where more students come to study than any place on Earth.

What's more, we are the first nation to be founded for the sake of an idea: the idea that each of us deserves the chance to shape our own destiny. That's why centuries of pioneers and immigrants have risked everything to come here. It's why our students don't just memorize equations, but answer questions like: "What do you think of that idea? What would you change about the world? What do you want to be when you grow up?"

The future is ours to win. But to get there, we can't just stand still. As Robert Kennedy told us: "The future is not a gift. It is an achievement." Sustaining the American Dream has never been about standing pat. It has required each generation to sacrifice and struggle and meet the demands of a new age.

And now it's our turn. We know what it takes to compete for the jobs and industries of our time. We need to outinnovate, outeducate, and outbuild the rest of the world. We have to make America the best place on Earth to do business. We need to take responsibility for our deficit and reform our Government. That's how our people will prosper. That's how we'll win the future. And tonight I'd like to talk about how we get there.

The first step in winning the future is encouraging American innovation. None of us can predict with certainty what the next big industry will be or where the new jobs will come from. Thirty years ago, we couldn't know that something called the Internet would lead to an economic revolution. What we can do–what America does better than anyone else– is spark the creativity and imagination of our people. We're the nation that put cars in driveways and computers in offices; the nation of Edison and the Wright brothers, of Google and Facebook. In America, innovation doesn't just change our lives. It is how we make our living.

Our free enterprise system is what drives innovation. But because it's not always profitable for companies to invest in basic research, throughout our history, our Government has provided cutting-edge scientists and inventors with the support that they need. That's what planted the seeds for the Internet. That's what helped make possible things like computer chips and GPS. Just think of all the good jobs– from manufacturing to retail–that have come from these breakthroughs.

Half a century ago, when the Soviets beat us into space with the launch of a satellite called Sputnik, we had no idea how we would beat them to the Moon. The science wasn't even there yet. NASA didn't exist. But after investing in better research and education, we didn't just surpass the Soviets, we unleashed a wave of innovation that created new industries and millions of new jobs.

This is our generation's Sputnik moment. Two years ago, I said that we needed to reach a level of research and development we haven't seen since the height of the space race. And in a few weeks, I will be sending a budget to Congress that helps us meet that goal. We'll invest in biomedical research, information technology, and especially clean energy technology, an investment that will strengthen our security, protect our planet, and create countless new jobs for our people.

Already, we're seeing the promise of renewable energy. Robert and Gary Allen are brothers who run a small Michigan roofing company. After September 11, they volunteered their best roofers to help repair the Pentagon. But half of their factory went unused, and the recession hit them hard. Today, with the help of a Government loan, that empty space is being used to manufacture solar shingles that are being sold all across the country. In Robert's words, "We reinvented ourselves."

That's what Americans have done for over 200 years: reinvented ourselves. And to spur on more success stories like the Allen Brothers, we've begun to reinvent our energy policy. We're not just handing out money. We're issuing a challenge. We're telling America's scientists and engineers that if they assemble teams of the best minds in their fields and focus on the hardest problems in clean energy, we'll fund the Apollo projects of our time.

At the California Institute of Technology, they're developing a way to turn sunlight and water into fuel for our cars. At Oak Ridge National Laboratory, they're using supercomputers to get a lot more power out of our nuclear facilities. With more research and incentives, we can break our dependence on oil with biofuels and become the first country to have a million electric vehicles on the road by 2015.

We need to get behind this innovation. And to help pay for it, I'm asking Congress to eliminate the billions in taxpayer dollars we currently give to oil companies. I don't know if you've noticed, but they're doing just fine on their own. [Laughter] So instead of subsidizing yesterday's energy, let's invest in tomorrow's.

Now, clean energy breakthroughs will only translate into clean energy jobs if businesses know there will be a market for what they're selling. So tonight I challenge you to join me in setting a new goal: By 2035, 80 percent of America's electricity will come from clean energy sources.

Some folks want wind and solar. Others want nuclear, clean coal, and natural gas. To meet this goal, we will need them all, and I urge Democrats and Republicans to work together to make it happen.

Maintaining our leadership in research and technology is crucial to America's success. But if we want to win the future, if we want innovation to produce jobs in America and not overseas, then we also have to win the race to educate our kids.

Think about it. Over the next 10 years, nearly half of all new jobs will require education that goes beyond a high school education. And yet as many as a quarter of our students aren't even finishing high school. The quality of our math and science education lags behind many other nations. America has fallen to ninth in the proportion of young people with a college degree. And so the question is whether all of us, as citizens and as parents, are willing to do what's necessary to give every child a chance to succeed.

That responsibility begins not in our classrooms, but in our homes and communities. It's family that first instills the love of learning in a child. Only parents can make sure the TV is turned off and homework gets done. We need to teach our kids that it's not just the winner of the Super Bowl who deserves to be celebrated, but the winner of the science fair. We need to teach them that success is not a function of fame or PR, but of hard work and discipline.

Our schools share this responsibility. When a child walks into a classroom, it should be a place of high expectations and high performance. But too many schools don't meet this test. That's why instead of just pouring money into a system that's not working, we launched a competition called Race to the Top. To all 50 States, we said, "If you show us the most innovative plans to improve teacher quality and student achievement, we'll show you the money."

Race to the Top is the most meaningful reform of our public schools in a generation. For less than 1 percent of what we spend on education each year, it has led over 40 States to raise their standards for teaching and learning. And these standards were developed, by the way, not by Washington, but by Republican and Democratic Governors throughout the country. And Race to the Top should be the approach we follow this year as we replace No Child Left Behind with a law that's more flexible and focused on what's best for our kids.

You see, we know what's possible from our children when reform isn't just a top-down mandate, but the work of local teachers and principals, school boards and communities. Take a school like Bruce Randolph in Denver. Three years ago, it was rated one of the worst schools in Colorado, located on turf between two rival gangs. But last May, 97 percent of the seniors received their diploma. Most will be the first in their families to go to college. And after the first year of the school's transformation, the principal who made it possible wiped away tears when a student said, "Thank you, Ms. Waters, for showing that we are smart and we can make it." That's what good schools can do, and we want good schools all across the country.

Let's also remember that after parents, the biggest impact on a child's success comes from the man or woman at the front of the classroom. In South Korea, teachers are known as nation builders. Here in America, it's time we treated the people who educate our children with the same level of respect. We want to reward good teachers and stop making excuses for bad ones. And over the next 10 years, with so many baby boomers retiring from our classrooms, we want to prepare 100,000 new teachers in the fields of science and technology and engineering and math.

In fact, to every young person listening tonight who's contemplating their career choice: If you want to make a difference in the life of our Nation, if you want to make a difference in the life of a child, become a teacher. Your country needs you.

Of course, the education race doesn't end with a high school diploma. To compete, higher education must be within the reach of every American. That's why we've ended the unwarranted taxpayer subsidies that went to banks and used the savings to make college affordable for millions of students. And this year, I ask Congress to go further and make permanent our tuition tax credit, worth $10,000 for 4 years of college. It's the right thing to do.

Because people need to be able to train for new jobs and careers in today's fast-changing economy, we're also revitalizing America's community colleges. Last month, I saw the promise of these schools at Forsyth Tech in North Carolina. Many of the students there used to work in the surrounding factories that have since left town. One mother of two, a woman named Kathy Proctor, had worked in the furniture industry since she was 18 years old. And she told me she's earning her degree in biotechnology now, at 55 years old, not just because the furniture jobs are gone, but because she wants to inspire her children to pursue their dreams too. As Kathy said, "I hope it tells them to never give up."

If we take these steps, if we raise expectations for every child and give them the best possible chance at an education, from the day they are born until the last job they take, we will reach the goal that I set 2 years ago: By the end of the decade, America will once again have the highest proportion of college graduates in the world.

One last point about education: Today, there are hundreds of thousands of students excelling in our schools who are not American citizens. Some are the children of undocumented workers, who had nothing to do with the actions of their parents. They grew up as Americans and pledge allegiance to our flag, and yet they live every day with the threat of deportation. Others come here from abroad to study in our colleges and universities. But as soon as they obtain advanced degrees, we send them back home to compete against us. It makes no sense.

Now, I strongly believe that we should take on, once and for all, the issue of illegal immigration. And I am prepared to work with Republicans and Democrats to protect our borders, enforce our laws, and address the millions of undocumented workers who are now living in the shadows. I know that debate will be difficult. I know it will take time. But tonight, let's agree to make that effort. And let's stop expelling talented, responsible young people who could be staffing our research labs or starting a new business, who could be further enriching this Nation.

The third step in winning the future is rebuilding America. To attract new businesses to our shores, we need the fastest, most reliable ways to move people, goods, and information, from high-speed rail to high- speed Internet.

Our infrastructure used to be the best, but our lead has slipped. South Korean homes now have greater Internet access than we do. Countries in Europe and Russia invest more in their roads and railways than we do. China is building faster trains and newer airports. Meanwhile, when our own engineers graded our Nation's infrastructure, they gave us a D.

We have to do better. America is the nation that built the transcontinental railroad, brought electricity to rural communities, constructed the Interstate Highway System. The jobs created by these projects didn't just come from laying down track or pavement. They came from businesses that opened near a town's new train station or the new off-ramp.

So over the last 2 years, we've begun rebuilding for the 21st century, a project that has meant thousands of good jobs for the hard-hit construction industry. And tonight I'm proposing that we redouble those efforts.

We'll put more Americans to work repairing crumbling roads and bridges. We'll make sure this is fully paid for, attract private investment, and pick projects based [on]* what's best for the economy, not politicians.

Within 25 years, our goal is to give 80 percent of Americans access to high-speed rail. This could allow you to go places in half the time it takes to travel by car. For some trips, it will be faster than flying, without the pat-down. [Laughter] As we speak, routes in California and the Midwest are already underway.

Within the next 5 years, we'll make it possible for businesses to deploy the next generation of high-speed wireless coverage to 98 percent of all Americans. This isn't just about–this isn't about faster Internet or fewer dropped calls. It's about connecting every part of America to the digital age. It's about a rural community in Iowa or Alabama where farmers and small-business owners will be able to sell their products all over the world. It's about a firefighter who can download the design of a burning building onto a handheld device, a student who can take classes with a digital text-book, or a patient who can have face-to-face video chats with her doctor.

All these investments–in innovation, education, and infrastructure– will make America a better place to do business and create jobs. But to help our companies compete, we also have to knock down barriers that stand in the way of their success.

For example, over the years, a parade of lobbyists has rigged the Tax Code to benefit particular companies and industries. Those with accountants or lawyers to work the system can end up paying no taxes at all. But all the rest are hit with one of the highest corporate tax rates in the world. It makes no sense, and it has to change.

So tonight I'm asking Democrats and Republicans to simplify the system, get rid of the loopholes, level the playing field, and use the savings to lower the corporate tax rate for the first time in 25 years without adding to our deficit. It can be done.

To help businesses sell more products abroad, we set a goal of doubling our exports by 2014. Because the more we export, the more jobs we create here at home. Already, our exports are up. Recently, we signed agreements with India and China that will support more than 250,000 jobs here in the United States. And last month, we finalized a trade agreement with South Korea that will support at least 70,000 American jobs. This agreement has unprecedented support from business and labor, Democrats and Republicans, and I ask this Congress to pass it as soon as possible.

Now, before I took office, I made it clear that we would enforce our trade agree-ments and that I would only sign deals that keep faith with American workers and promote American jobs. That's what we did with Korea, and that's what I intend to do as we pursue agreements with Panama and Colombia and continue our Asia-Pacific and global trade talks.

To reduce barriers to growth and investment, I've ordered a review of Govern-ment regulations. When we find rules that put an unnecessary burden on businesses, we will fix them. But I will not hesitate to create or enforce commonsense safeguards to protect the American people. That's what we've done in this country for more than a century. It's why our food is safe to eat, our water is safe to drink, and our air is safe to breathe. It's why we have speed limits and child labor laws. It's why last year, we put in place consumer protections against hidden fees and penalties by credit card companies and new rules to prevent another financial crisis. And it's why we passed reform that finally prevents the health insurance industry from exploiting patients.

Now, I have heard rumors that a few of you still have concerns about our new health care law. [Laughter] So let me be the first to say that anything can be improved. If you have ideas about how to improve this law by making care better or more affordable, I am eager to work with you. We can start right now by correcting a flaw in the legislation that has placed an unnecessary bookkeeping burden on small businesses.

What I'm not willing to do–what I'm not willing to do–is go back to the days when insurance companies could deny someone coverage because of a preexisting condition.

I'm not willing to tell James Howard, a brain cancer patient from Texas, that his treatment might not be covered. I'm not willing to tell Jim Houser, a small-businessman from Oregon, that he has to go back to paying $5,000 more to cover his employees. As we speak, this law is making prescription drugs cheaper for seniors and giving uninsured students a chance to stay on their patients'–parents' coverage.

So I say to this Chamber tonight: Instead of refighting the battles of the last 2 years, let's fix what needs fixing, and let's move forward.

Now, the final critical step in winning the future is to make sure we aren't buried under a mountain of debt.

We are living with a legacy of deficit spending that began almost a decade ago. And in the wake of the financial crisis, some of that was necessary to keep credit flowing, save jobs, and put money in people's pockets.

But now that the worst of the recession is over, we have to confront the fact that our Government spends more than it takes in. That is not sustainable. Every day, families sacrifice to live within their means. They deserve a Government that does the same.

So tonight I am proposing that starting this year, we freeze annual domestic spending for the next 5 years. Now, this would reduce the deficit by more than $400 billion over the next decade and will bring discretionary spending to the lowest share of our economy since Dwight Eisenhower was President.

This freeze will require painful cuts. Already, we've frozen the salaries of hard-working Federal employees for the next 2 years. I've proposed cuts to things I care deeply about, like community action programs. The Secretary of Defense has also agreed to cut tens of billions of dollars in spending that he and his generals believe our military can do without.

Now, I recognize that some in this Chamber have already proposed deeper cuts, and I'm willing to eliminate whatever we can honestly afford to do without. But let's make sure that we're not doing it on the backs of our most vulnerable citizens. And let's make sure that what we're cutting is really excess weight. Cutting the deficit by gutting our investments in innovation and education is like lightening an overloaded airplane by removing its engine. It may make you feel like you're flying high at first, but it won't take long before you feel the impact. [Laughter]

Now, most of the cuts and savings I've proposed only address annual domestic spending, which represents a little more than 12 percent of our budget. To make further progress, we have to stop pretending that cutting this kind of spending alone will be enough. It won't.

The bipartisan fiscal commission I created last year made this crystal clear. I don't agree with all their proposals, but they made important progress. And their conclusion is that the only way to tackle our deficit is to cut excessive spending wherever we find it, in domestic spending, defense spending, health care spending, and spending through tax breaks and loopholes.

This means further reducing health care costs, including programs like Medicare and Medicaid, which are the single biggest contributor to our long-term deficit. The health insurance law we passed last year will slow these rising costs, which is part of the reason that nonpartisan economists have said that repealing the health care law would add a quarter of a trillion dollars to our deficit. Still, I'm willing to look at other ideas to bring down costs, including one that Republicans suggested last year: medical malpractice reform to rein in frivolous lawsuits.

To put us on solid ground, we should also find a bipartisan solution to strengthen Social Security for future generations. We must do it without putting at risk current retirees, the most vulnerable, or people with disabilities, without slashing benefits for future generations, and without subjecting Americans' guaranteed retirement income to the whims of the stock market.

And if we truly care about our deficit, we simply can't afford a permanent extension of the tax cuts for the wealthiest 2 percent of Americans. Before we take money away from our schools or scholarships away from our students, we should ask millionaires to give up their tax break. It's not a matter of punishing their success, it's about promoting America's success.

In fact, the best thing we could do on taxes for all Americans is to simplify the individual Tax Code. This will be a tough job, but members of both parties have expressed an interest in doing this, and I am prepared to join them.

So now is the time to act. Now is the time for both sides and both Houses of Congress, Democrats and Republicans, to forge a principled compromise that gets the job done. If we make the hard choices now to rein in our deficits, we can make the investments we need to win the future.

Let me take this one step further. We shouldn't just give our people a Government that's more affordable, we should give them a Government that's more competent and more efficient. We can't win the future with a Government of the past.

We live and do business in the Information Age, but the last major reorganization of the Government happened in the age of black-and-white TV. There are 12 different agencies that deal with exports. There are at least five different agencies that deal with housing policy. Then there's my favorite example: The Interior Department is in charge of salmon while they're in fresh water, but the Commerce Department handles them when they're in saltwater. [Laughter] I hear it gets even more complicated once they're smoked. [Laughter]

Now, we've made great strides over the last 2 years in using technology and getting rid of waste. Veterans can now download their electronic medical records with a click of the mouse. We're selling acres of Federal office space that hasn't been used in years, and we'll cut through redtape to get rid of more. But we need to think bigger. In the coming months, my administration will develop a proposal to merge, consolidate, and reorganize the Federal Government in a way that best serves the goal of a more competitive America. I will submit that proposal to Congress for a vote, and we will push to get it passed.

In the coming year, we'll also work to rebuild people's faith in the institution of

Government. Because you deserve to know exactly how and where your tax dollars are being spent, you'll be able to go to a web site and get that information for the very first time in history. Because you deserve to know when your elected officials are meeting with lobbyists, I ask Congress to do what the White House has already done: put that information online. And because the American people deserve to know that special interests aren't larding up legislation with pet projects, both parties in Congress should know this: If a bill comes to my desk with earmarks inside, I will veto it. I will veto it.

The 21st-century Government that's open and competent, a government that lives within its means, an economy that's driven by new skills and new ideas–our success in this new and changing world will require reform, responsibility, and innovation. It will also require us to approach that world with a new level of engagement in our foreign affairs.

Just as jobs and businesses can now race across borders, so can new threats and new challenges. No single wall separates East and West. No one rival superpower is aligned against us.

And so we must defeat determined enemies, wherever they are, and build coalitions that cut across lines of region and race and religion. And America's moral example must always shine for all who yearn for freedom and justice and dignity. And because we've begun this work, tonight we can say that American leadership has been renewed and America's standing has been restored.

Look to Iraq, where nearly 100,000 of our brave men and women have left with their heads held high. American combat patrols have ended, violence is down, and a new Government has been formed. This year, our civilians will forge a lasting partnership with the Iraqi people, while we finish the job of bringing our troops out of Iraq. America's commitment has been kept. The Iraq war is coming to an end.

Of course, as we speak, Al Qaida and their affiliates continue to plan attacks against us. Thanks to our intelligence and law enforcement professionals, we're disrupting plots and securing our cities and skies. And as extremists try to inspire acts of violence within our borders, we are responding with the strength of our communities, with respect for the rule of law, and with the conviction that American Muslims are a part of our American family.

We've also taken the fight to Al Qaida and their allies abroad. In Afghanistan, our troops have taken Taliban strongholds and trained Afghan security forces. Our purpose is clear: By preventing the Taliban from reestablishing a stranglehold over the Afghan people, we will deny Al Qaida the safe haven that served as a launching pad for 9/11.

Thanks to our heroic troops and civilians, fewer Afghans are under the control of the insurgency. There will be tough fighting ahead, and the Afghan Government will need to deliver better governance. But we are strengthening the capacity of the Afghan people and building an enduring partnership with them. This year, we will work with nearly 50 countries to begin a transition to an Afghan lead, and this July, we will begin to bring our troops home.

In Pakistan, Al Qaida's leadership is under more pressure than at any point since 2001. Their leaders and operatives are being removed from the battlefield. Their safe havens are shrinking. And we've sent a message from the Afghan border to the Arabian Peninsula to all parts of the globe: We will not relent, we will not waver, and we will defeat you.

American leadership can also be seen in the effort to secure the worst weapons of war. Because Republicans and Democrats approved the new START Treaty, far fewer nuclear weapons and launchers will be deployed. Because we rallied the world, nuclear materials are being locked down on every continent so they never fall into the hands of terrorists.

Because of a diplomatic effort to insist that Iran meet its obligations, the Iranian Government now faces tougher sanctions, tighter sanctions than ever before. And on the Korean Peninsula, we stand with our ally South Korea and insist that North Korea keeps its commitment to abandon nuclear weapons.

This is just a part of how we're shaping a world that favors peace and prosperity. With our European allies, we revitalized NATO and increased our cooperation on everything from counterterrorism to missile defense. We've reset our relationship with Russia, strengthened Asian alliances, built new partnerships with nations like India.

This March, I will travel to Brazil, Chile, and El Salvador to forge new alliances across the Americas. Around the globe, we're standing with those who take responsibility, helping farmers grow more food, supporting doctors who care for the sick, and combating the corruption that can rot a society and rob people of opportunity.

Recent events have shown us that what sets us apart must not just be our power; it must also be the purpose behind it. In south Sudan—with our assistance—the people were finally able to vote for independence after years of war. Thousands lined up before dawn. People danced in the streets. One man who lost four of his brothers at war summed up the scene around him. "This was a battlefield for most of my life," he said. "Now we want to be free."

And we saw that same desire to be free in Tunisia, where the will of the people proved more powerful than the writ of a dictator. And tonight let us be clear: The United States of America stands with the people of Tunisia and supports the democratic aspirations of all people.

We must never forget that the things we've struggled for and fought for live in the hearts of people everywhere. And we must always remember that the Americans who have borne the greatest burden in this struggle are the men and women who serve our country.

Tonight let us speak with one voice in reaffirming that our Nation is united in support of our troops and their families. Let us serve them as well as they've served us, by giving them the equipment they need, by providing them with the care and benefits that they have earned, and by enlisting our veterans in the great task of building our own Nation.

Our troops come from every corner of this country. They're Black, White, Latino, Asian, Native American. They are Christian and Hindu, Jewish and Muslim. And yes, we know that some of them are gay. Starting this year, no American will be forbidden from serving the country they love because of who they love. And with that change, I call on all our college campuses to open their doors to our military recruiters and ROTC. It is time to leave behind the divisive battles of the past. It is time to move forward as one Nation.

We should have no illusions about the work ahead of us. Reforming our schools, changing the way we use energy, reducing our deficit, none of this will be easy. All of it will take time. And it will be harder because we will argue about everything: the costs, the details, the letter of every law.

Of course, some countries don't have this problem. If the central government wants a railroad, they build a railroad, no matter how many homes get bulldozed. If they don't want a bad story in the newspaper, it doesn't get written.

And yet, as contentious and frustrating and messy as our democracy can sometimes be, I know there isn't a person here who would trade places with any other nation on Earth.

We may have differences in policy, but we all believe in the rights enshrined in our Constitution. We may have different opinions, but we believe in the same promise that says this is a place where you can make it if you try. We may have different backgrounds, but we believe in the same dream that says this is a country where anything is possible, no matter who you are, no matter where you come from.

That dream is why I can stand here before you tonight. That dream is why a working class kid from Scranton can sit behind me. [Laughter] That dream is why someone who began by sweeping the floors of his father's Cincinnati bar can preside as Speaker of the House in the greatest nation on Earth.

That dream–that American Dream–is what drove the Allen Brothers to reinvent their roofing company for a new era. It's what drove those students at Forsyth Tech to learn a new skill and work towards the future. And that dream is the story of a small-business owner named Brandon Fisher.

Brandon started a company in Berlin, Pennsylvania, that specializes in a new kind of drilling technology. And one day last summer, he saw the news that halfway across the world, 33 men were trapped in a Chilean mine, and no one knew how to save them.

But Brandon thought his company could help. And so he designed a rescue that would come to be known as Plan B. His employees worked around the clock to manufacture the necessary drilling equipment, and Brandon left for Chile.

Along with others, he began drilling a 2,000-foot hole into the ground, working 3 or 4 hour–3 or 4 days at a time without any sleep. Thirty- seven days later, Plan B succeeded and the miners were rescued. But because he didn't want all of the attention, Brandon wasn't there when the miners emerged. He'd already gone back home, back to work on his next project.

And later, one of his employees said of the rescue, "We proved that Center Rock is a little company, but we do big things."

We do big things.

From the earliest days of our founding, America has been the story of ordinary people who dare to dream. That's how we win the future.

We're a nation that says, "I might not have a lot of money, but I have this great idea for a new company." "I might not come from a family of college graduates, but I will be the first to get my degree." "I might not know those people in trouble, but I think I can help them, and I need to try." "I'm not sure how we'll reach that better place beyond the horizon, but I know we'll get there. I know we will."

We do big things.

The idea of America endures. Our destiny remains our choice. And tonight, more than two centuries later, it's because of our people that our future is hopeful, our journey goes forward, and the state of our Union is strong.

Thank you. God bless you, and may God bless the United States of America.

8

REMARKS REGARDING HIS BIRTH CERTIFICATE

APRIL 27, 2011

Hello, everybody. Now, let me just comment, first of all, on the fact that I can't get the networks to break in on all kinds of other discussions. I was just back there listening to Chuck – he was saying, it's amazing that he's not going to be talking about national security. I would not have the networks breaking in if I was talking about that, Chuck, and you know it.

[…] As many of you have been briefed, we provided additional information today about the site of my birth. Now, this issue has been going on for two, two and a half years now. I think it started during the campaign. And I have to say that over the last two and a half years I have watched with bemusement, I've been puzzled at the degree to which this thing just kept on going. We've had every official in Hawaii, Democrat and Republican, every news outlet that has investigated this, confirm that, yes, in fact, I was born in Hawaii, August 4, 1961, in Kapiolani Hospital.

We've posted the certification that is given by the state of Hawaii on the Internet for everybody to see. People have provided affidavits that they, in fact, have seen this birth certificate. And yet this thing just keeps on going.

Now, normally I would not comment on something like this, because obviously there's a lot of stuff swirling in the press on at any given day and I've got other things to do. But two weeks ago, when the Republican House had put forward a budget that will have huge consequences potentially to the country, and when I gave a speech about my budget and how I felt that we needed to invest in education and infrastructure and making sure that we had a strong safety net for our seniors even as we were closing the deficit, during that entire week the dominant news story wasn't about these huge, monumental choices that we're going to have to make as a nation. It was about my birth certificate. And that was true on most of the news outlets that were represented here.

And so I just want to make a larger point here. We've got some enormous challenges out there. There are a lot of folks out there who are still looking for work.

Everybody is still suffering under high gas prices. We're going to have to make a series of very difficult decisions about how we invest in our future but also get a hold of our deficit and our debt – how do we do that in a balanced way.

And this is going to generate huge and serious debates, important debates. And there are going to be some fierce disagreements – and that's good. That's how democracy is supposed to work. And I am confident that the American people and America's political leaders can come together in a bipartisan way and solve these problems. We always have.

But we're not going to be able to do it if we are distracted. We're not going to be able to do it if we spend time vilifying each other. We're not going to be able to do it if we just make stuff up and pretend that facts are not facts. We're not going to be able to solve our problems if we get distracted by sideshows and carnival barkers.

We live in a serious time right now and we have the potential to deal with the issues that we confront in a way that will make our kids and our grandkids and our great grandkids proud. And I have every confidence that America in the 21st century is going to be able to come out on top just like we always have. But we're going to have to get serious to do it.

I know that there's going to be a segment of people for which, no matter what we put out, this issue will not be put to rest. But I'm speaking to the vast majority of the American people, as well as to the press. We do not have time for this kind of silliness. We've got better stuff to do. I've got better stuff to do. We've got big problems to solve. And I'm confident we can solve them, but we're going to have to focus on them – not on this.

Thanks very much, everybody.

❄ 9 ❀

REMARKS AT A MEMORIAL SERVICE FOR THE VICTIMS OF THE SHOOTING IN TUCSON, ARIZONA

JUNE 12, 2011

T hank you. Thank you very much. Please, please be seated.

To the families of those we've lost; to all who called them friends; to the students of this university, the public servants who are gathered here, the people of Tucson and the people of Arizona: I have come here tonight as an American who, like all Americans, kneels to pray with you today and will stand by you tomorrow.

There is nothing I can say that will fill the sudden hole torn in your hearts. But know this: The hopes of a nation are here tonight. We mourn with you for the fallen. We join you in your grief. And we add our faith to yours that Representative Gabrielle Giffords and the other living victims of this tragedy will pull through.

Scripture tells us:

There is a river whose streams make glad the city of God,

the holy place where the Most High dwells.

God is within her, she will not fall;

God will help her at break of day.

On Saturday morning, Gabby, her staff and many of her constituents gathered outside a supermarket to exercise their right to peaceful assembly and free speech. They were fulfilling a central tenet of the democracy envisioned by our founders -- representatives of the people answering questions to their constituents, so as to carry their concerns back to our nation's capital. Gabby called it "Congress on Your Corner" -- just an updated version of government of and by and for the people.

And that quintessentially American scene, that was the scene that was shattered by a gunman's bullets. And the six people who lost their lives on Saturday — they, too, represented what is best in us, what is best in America.

Judge John Roll served our legal system for nearly 40 years. A graduate of this university and a graduate of this law school – Judge Roll was recommended for the federal bench by John McCain 20 years ago – appointed by President George H.W. Bush and rose to become Arizona's chief federal judge.

His colleagues described him as the hardest-working judge within the Ninth Circuit. He was on his way back from attending Mass, as he did every day, when he decided to stop by and say hi to his representative. John is survived by his loving wife, Maureen, his three sons and his five beautiful grandchildren.

George and Dorothy Morris -- "Dot" to her friends -- were high school sweethearts who got married and had two daughters. They did everything together – traveling the open road in their RV, enjoying what their friends called a 50-year honeymoon. Saturday morning, they went by the Safeway to hear what their congresswoman had to say. When gunfire rang out, George, a former Marine, instinctively tried to shield his wife. Both were shot. Dot passed away.

A New Jersey native, Phyllis Schneck retired to Tucson to beat the snow. But in the summer, she would return East, where her world revolved around her three children, her seven grandchildren and 2-year-old great-granddaughter. A gifted quilter, she'd often work under a favorite tree, or sometimes she'd sew aprons with the logos of the Jets and the Giants – to give out at the church where she volunteered. A Republican, she took a liking to Gabby, and wanted to get to know her better.

Dorwan and Mavy Stoddard grew up in Tucson together -- about 70 years ago. They moved apart and started their own respective families. But after both were widowed they found their way back here, to, as one of Mavy's daughters put it, "be boyfriend and girlfriend again."

When they weren't out on the road in their motor home, you could find them just up the road, helping folks in need at the Mountain Avenue Church of Christ. A retired construction worker, Dorwan spent his spare time fixing up the church along with his dog, Tux. His final act of selflessness was to dive on top of his wife, sacrificing his life for hers.

Everything – everything – Gabe Zimmerman did, he did with passion. But his true passion was helping people. As Gabby's outreach director, he made the cares of thousands of her constituents his own, seeing to it that seniors got the Medicare benefits that they had earned, that veterans got the medals and the care that they deserved, that government was working for ordinary folks. He died doing what he loved -- talking with people and seeing how he could help. And Gabe is survived by his parents, Ross and Emily, his brother, Ben, and his fiancée, Kelly, who he planned to marry next year.

And then there is nine-year-old Christina Taylor Green. Christina was an A student; she was a dancer; she was a gymnast; she was a swimmer. She decided that she wanted to be the first woman to play in the Major Leagues, and as the only girl on her Little League team, no one put it past her.

She showed an appreciation for life uncommon for a girl her age. She'd remind her mother, "We are so blessed. We have the best life." And she'd pay those blessings back by participating in a charity that helped children who were less fortunate.

Our hearts are broken by their sudden passing. Our hearts are broken -- and yet, our hearts also have reason for fullness.

Our hearts are full of hope and thanks for the 13 Americans who survived the shooting, including the congresswoman many of them went to see on Saturday.

I have just come from the University Medical Center, just a mile from here, where our friend Gabby courageously fights to recover even as we speak. And I want to tell you – her husband Mark is here and he allows me to share this with you – right after we went to visit, a few minutes after we left her room and some of her colleagues in Congress were in the room, Gabby opened her eyes for the first time. Gabby opened her eyes for the first time.

Gabby opened her eyes. Gabby opened her eyes, so I can tell you she knows we are here. She knows we love her. And she knows that we are rooting for her through what is undoubtedly going to be a difficult journey. We are there for her.

Our hearts are full of thanks for that good news, and our hearts are full of gratitude for those who saved others. We are grateful to Daniel Hernandez – a volunteer in Gabby's office.

And, Daniel, I'm sorry, you may deny it, but we've decided you are a hero because – you ran through the chaos to minister to your boss, and tended to her wounds and helped keep her alive.

We are grateful to the men who tackled the gunman as he stopped to reload. Right over there. We are grateful for petite Patricia Maisch, who wrestled away the killer's ammunition, and undoubtedly saved some lives. And we are grateful for the doctors and nurses and first responders who worked wonders to heal those who'd been hurt. We are grateful to them.

These men and women remind us that heroism is found not only on the fields of battle. They remind us that heroism does not require special training or physical strength. Heroism is here, in the hearts of so many of our fellow citizens, all around us, just waiting to be summoned –– as it was on Saturday morning. Their actions, their selflessness poses a challenge to each of us. It raises a question of what, beyond prayers and expressions of concern, is required of us going forward. How can we honor the fallen? How can we be true to their memory?

You see, when a tragedy like this strikes, it is part of our nature to demand explanations –– to try and pose some order on the chaos and make sense out of that which seems senseless. Already we've seen a national conversation commence, not only about the motivations behind these killings, but about everything from the merits of gun safety laws to the adequacy of our mental health system. And much of this process, of debating what might be done to prevent such tragedies in the future, is an essential ingredient in our exercise of self-government.

But at a time when our discourse has become so sharply polarized –– at a time when we are far too eager to lay the blame for all that ails the world at the feet of those who happen to think differently than we do –– it's important for us to pause for a moment and make sure that we're talking with each other in a way that heals, not in a way that wounds.

Scripture tells us that there is evil in the world, and that terrible things happen for reasons that defy human understanding. In the words of Job, "When I looked for light, then came darkness." Bad things happen, and we have to guard against simple explanations in the aftermath.

For the truth is none of us can know exactly what triggered this vicious attack. None of us can know with any certainty what might have stopped these shots from being fired, or what thoughts lurked in the inner recesses of a violent man's mind. Yes, we have to examine all the facts behind this tragedy. We cannot and will not be passive in the face of such violence. We should be willing to challenge old assumptions in order to lessen the prospects of such violence in the future. But what we cannot do is use this tragedy as one more occasion to turn on each other. That we cannot do. That we cannot do.

As we discuss these issues, let each of us do so with a good dose of humility. Rather than pointing fingers or assigning blame, let's use this occasion to expand our moral imaginations, to listen to each other more carefully, to sharpen our instincts for empathy and remind ourselves of all the ways that our hopes and dreams are bound together.

After all, that's what most of us do when we lose somebody in our family — especially if the loss is unexpected. We're shaken out of our routines. We're forced to look inward. We reflect on the past: Did we spend enough time with an aging parent, we wonder. Did we express our gratitude for all the sacrifices that they made for us? Did we tell a spouse just how desperately we loved them, not just once in a while but every single day?

So sudden loss causes us to look backward — but it also forces us to look forward; to reflect on the present and the future, on the manner in which we live our lives and nurture our relationships with those who are still with us.

We may ask ourselves if we've shown enough kindness and generosity and compassion to the people in our lives. Perhaps we question whether we're doing right by our children, or our community, whether our priorities are in order.

We recognize our own mortality, and we are reminded that in the fleeting time we have on this Earth, what matters is not wealth, or status, or power, or fame — but rather, how well we have loved – and what small part we have played in making the lives of other people better.

And that process – that process of reflection, of making sure we align our values with our actions — that, I believe, is what a tragedy like this requires.

For those who were harmed, those who were killed — they are part of our family, an American family 300 million strong. We may not have known them personally, but surely we see ourselves in them. In George and Dot, in Dorwan and Mavy, we sense the abiding love we have for our own husbands, our own wives, our own life partners. Phyllis — she's our mom or our grandma; Gabe our brother or son. In Judge Roll, we recognize not only a man who prized his family and doing his job well, but also a man who embodied America's fidelity to the law.

And in Gabby – in Gabby, we see a reflection of our public-spiritedness; that desire to participate in that sometimes frustrating, sometimes contentious, but always necessary and never-ending process to form a more perfect union.

And in Christina – in Christina we see all of our children. So curious, so trusting, so energetic, so full of magic. So deserving of our love. And so deserving of our good example.

If this tragedy prompts reflection and debate – as it should – let's make sure it's worthy of those we have lost. Let's make sure it's not on the usual plane of politics and point-scoring and pettiness that drifts away in the next news cycle.

The loss of these wonderful people should make every one of us strive to be better. To be better in our private lives, to be better friends and neighbors and coworkers and parents. And if, as has been discussed in recent days, their death helps usher in more civility in our public discourse, let us remember it is not because a simple lack of civility caused this tragedy – it did not – but rather because only a more civil and honest public discourse can help us face up to the challenges of our nation in a way that would make them proud.

We should be civil because we want to live up to the example of public servants like John Roll and Gabby Giffords, who knew first and foremost that we are all Americans, and that we can question each other's ideas without questioning each other's love of country and that our task, working together, is to constantly widen the circle of our concern so that we bequeath the American Dream to future generations.

They believed – they believed, and I believe that we can be better. Those who died here, those who saved life here — they help me believe. We may not be able to stop all evil in the world, but I know that how we treat one another, that's entirely up to us.

And I believe that for all our imperfections, we are full of decency and goodness, and that the forces that divide us are not as strong as those that unite us.

That's what I believe, in part because that's what a child like Christina Taylor Green believed.

Imagine – imagine for a moment, here was a young girl who was just becoming aware of our democracy; just beginning to understand the obligations of citizenship; just starting to glimpse the fact that some day she, too, might play a part in shaping her nation's future. She had been elected to her student council. She saw public service as something exciting and hopeful. She was off to meet her congresswoman, someone she was sure was good and important and might be a role model. She saw all this through the eyes of a child, undimmed by the cynicism or vitriol that we adults all too often just take for granted.

I want to live up to her expectations. I want our democracy to be as good as Christina imagined it. I want America to be as good as she imagined it. All of us — we should do everything we can to make sure this country lives up to our children's expectations.

As has already been mentioned, Christina was given to us on September 11th, 2001, one of 50 babies born that day to be pictured in a book called "Faces of Hope." On either side of her photo in that book were simple wishes for a child's life. "I hope you help those in need," read one. "I hope you know all the words to the National Anthem and sing it with your hand over your heart." "I hope you jump in rain puddles."

If there are rain puddles in Heaven, Christina is jumping in them today. And here on this Earth – here on this Earth, we place our hands over our hearts, and we commit ourselves as Americans to forging a country that is forever worthy of her gentle, happy spirit.

May God bless and keep those we've lost in restful and eternal peace. May He love and watch over the survivors. And may He bless the United States of America.

2012 STATE OF THE UNION ADDRESS
JANUARY 24, 2012

M r. Speaker, Mr. Vice President, Members of Congress, distinguished guests, and fellow Americans: Last month, I went to Andrews Air Force Base and welcomed home some of our last troops to serve in Iraq. Together, we offered a final, proud salute to the colors under which more than a million of our fellow citizens fought and several thousand gave their lives.

We gather tonight knowing that this generation of heroes has made the United States safer and more respected around the world. For the first time in 9 years, there are no Americans fighting in Iraq. For the first time in two decades, Usama bin Laden is not a threat to this country. Most of Al Qaida's top lieutenants have been defeated. The Taliban's momentum has been broken, and some troops in Afghanistan have begun to come home.

These achievements are a testament to the courage, selflessness, and teamwork of America's Armed Forces. At a time when too many of our institutions have let us down, they exceed all expectations. They're not consumed with personal ambition. They don't obsess over their differences. They focus on the mission at hand. They work together.

Imagine what we could accomplish if we followed their example. Think about the America within our reach: a country that leads the world in educating its people; an America that attracts a new generation of high-tech manufacturing and high-paying jobs; a future where we're in control of our own energy and our security and prosperity aren't so tied to unstable parts of the world; an economy built to last, where hard work pays off and responsibility is rewarded.

We can do this. I know we can, because we've done it before. At the end of World War II, when another generation of heroes returned home from combat, they built the strongest economy and middle class the world has ever known. My grandfather, a veteran of Patton's army, got the chance to go to college on the GI bill. My grandmother, who worked on a bomber assembly line, was part of a workforce that turned out the best products on Earth.

The two of them shared the optimism of a nation that had triumphed over a depression and fascism. They understood they were part of something larger, that they were contributing to a story of success that every American had a chance to share, the basic American promise that if you worked hard, you could do well enough to raise a family, own a home, send your kids to college, and put a little away for retirement.

The defining issue of our time is how to keep that promise alive. No challenge is more urgent. No debate is more important. We can either settle for a country where a shrinking number of people do really well while a growing number of Americans barely get by. Or we can restore an economy where everyone gets a fair shot and everyone does their fair share and everyone plays by the same set of rules. What's at stake aren't Democratic values or Republican values, but American values. And we have to reclaim them.

Let's remember how we got here. Long before the recession, jobs and manufacturing began leaving our shores. Technology made businesses more efficient, but also made some jobs obsolete. Folks at the top saw their incomes rise like never before, but most hard-working Americans struggled with costs that were growing, paychecks that weren't, and personal debt that kept piling up.

In 2008, the house of cards collapsed. We learned that mortgages had been sold to people who couldn't afford or understand them. Banks had made huge bets and bonuses with other people's money. Regulators had looked the other way or didn't have the authority to stop the bad behavior.

It was wrong, it was irresponsible, and it plunged our economy into a crisis that put millions out of work, saddled us with more debt, and left innocent, hard-working Americans holding the bag. In the 6 months before I took office, we lost nearly 4 million jobs. And we lost another 4 million before our policies were in full effect.

Those are the facts. But so are these: In the last 22 months, businesses have created more than 3 million jobs. Last year, they created the most jobs since 2005. American manufacturers are hiring again, creating jobs for the first time since the late 1990s. Together, we've agreed to cut the deficit by more than $2 trillion. And we've put in place new rules to hold Wall Street accountable so a crisis like this never happens again.

The state of our Union is getting stronger. And we've come too far to turn back now. As long as I'm President, I will work with anyone in this Chamber to build on this momentum. But I intend to fight obstruction with action, and I will oppose any effort to return to the very same policies that brought on this economic crisis in the first place.

No, we will not go back to an economy weakened by outsourcing, bad debt, and phony financial profits. Tonight I want to speak about how we move forward and lay out a blueprint for an economy that's built to last, an economy built on American manufacturing, American energy, skills for American workers, and a renewal of American values.

Now, this blueprint begins with American manufacturing.

On the day I took office, our auto industry was on the verge of collapse. Some even said we should let it die. With a million jobs at stake, I refused to let that happen. In exchange for help, we demanded responsibility. We got workers and automakers to settle their differences. We got the industry to retool and restructure. Today, General Motors is back on top as the world's number-one automaker. Chrysler has grown faster in the U.S. than any major car company. Ford is investing billions in U.S. plants and factories. And together, the entire industry added nearly a hundred and sixty thousand jobs.

We bet on American workers. We bet on American ingenuity. And tonight, the American auto industry is back.

What's happening in Detroit can happen in other industries. It can happen in Cleveland and Pittsburgh and Raleigh. We can't bring every job back that's left our shore. But right now it's getting more expensive to do business in places like China. Meanwhile, America is more productive. A few weeks ago, the CEO of Master Lock told me that it now makes business sense for him to bring jobs back home. Today, for the first time in 15 years, Master Lock's unionized plant in Milwaukee is running at full capacity.

So we have a huge opportunity at this moment to bring manufacturing back. But we have to seize it. Tonight my message to business leaders is simple: Ask yourselves what you can do to bring jobs back to your country, and your country will do everything we can to help you succeed.

We should start with our Tax Code. Right now companies get tax breaks for moving jobs and profits overseas. Meanwhile, companies that choose to stay in America get hit with one of the highest tax rates in the world. It makes no sense, and everyone knows it. So let's change it.

First, if you're a business that wants to outsource jobs, you shouldn't get a tax deduction for doing it. That money should be used to cover moving expenses for companies like Master Lock that decide to bring jobs home.

Second, no American company should be able to avoid paying its fair share of taxes by moving jobs and profits overseas. From now on, every multinational company should have to pay a basic minimum tax. And every penny should go towards lowering taxes for companies that choose to stay here and hire here in America.

Third, if you're an American manufacturer, you should get a bigger tax cut. If you're a high-tech manufacturer, we should double the tax deduction you get for making your products here. And if you want to relocate in a community that was hit hard when a factory left town, you should get help financing a new plant, equipment, or training for new workers.

So my message is simple: It is time to stop rewarding businesses that ship jobs overseas, and start rewarding companies that create jobs right here in America. Send me these tax reforms, and I will sign them right away.

We're also making it easier for American businesses to sell products all over the world. Two years ago, I set a goal of doubling U.S. exports over 5 years. With the bipartisan trade agreements we signed into law, we're on track to meet that goal ahead of schedule. And soon there will be millions of new customers for American goods in Panama, Colombia, and South Korea. Soon there will be new cars on the streets of Seoul imported from Detroit and Toledo and Chicago.

I will go anywhere in the world to open new markets for American products. And I will not stand by when our competitors don't play by the rules. We've brought trade cases against China at nearly twice the rate as the last administration, and it's made a difference. Over a thousand Americans are working today because we stopped a surge in Chinese tires. But we need to do more. It's not right when another country lets our movies, music, and software be pirated. It's not fair when foreign manufacturers have a leg up on ours only because they're heavily subsidized.

Tonight I'm announcing the creation of a trade enforcement unit that will be charged with investigating unfair trading practices in countries like China. There will be more inspections to prevent counterfeit or unsafe goods from crossing our borders. And this Congress should make sure that no foreign company has an advantage over American manufacturing when it comes to accessing financing or new markets like Russia. Our workers are the most productive on Earth, and if the playing field is level, I promise you, America will always win.

I also hear from many business leaders who want to hire in the United States, but can't find workers with the right skills. Growing industries in science and technology have twice as many openings as we have workers who can do the job. Think about that: openings at a time when millions of Americans are looking for work. It's inexcusable, and we know how to fix it.

Jackie Bray is a single mom from North Carolina who was laid off from her job as a mechanic. Then Siemens opened a gas turbine factory in Charlotte and formed a partnership with Central Piedmont Community College. The company helped the college design courses in laser and robotics training. It paid Jackie's tuition, then hired her to help operate their plant.

I want every American looking for work to have the same opportunity as Jackie did. Join me in a national commitment to train 2 million Americans with skills that will lead directly to a job. My administration has already lined up more companies that want to help. Model partnerships between businesses like Siemens and community colleges in places like Charlotte and Orlando and Louisville are up and running. Now you need to give more community colleges the resources they need to become community career centers, places that teach people skills that businesses are looking for right now, from data management to high-tech manufacturing.

And I want to cut through the maze of confusing training programs so that from now on, people like Jackie have one program, one web site, and one place to go for all the information and help that they need. It is time to turn our unemployment system into a reemployment system that puts people to work.

These reforms will help people get jobs that are open today. But to prepare for the jobs of tomorrow, our commitment to skills and education has to start earlier.

For less than 1 percent of what our Nation spends on education each year, we've convinced nearly every State in the country to raise their standards for teaching and learning, the first time that's happened in a generation. But challenges remain, and we know how to solve them.

At a time when other countries are doubling down on education, tight budgets have forced States to lay off thousands of teachers. We know a good teacher can increase the lifetime income of a classroom by over $250,000. A great teacher can offer an escape from poverty to the child who dreams beyond his circumstance. Every person in this Chamber can point to a teacher who changed the trajectory of their lives. Most teachers work tirelessly, with modest pay, sometimes digging into their own pocket for school supplies, just to make a difference.

Teachers matter. So instead of bashing them or defending the status quo, let's offer schools a deal. Give them the resources to keep good teachers on the job and reward the best ones. And in return, grant schools flexibility to teach with creativity and passion, to stop teaching to the test, and to replace teachers who just aren't helping kids learn. That's a bargain worth making.

We also know that when students don't walk away from their education, more of them walk the stage to get their diploma. When students are not allowed to drop out, they do better. So tonight I am proposing that every State–every State–requires that all students stay in high school until they graduate or turn 18.

When kids do graduate, the most daunting challenge can be the cost of college. At a time when Americans owe more in tuition debt than credit card debt, this Congress needs to stop the interest rates on student loans from doubling in July.

Extend the tuition tax credit we started that saves millions of middle class families thousands of dollars and give more young people the chance to earn their way through college by doubling the number of work-study jobs in the next 5 years.

Of course, it's not enough for us to increase student aid. We can't just keep subsidizing skyrocketing tuition; we'll run out of money. States also need to do their part by making higher education a higher priority in their budgets. And colleges and universities have to do their part by working to keep costs down.

Recently, I spoke with a group of college presidents who have done just that. Some schools redesign courses to help students finish more quickly. Some use better technology. The point is, it's possible. So let me put colleges and universities on notice: If you can't stop tuition from going up, the funding you get from taxpayers will go down. Higher education can't be a luxury. It is an economic imperative that every family in America should be able to afford.

Let's also remember that hundreds of thousands of talented, hard- working students in this country face another challenge: the fact that they aren't yet American citizens. Many were brought here as small children, are American through and through, yet they live every day with the threat of deportation. Others came more recently, to study business and science and engineering, but as soon as they get their degree, we send them home to invent new products and create new jobs somewhere else. That doesn't make sense.

I believe as strongly as ever that we should take on illegal immigration. That's why my administration has put more boots on the border than ever before. That's why there are fewer illegal crossings than when I took office. The opponents of action are out of excuses. We should be working on comprehensive immigration reform right now.

But if election-year politics keeps Congress from acting on a comprehensive plan, let's at least agree to stop expelling responsible young people who want to staff our labs, start new businesses, defend this country. Send me a law that gives them the chance to earn their citizenship. I will sign it right away.

You see, an economy built to last is one where we encourage the talent and ingenuity of every person in this country. That means women should earn equal pay for equal work. It means we should support everyone who's willing to work and every risk taker and entrepreneur who aspires to become the next Steve Jobs.

After all, innovation is what America has always been about. Most new jobs are created in startups and small businesses. So let's pass an agenda that helps them succeed. Tear down regulations that prevent aspiring entrepreneurs from getting the financing to grow. Expand tax relief to small businesses that are raising wages and creating good jobs. Both parties agree on these ideas. So put them in a bill and get it on my desk this year.

Innovation also demands basic research. Today, the discoveries taking place in our federally financed labs and universities could lead to new treatments that kill cancer cells, but leave healthy ones untouched, new lightweight vests for cops and soldiers that can stop any bullet. Don't gut these investments in our budget. Don't let other countries win the race for the future. Support the same kind of research and innovation that led to the computer chip and the Internet, to new American jobs and new American industries.

And nowhere is the promise of innovation greater than in American-made energy. Over the last 3 years, we've opened millions of new acres for oil and gas exploration, and tonight I'm directing my administration to open more than 75 percent of our potential offshore oil and gas resources. Right now—right now—American oil production is the highest that it's been in 8 years. That's right, 8 years. Not only that, last year, we relied less on foreign oil than in any of the past 16 years.

But with only 2 percent of the world's oil reserves, oil isn't enough. This country needs an all-out, all-of-the-above strategy that develops every available source of American energy, a strategy that's cleaner, cheaper, and full of new jobs.

We have a supply of natural gas that can last America nearly 100 years. And my administration will take every possible action to safely develop this energy. Experts believe this will support more than 600,000 jobs by the end of the decade. And I'm requiring all companies that drill for gas on public lands to disclose the chemicals they use. Because America will develop this resource without putting the health and safety of our citizens at risk.

The development of natural gas will create jobs and power trucks and factories that are cleaner and cheaper, proving that we don't have to choose between our environment and our economy. And by the way, it was public research dollars, over the course of 30 years, that helped develop the technologies to extract all this natural gas out of shale rock, reminding us that Government support is critical in helping businesses get new energy ideas off the ground.

Now, what's true for natural gas is just as true for clean energy. In 3 years, our partnership with the private sector has already positioned America to be the world's leading manufacturer of high-tech batteries. Because of Federal investments, renewable energy use has nearly doubled, and thousands of Americans have jobs because of it.

When Bryan Ritterby was laid off from his job making furniture, he said he worried that at 55 no one would give him a second chance. But he found work at Energetx, a wind turbine manufacturer in Michigan. Before the recession, the factory only made luxury yachts. Today, it's hiring workers like Bryan, who said, "I'm proud to be working in the industry of the future."

Our experience with shale gas, our experience with natural gas, shows us that the payoffs on these public investments don't always come right away. Some technologies don't pan out, some companies fail. But I will not walk away from the promise of clean energy. I will not walk away from workers like Bryan. I will not cede the wind or solar or battery industry to China or Germany because we refuse to make the same commitment here.

We've subsidized oil companies for a century. That's long enough. It's time to end the taxpayer giveaways to an industry that rarely has been more profitable and double down on a clean energy industry that never has been more promising. Pass clean energy tax credits. Create these jobs.

We can also spur energy innovation with new incentives. The differences in this Chamber may be too deep right now to pass a comprehensive plan to fight climate change. But there's no reason why Congress shouldn't at least set a clean energy standard that creates a market for innovation. So far, you haven't acted. Well, tonight I will. I'm directing my administration to allow the development of clean energy on enough public land to power 3 million homes. And I'm proud to announce that the Department of Defense, working with us, the world's largest consumer of energy, will make one of the largest commitments to clean energy in history, with the Navy purchasing enough capacity to power a quarter of a million homes a year.

Of course, the easiest way to save money is to waste less energy. So here's a proposal: Help manufacturers eliminate energy waste in their factories and give businesses incentives to upgrade their buildings. Their energy bills will be a hundred billion dollars lower over the next decade, and America will have less pollution, more manufacturing, more jobs for construction workers who need them. Send me a bill that creates these jobs.

Building this new energy future should be just one part of a broader agenda to repair America's infrastructure. So much of America needs to be rebuilt. We've got crumbling roads and bridges, a power grid that wastes too much energy, an incomplete high-speed broadband network that prevents a small-business owner in rural America from selling her products all over the world.

During the Great Depression, America built the Hoover Dam and the Golden Gate Bridge. After World War II, we connected our States with a system of highways. Democratic and Republican administrations invested in great projects that benefited everybody, from the workers who built them to the businesses that still use them today.

In the next few weeks, I will sign an Executive order clearing away the redtape that slows down too many construction projects. But you need to fund these projects. Take the money we're no longer spending at war, use half of it to pay down our debt, and use the rest to do some nation-building right here at home.

There's never been a better time to build, especially since the construction industry was one of the hardest hit when the housing bubble burst. Of course, construction workers weren't the only ones who were hurt. So were millions of innocent Americans who've seen their home values decline. And while Government can't fix the problem on its own, responsible homeowners shouldn't have to sit and wait for the housing market to hit bottom to get some relief.

And that's why I'm sending this Congress a plan that gives every responsible homeowner the chance to save about $3,000 a year on their mortgage by refinancing at historically low rates. No more redtape. No more runaround from the banks. A small fee on the largest financial institutions will ensure that it won't add to the deficit and will give those banks that were rescued by taxpayers a chance to repay a deficit of trust.

Let's never forget: Millions of Americans who work hard and play by the rules every day deserve a Government and a financial system that do the same. It's time to apply the same rules from top to bottom. No bailouts, no handouts, and no copouts. An America built to last insists on responsibility from everybody.

We've all paid the price for lenders who sold mortgages to people who couldn't afford them and buyers who knew they couldn't afford them. That's why we need smart regulations to prevent irresponsible behavior. Rules to prevent financial fraud or toxic dumping or faulty medical devices, these don't destroy the free market. They make the free market work better.

There's no question that some regulations are outdated, unnecessary, or too costly. In fact, I've approved fewer regulations in the first 3 years of my Presidency than my Republican predecessor did in his. I've ordered every Federal agency to eliminate rules that don't make sense. We've already announced over 500 reforms, and just a fraction of them will save business and citizens more than $10 billion over the next 5 years. We got rid of one rule from 40 years ago that could have forced some dairy farmers to spend $10,000 a year proving that they could contain a spill, because milk was somehow classified as an oil. With a rule like that, I guess it was worth crying over spilled milk. [Laughter]

Now, I'm confident a farmer can contain a milk spill without a Federal agency looking over his shoulder. Absolutely. But I will not back down from making sure an oil company can contain the kind of oil spill we saw in the Gulf 2 years ago. I will not back down from protecting our kids from mercury poisoning or making sure that our food is safe and our water is clean. I will not go back to the days when health insurance companies had unchecked power to cancel your policy, deny your coverage, or charge women differently than men.

And I will not go back to the days when Wall Street was allowed to play by its own set of rules. The new rules we passed restore what should be any financial system's core purpose: getting funding to entrepreneurs with the best ideas and getting loans to responsible families who want to buy a home or start a business or send their kids to college.

So if you are a big bank or financial institution, you're no longer allowed to make risky bets with your customers' deposits. You're required to write out a "living will" that details exactly how you'll pay the bills if you fail, because the rest of us are not bailing you out ever again. And if you're a mortgage lender or a payday lender or a credit card company, the days of signing people up for products they can't afford with confusing forms and deceptive practices, those days are over. Today, American consumers finally have a watchdog in Richard Cordray, with one job: to look out for them.

We'll also establish a financial crimes unit of highly trained investigators to crack down on large-scale fraud and protect people's investments. Some financial firms violate major antifraud laws because there's no real penalty for being a repeat offender. That's bad for consumers, and it's bad for the vast majority of bankers and financial service professionals who do the right thing. So pass legislation that makes the penalties for fraud count.

And tonight I'm asking my Attorney General to create a special unit of Federal prosecutors and leading State attorney general to expand our investigations into the abusive lending and packaging of risky mortgages that led to the housing crisis. This new unit will hold accountable those who broke the law, speed assistance to home-owners, and help turn the page on an era of recklessness that hurt so many Americans.

Now, a return to the American values of fair play and shared responsibility will help protect our people and our economy. But it should also guide us as we look to pay down our debt and invest in our future.

Right now our most immediate priority is stopping a tax hike on a hundred and sixty million working Americans while the recovery is still fragile. People cannot afford losing $40 out of each paycheck this year. There are plenty of ways to get this done. So let's agree right here, right now. No side issues. No drama. Pass the payroll tax cut without delay. Let's get it done.

When it comes to the deficit, we've already agreed to more than $2 trillion in cuts and savings. But we need to do more, and that means making choices. Right now we're poised to spend nearly $1 trillion more on what was supposed to be a tempo-rary tax break for the wealthiest 2 percent of Americans. Right now because of loop-holes and shelters in the Tax Code, a quarter of all millionaires pay lower tax rates than millions of middle class households. Right now Warren Buffett pays a lower tax rate than his secretary.

Do we want to keep these tax cuts for the wealthiest Americans? Or do we want to keep our investments in everything else, like education and medical research, a strong military and care for our veterans? Because if we're serious about paying down our debt, we can't do both.

The American people know what the right choice is. So do I. As I told the Speaker this summer, I'm prepared to make more reforms that rein in the long-term costs of Medicare and Medicaid and strengthen Social Security, so long as those programs remain a guarantee of security for seniors. But in return, we need to change our Tax Code so that people like me, and an awful lot of Members of Congress, pay our fair share of taxes.

Tax reform should follow the Buffett rule. If you make more than a million dollars a year, you should not pay less than 30 percent in taxes. And my Republican friend Tom Coburn is right: Washington should stop subsidizing millionaires. In fact, if you're earning a million dollars a year, you shouldn't get special tax subsidies or deductions. On the other hand, if you make under $250,000 a year, like 98 percent of American families, your taxes shouldn't go up. You're the ones struggling with rising costs and stagnant wages. You're the ones who need relief.

Now, you can call this class warfare all you want. But asking a billionaire to pay at least as much as his secretary in taxes? Most Americans would call that common sense.

We don't begrudge financial success in this country. We admire it. When Americans talk about folks like me paying my fair share of taxes, it's not because they envy the rich. It's because they understand that when I get a tax break I don't need and the country can't afford, it either adds to the deficit or somebody else has to make up the difference, like a senior on a fixed income or a student trying to get through school or a family trying to make ends meet. That's not right. Americans know that's not right. They know that this generation's success is only possible because past generations felt a responsibility to each other and to the future of their country, and they know our way of life will only endure if we feel that same sense of shared responsibility. That's how we'll reduce our deficit. That's an America built to last.

Now, I recognize that people watching tonight have differing views about taxes and debt, energy and health care. But no matter what party they belong to, I bet most Americans are thinking the same thing right about now: Nothing will get done in Washington this year or next year or maybe even the year after that, because Washington is broken.

Can you blame them for feeling a little cynical?

The greatest blow to our confidence in our economy last year didn't come from events beyond our control. It came from a debate in Washington over whether the United States would pay its bills or not. Who benefited from that fiasco?

I've talked tonight about the deficit of trust between Main Street and Wall Street. But the divide between this city and the rest of the country is at least as bad, and it seems to get worse every year.

Now, some of this has to do with the corrosive influence of money in politics. So together, let's take some steps to fix that. Send me a bill that bans insider trading by Members of Congress. I will sign it tomorrow. Let's limit any elected official from owning stocks in industries they impact. Let's make sure people who bundle campaign contributions for Congress can't lobby Congress and vice versa, an idea that has bipartisan support, at least outside of Washington.

Some of what's broken has to do with the way Congress does its business these days. A simple majority is no longer enough to get anything–even routine business– passed through the Senate. Neither party has been blameless in these tactics. Now both parties should put an end to it. For starters, I ask the Senate to pass a simple rule that all judicial and public service nominations receive a simple up-or-down vote within 90 days.

The executive branch also needs to change. Too often, it's inefficient, outdated, and remote. That's why I've asked this Congress to grant me the authority to consolidate the Federal bureaucracy so that our Government is leaner, quicker, and more responsive to the needs of the American people.

Finally, none of this can happen unless we also lower the temperature in this town. We need to end the notion that the two parties must be locked in a perpetual campaign of mutual destruction, that politics is about clinging to rigid ideologies instead of building consensus around commonsense ideas.

I'm a Democrat, but I believe what Republican Abraham Lincoln believed: That Government should do for people only what they cannot do better by themselves and no more. That's why my education reform offers more competition and more control for schools and States. That's why we're getting rid of regulations that don't work. That's why our health care law relies on a reformed private market, not a Government program.

On the other hand, even my Republican friends who complain the most about Government spending have supported federally financed roads and clean energy projects and Federal offices for the folks back home.

The point is, we should all want a smarter, more effective Government. And while we may not be able to bridge our biggest philosophical differences this year, we can make real progress. With or without this Congress, I will keep taking actions that help the economy grow. But I can do a whole lot more with your help. Because when we act together, there's nothing the United States of America can't achieve.

That's the lesson we've learned from our actions abroad over the last few years. Ending the Iraq war has allowed us to strike decisive blows against our enemies. From Pakistan to Yemen, the Al Qaida operatives who remain are scrambling, knowing that they can't escape the reach of the United States of America.

From this position of strength, we've begun to wind down the war in Afghanistan. Ten thousand of our troops have come home. Twenty-three thousand more will leave by the end of this summer. This transition to Afghan lead will continue, and we will build an enduring partnership with Afghanistan so that it is never again a source of attacks against America.

As the tide of war recedes, a wave of change has washed across the Middle East and North Africa, from Tunis to Cairo, from Sana'a to Tripoli. A year ago, Qadhafi was one of the world's longest serving dictators, a murderer with American blood on his hands. Today, he is gone. And in Syria, I have no doubt that the Asad regime will soon discover that the forces of change cannot be reversed and that human dignity cannot be denied.

How this incredible transformation will end remains uncertain. But we have a huge stake in the outcome. And while it's ultimately up to the people of the region to decide their fate, we will advocate for those values that have served our own country so well. We will stand against violence and intimidation. We will stand for the rights and dignity of all human beings: men and women; Christians, Muslims, and Jews. We will support policies that lead to strong and stable democracies and open markets, because tyranny is no match for liberty.

And we will safeguard America's own security against those who threaten our citizens, our friends, and our interests. Look at Iran. Through the power of our diplomacy, a world that was once divided about how to deal with Iran's nuclear program now stands as one. The regime is more isolated than ever before. Its leaders are faced with crippling sanctions, and as long as they shirk their responsibilities, this pressure will not relent.

88

Let there be no doubt: America is determined to prevent Iran from getting a nuclear weapon, and I will take no options off the table to achieve that goal. But a peaceful resolution of this issue is still possible, and far better. And if Iran changes course and meets its obligations, it can rejoin the community of nations.

The renewal of American leadership can be felt across the globe. Our oldest alliances in Europe and Asia are stronger than ever. Our ties to the Americas are deeper. Our ironclad commitment–and I mean ironclad–to Israel's security has meant the closest military cooperation between our two countries in history.

We've made it clear that America is a Pacific power, and a new beginning in Burma has lit a new hope. From the coalitions we've built to secure nuclear materials, to the missions we've led against hunger and disease, from the blows we've dealt to our enemies, to the enduring power of our moral example, America is back.

Anyone who tells you otherwise, anyone who tells you that America is in decline or that our influence has waned, doesn't know what they're talking about. That's not the message we get from leaders around the world who are eager to work with us. That's not how people feel from Tokyo to Berlin, from Cape Town to Rio, where opinions of America are higher than they've been in years. Yes, the world is changing. No, we can't control every event. But America remains the one indispensable nation in world affairs, and as long as I'm President, I intend to keep it that way.

That's why, working with our military leaders, I've proposed a new defense strategy that ensures we maintain the finest military in the world, while saving nearly half a trillion dollars in our budget. To stay one step ahead of our adversaries, I've already sent this Congress legislation that will secure our country from the growing dangers of cyber threats.

Above all, our freedom endures because of the men and women in uniform who defend it. As they come home, we must serve them as well as they've served us. That includes giving them the care and the benefits they have earned, which is why we've increased annual VA spending every year I've been President. And it means enlisting our veterans in the work of rebuilding our Nation.

With the bipartisan support of this Congress, we're providing new tax credits to companies that hire vets. Michelle and Jill Biden have worked with American businesses to secure a pledge of 135,000 jobs for veterans and their families. And tonight I'm proposing a veterans jobs corps that will help our communities hire veterans as cops and firefighters, so that America is as strong as those who defend her.

Which brings me back to where I began. Those of us who've been sent here to serve can learn a thing or two from the service of our troops. When you put on that uniform, it doesn't matter if you're Black or White, Asian, Latino, Native American; conservative, liberal; rich, poor; gay, straight. When you're marching into battle, you look out for the person next to you or the mission fails. When you're in the thick of the fight, you rise or fall as one unit, serving one nation, leaving no one behind.

You know, one of my proudest possessions is the flag that the SEAL team took with them on the mission to get bin Laden. On it are each of their names. Some may be Democrats, some may be Republicans, but that doesn't matter. Just like it didn't matter that day in the Situation Room, when I sat next to Bob Gates, a man who was

George Bush's Defense Secretary, and Hillary Clinton, a woman who ran against me for President.

All that mattered that day was the mission. No one thought about politics. No one thought about themselves. One of the young men involved in the raid later told me that he didn't deserve credit for the mission. It only succeeded, he said, because every single member of that unit did their job: the pilot who landed the helicopter that spun out of control, the translator who kept others from entering the compound, the troops who separated the women and children from the fight, the SEALs who charged up the stairs. More than that, the mission only succeeded because every member of that unit trusted each other, because you can't charge up those stairs into darkness and danger unless you know that there's somebody behind you, watching your back.

So it is with America. Each time I look at that flag, I'm reminded that our destiny is stitched together like those 50 stars and those 13 stripes. No one built this country on their own. This Nation is great because we built it together. This Nation is great because we worked as a team. This Nation is great because we get each other's backs. And if we hold fast to that truth, in this moment of trial, there is no challenge too great, no mission too hard. As long as we are joined in common purpose, as long as we maintain our common resolve, our journey moves forward, and our future is hopeful, and the state of our Union will always be strong.

Thank you, God bless you, and God bless the United States of America.

❦ II ❦

"YOU DIDN'T BUILD THAT." REMARKS AT A CAMPAIGN EVENT IN ROANOKE, VIRGINIA

JULY 13, 2012

Hello, Roanoke! It is good to be back in Roanoke! Good to be back in Virginia. Back in the Star City.

There are a couple of people I want to acknowledge. First of all, you've got one of the finest senators and public servants in the country in Mark Warner. Give it up for Mark Warner. Now, Mark was a great governor for the Commonwealth of Virginia, and now he's a great senator. I just want to point out we've got another great governor of the Commonwealth of Virginia who is going to be a great senator in Tim Kaine. We are thrilled to have them both with us today.

I want to thank Mayor David Bowers who's here. City Manager, Christopher Morrill. Fire Chief, David Hoback. And we've got former Majority Leader of the House of Delegates, Dick Cranwell is here.

And all of you are here. Couldn't ask for a nicer setting. It is beautiful flying in to Roanoke.

Now, let me just say, unless you have managed to break your television set – you're probably aware that it is campaign season. And I know it's not always pretty to watch. We're seeing more money flooding into the system than ever before, more negative ads, more cynicism. A lot of the reporting is just about who's up and who's down in the polls instead of talking about the things that matter in your day-to-day life.

So I know all this kind of makes it tempting to just turn off the TV set, and turn away from politics. And there are some people who are betting that you lose interest.

[…] But the fact that you are here tells me that you're still ready to work to make this a better country. You're still betting on hope and you're still betting on change – and I am still betting on you.

[…] And the reason you're here tonight is because no matter how petty and small politics seems sometimes, you recognize that the stakes could not be bigger. In some ways, the stakes are even bigger now than they were in 2008, because what's at stake is not just two people or two political parties. What's at stake is a decision between two fundamentally different views about where we take the country right now. And the choice is up to you.

Now, this is my last political campaign.

[…] There is a term limit for Presidents. You get two. So no matter what happens, this will be my last campaign. And it makes you nostalgic sometimes, and I started thinking about some of my first campaigns.

When I was traveling across Illinois – and Illinois is a big state. And it's got big cities like Chicago and it's got small towns, and it's got rural areas and suburban areas, and you meet people from every walk of life – black, white, Latino, Asian, Native American. You stop in VFW halls, you stop in diners, you go to churches, you go to synagogues. Wherever you go, you're going to have a chance to meet people from different walks of life. And when I think about that first campaign, what strikes me is no matter where I went, no matter who I was talking to, I could see my own life in the life of the people whose vote I was asking for.

So I would meet an elderly vet and I'd think about my grandfather who fought in World War II, and my grandmother who worked on a bomber assembly line during the war. And I'd think about how, when my grandfather came back home, because of this country he was able to get an education on the GI Bill and they were able to buy their first home using an FHA loan.

And then I'd meet a single mom somewhere and I'd think about my mom. I never knew my dad. He left when I was just barely a baby, and so – and my mother didn't have a lot of money and she was struggling, and she had to go back to school raising a kid, later raising my sister, and she had to work while she was in school. But despite all that, because she was in America, she was able to get grants and scholarships and her kids were able to get grants and scholarships. And they could go as far as their dreams could take them.

And then I'd talk to some working folks, and I'd think about Michelle's family – her dad who was a blue-collar worker, worked at a water filtration plant in Chicago, and her mom was a secretary. And yet, despite never having a lot, there was so much love and so much passion – and her dad had MS, so he had to wake up an hour earlier than everybody else just to get to work because it took him that long to get dressed, and he could barely walk. But he never missed a day's work – because he took pride in the idea that, you know what, I'm going to earn my way and look after my family. And I'd see that same pride in the people I was talking to.

And what this reminded me of was that, at the heart of this country, its central idea is the idea that in this country, if you're willing to work hard, if you're willing to take responsibility, you can make it if you try. That you can find a job that supports a family and find a home you can make your own; that you won't go bankrupt when you get sick. That maybe you can take a little vacation with your family once in a while – nothing fancy, but just time to spend with those you love. Maybe see the country a little bit, maybe come down to Roanoke. That your kids can get a great education, and if they're willing to work hard, then they can achieve things that you wouldn't have even imagined achieving. And then you can maybe retire with some dignity and some respect, and be part of a community and give something back.

That's the idea of America. It doesn't matter what you look like. It doesn't matter where you come from. It doesn't matter what your last name is. You can live out the American Dream. That's what binds us all together.

Now, the reason that I think so many of us came together in 2008 was because we saw that for a decade that dream was fraying, that it was slipping away; that there were too many people who were working hard but not seeing their incomes or wages go up; that we had taken a surplus and turned it into a deficit – we were running two wars on a credit card; that job growth was the most sluggish it had been in 50 years. There was a sense that those who were in charge didn't feel responsible.

And so we came together to say we are going to bring about the kinds of changes that allow us to get back to those basics, allow us to restore and live out those values. What we didn't realize was that some of that recklessness, some of that irresponsibility would lead to the worst financial crisis we've seen since the Great Depression. And I don't need to tell you what we've been through over the last three and a half years because you've lived it. Too many folks lost jobs. Too many people saw their homes lose value. Too many folks saw their savings take a hit.

But you know what's given me confidence and faith is that fact that as I've traveled around the country now, just like I used to travel around Illinois, that same decency, those same values – they're still alive, at least outside Washington. Times have been tough, but America's character hasn't changed. The core decency of the American people is undiminished. Our willingness to fight through and work through the tough times and come together, that's still there.

And so, just as we came together in the last campaign – not just Democrats, by the way, but Republicans and independents, because we're not Democrats or Republicans first, we're Americans first. Just like we came together in 2008, we know that we've got to keep working, we got to keep moving forward in 2012. And we knew back then that it wasn't going to be easy. These problems we're facing, they didn't happen overnight, and they're not going to be solved overnight. We understood it might take more than one year or one term or even one President. But what we also understood was that we weren't going to stop until we had restored that basic American bargain that makes us the greatest country on Earth.

Our goal isn't just to put people back to work – although that's priority number one – it is to build an economy where that work pays off. An economy where everyone, whether you are starting a business or punching a clock, can see your hard work and responsibility rewarded. That's what this campaign's about, Roanoke. And that's why I'm running for a second term as President of the United States of America.

[…] Now, let me say this. It's fashionable among some pundits – and this happens every time America hits a rough patch – it's fashionable to be saying, well, this time it's different, this time we really are in the soup; it's going to be hard to solve our problems. Let me tell you something. What's missing is not big ideas. What's missing is not that we've got an absence of technical solutions to deal with issues like education or energy or our deficit. The problem we've got right now is we've just got a stalemate in Washington.

And the outcome of this debate that we're having is going to set the stage not just for the next year or five years, but for the next twenty. On the one side you've got my opponent in this presidential race and his Republican allies who [...] I mean, we're having a good, healthy, democratic debate. That's how this works. And on their side, they've got a basic theory about how you grow the economy. And the theory is very simple: They think that the economy grows from the top down. So their basic theory is, if wealthy investors are doing well then everybody does well. So if we spend trillions of dollars on more tax cuts mostly for the wealthy, that that's somehow going to create jobs, even if we have to pay for it by gutting education and gutting job-training programs and gutting transportation projects, and maybe even seeing middle-class folks have a higher tax burden.

[...] So that's part number one, right. More tax cuts for those at the top.

Part number two is they believe if you tear down all the regulations that we've put in place – for example, on Wall Street banks or on insurance companies or on credit card companies or on polluters – that somehow the economy is going to do much, much better. So those are their two theories. They've got the tax cuts for the high end, and they've got rollback regulation.

Now, here's the problem. You may have guessed – we tried this. We tried this in the last decade and it did not work.

[...] Now, before I finish, can I say, by the way, that some of you have been standing for a while and I see a couple folks slumping down a little bit. Make sure you're drinking water. Bend your knees. Don't stand up too straight. The paralegals will be – the paralegals? You don't need lawyers. The paramedics will be coming by, so just give folks a little bit of room, they'll be fine. This happens at every event.

[...] I just want to point out that we tried their theory for almost 10 years, and here's what it got us: We got the slowest job growth in decades. We got deficits as far as the eye can see. Your incomes and your wages didn't go up. And it culminated in a crisis because there weren't enough regulations on Wall Street and they could make reckless bets with other people's money that resulted in this financial crisis, and you had to foot the bill. So that's where their theory turned out.

Now, we don't need more top-down economics. I've got a different view. I believe that the way you grow the economy is from the middle out. I believe that you grow the economy from the bottom up. I believe that when working people are doing well, the country does well.

I believe in fighting for the middle class because if they're prospering, all of us will prosper. That's what I'm fighting for, and that's why I'm running for a second term as President of the United States.

Now, this is what I've been focused on since I've been in office. In 2008, I promised to make sure that middle-class taxes didn't go up. And in fact, because of the recession, you needed some help, so we cut the typical family's income taxes by $3,600. So if you hear somebody say that I'm a big tax guy, just remember $3,600 for the typical family. That's the tax break you've gotten since I've been in office.

Four years later, I'm running to keep middle-class taxes low. So this week, I called on Congress to immediately extend income tax cuts on the first $250,000 of income. Now, what that means is 98 percent of Americans make less than $250,000, so 98 percent of folks would have the certainty and security that your taxes, your income taxes would not go up a dime. And, by the way, this is not a hypothetical. This wasn't some campaign promise. The reason I called on Congress to act now is because if they don't do anything, on January 1st, almost everybody here, your taxes will go up an average of $1,600.

[…] So we need to stop that tax hike from happening.

So you would think that this makes sense, right, because the Republicans say they're the party of no new taxes, right? That's what they always say. Except so far, they've refused to act. And this might confuse you. You might say, why would they not want to give 98 percent of Americans the certainty of this income tax cut?

Well, it turns out they don't want you to get your tax break unless the other 2 percent, the top 2 percent, they get their tax break as well.

Now, understand, the top 2 percent, folks like me, we're the ones who most bene-fited over the last decade from not only tax breaks, but also a lot of the money from increased profits and productivity went up to that top 2 percent. So the bottom line is, the top 2 percent doesn't need help. They're doing just fine.

And I understand why they wouldn't want to pay more in taxes. Nobody likes to pay more in taxes. Here's the problem: If you continue their tax breaks, that costs a trillion dollars. And since we're trying to bring down our deficit and our debt, if we spend a trillion dollars on tax cuts for them, we're going to have to find that trillion dollars someplace else. That means we're going to have to maybe make student loans more expensive for students. Or we might have to cut back on the services we're providing our brave veterans when they come home.

[…] Or we might have to stop investing in basic science and research that keeps us as a leading-edge economy. Or, as they suggested, maybe you would have to turn Medicare into a voucher program.

[…] I don't think those are good ideas. So what I've said to the Republicans is, look, all right, let's have this debate about the tax cuts for the wealthiest folks. I don't mind having that debate. But in the meantime, let's go ahead and do what we agree on, which is give 98 percent of Americans some certainty and some security. So far, they haven't taken me up on my offer.

Now, this gives you a sense of how Congress works these days – you've got the possibility of your taxes going up in four months, five months, and instead of working on that, guess what they worked on this week? They worked […] – they voted for the 33rd time to try to repeal a health care bill we passed two years ago, after the Supreme Court said it's constitutional and we are going to go ahead and implement that law. I don't know about you, Virginia, but I think they've got a better way to use their time. I think helping you make sure your taxes don't go up, that would be a good use of congressional time.

Now, this is just a small example of the difference between myself and Mr. Romney, between myself and some of the Republicans who are running Congress. And look, Virginia, I want to repeat – this is a choice. If you think their way of doing things is a recipe for economic growth and helping the middle class, then you should vote for them.

[…] You can send those folks to Washington. I promise you they will carry out what they promise to do.

But that's not why I went to Washington. I went to Washington to fight for the middle class. I went to Washington to fight for working people who are trying to get into the middle class, and have some sense of security in their lives. People like me and Mr. Romney don't need another tax cut. You need some help right now to make sure your kids are living the kind of life you want for them. And that's why I'm running for a second term as President of the United States.

On almost every issue, you've got the same kind of choice. When the auto industry was about to go under, a million jobs lost, and my opponent said, "let's let Detroit go bankrupt," what did I say? I said –

[…] I said I'm betting on America's workers. I'm betting on American industry. And guess what? Three years later, GM is number one again and the American auto industry has come roaring back.

So I believe in American manufacturing. I believe in making stuff here in America. My opponent, he invested in companies who are called "pioneers" of outsourcing. I don't believe in outsourcing – I believe in insourcing. I want to stop giving tax breaks to companies that ship jobs overseas; let's give tax breaks to companies that are investing right here in Roanoke, right here in the United States of America. Let's invest in American workers so they can make products and ship them around the world with those three proud words: Made in America.

I'm running because our men and women in uniform have sacrificed so much. We could not be prouder of them and we could not be prouder of our veterans. And because of their efforts, I was able to keep my promise and end the war in Iraq.

And I now intend to transition out of Afghanistan and bring our troops home. And what I said is, because of their outstanding work, we've been able to decimate al Qaeda and take out bin Laden. And so now it's time for us to take half of the money we were saving on war and pay down our deficit, and use the other half to do some nation-building here at home.

Roanoke knows something about transportation – this was a railroad hub for a long time. So you know how important that is to growing an economy. Let's take some of that money and rebuild our roads and our bridges and our rail systems, and let's build wireless networks into rural communities so everybody can tap into world markets. Let's put construction workers back to work doing what they do best and that is rebuilding America. That's why I'm running for a second term as President of the United States. That's the choice you face.

I'm running to make sure that our kids are getting the best education in the world. When I came into office, we passed a tuition tax credit that has saved millions of families thousands of dollars, and now I want to extend it. But I don't want to stop there. We just won a fight thanks to some of the folks who are here, including students from VT that – we just won a fight to make sure that student loan interest rates would not double.

But that's not enough. I want to lower tuition to make it more affordable for all young people. I want to help our elementary schools and our middle schools and our high schools hire more teachers, especially in math and science. I want 2 million more people to be able to go to community colleges to get trained in the jobs that businesses are hiring for right now – because a higher education, a good education is not a luxury, it is an economic necessity. That's how we're going to win the race for the future. And that's why I'm running for a second term as President – to finish the job we started in 2008.

We've got to deal with homeownership, and the fact of the matter is that my opponent's philosophy when it comes to dealing with homeowners is, let the market bottom out and let as many foreclosures happen as it takes. I don't think that's part of a solution – that's part of the problem.

So what I want to do is, I want to let every single person refinance their homes and save about $3,000 a year because you'll spend that $3,000 on some of these stores right here in downtown. You'll help small businesses and large businesses grow because they'll have more customers. It will be good for you and it will be good for the economy. And that's why I'm running for a second term as President – because I want to help America's homeowners.

I am running because I still believe that you shouldn't go bankrupt when you get sick. We passed that health care law because it was the right thing to do. And because we did, 30 million people who don't have health insurance are going to get help getting health insurance. Six million young people who didn't have health insurance can now stay on their parent's plan and get health insurance.

Seniors are seeing their prescription drug costs go down. And, by the way, if you've got health insurance, you're not getting hit by a tax. The only thing that's happening to you is that you now have more security because insurance companies can't drop you when you get sick. And they can't mess around with you because of some fine print in your policy. If you're paying your policy, you will get the deal that you paid for. That's why we passed health care reform.

Now, one last thing – one of the biggest differences is how we pay down our debt and our deficit. My opponent, Mr. Romney's plan is he wants to cut taxes another $5 trillion on top of the Bush tax cuts.

[…] Well, first of all, like I said, the only way you can pay for that – if you're actually saying you're bringing down the deficit – is to cut transportation, cut education, cut basic research, voucherize Medicare, and you're still going to end up having to raise taxes on middle-class families to pay for this $5 trillion tax cut. That's not a deficit reduction plan. That's a deficit expansion plan.

I've got a different idea. I do believe we can cut – we've already made a trillion dollars' worth of cuts. We can make some more cuts in programs that don't work, and make government work more efficiently. Not every government program works the way it's supposed to. And frankly, government can't solve every problem. If somebody doesn't want to be helped, government can't always help them. Parents – we can put more money into schools, but if your kids don't want to learn it's hard to teach them.

But you know what, I'm not going to see us gut the investments that grow our economy to give tax breaks to me or Mr. Romney or folks who don't need them. So I'm going to reduce the deficit in a balanced way. We've already made a trillion dollars' worth of cuts. We can make another trillion or trillion-two, and what we then do is ask for the wealthy to pay a little bit more. And, by the way, we've tried that before – a guy named Bill Clinton did it. We created 23 million new jobs, turned a deficit into a surplus, and rich people did just fine. We created a lot of millionaires.

There are a lot of wealthy, successful Americans who agree with me – because they want to give something back. They know they didn't – look, if you've been successful, you didn't get there on your own. You didn't get there on your own. I'm always struck by people who think, well, it must be because I was just so smart. There are a lot of smart people out there. It must be because I worked harder than everybody else. Let me tell you something – there are a whole bunch of hardworking people out there.

If you were successful, somebody along the line gave you some help. There was a great teacher somewhere in your life. Somebody helped to create this unbelievable American system that we have that allowed you to thrive. Somebody invested in roads and bridges. If you've got a business – you didn't build that. Somebody else made that happen. The Internet didn't get invented on its own. Government research created the Internet so that all the companies could make money off the Internet.

The point is, is that when we succeed, we succeed because of our individual initiative, but also because we do things together. There are some things, just like fighting fires, we don't do on our own. I mean, imagine if everybody had their own fire service. That would be a hard way to organize fighting fires.

So we say to ourselves, ever since the founding of this country, you know what, there are some things we do better together. That's how we funded the GI Bill. That's how we created the middle class. That's how we built the Golden Gate Bridge or the Hoover Dam. That's how we invented the Internet. That's how we sent a man to the moon. We rise or fall together as one nation and as one people, and that's the reason I'm running for President – because I still believe in that idea. You're not on your own, we're in this together.

So all these issues go back to that first campaign that I talked about, because everything has to do with how do we help middle-class families, working people, strivers, doers – how do we help them succeed? How do we make sure that their hard work pays off? That's what I've been thinking about the entire time I've been President.

Now, over the next four months, the other side is going to spend more money than we've even seen in history. And they don't really have a good argument for how they would do better, but they're thinking they can win the election if they just remind people that a lot of people are still out of work, and the economy is not growing as fast as it needs to, and it's all Obama's fault. That's basically their pitch. […] No, no, I mean, I'm just telling you. You've seen the ads, and they're going to run more of them, and there will be all kinds of variations on the same theme. But it will be the same basic message over and over and over and over and over again.

Now, their ads may be a plan to win an election, but it's not a plan to put people back to work. It's not a plan to strengthen the middle class. And the reason it doesn't worry me is because we've been outspent before. We've been counted out before. The pundits, they didn't think I could win Virginia the last time. The last time I came to this part of Virginia, all the political writers, they're all like, well, he's not serious, he's just making a tactical move. No, I'm serious – I'm going to get some votes down here.

And so the reason that I continue to have confidence is because when I look at you, I see my grandparents. When I see your kids, I see my kids. And I think about

98

all those previous generations – our parents and grandparents and great-grandparents. Some of them came here as immigrants, some were brought here against their will. Some of them worked on farms, and some worked in mills, and some worked in mines, and some worked on the railroad.

But no matter where they worked, no matter how times were tough, they always had faith that there was something different about this country; that in this country, you have some God-given rights: a life in liberty and the pursuit of happiness, and a belief that all of us are equal – and that we're not guaranteed success, but we're guaranteed the right to work hard for success.

They understood that, and they understood that succeeding in America wasn't about how much money was in your bank account, but it was about whether you were doing right by your people, doing right by your family, doing right by your neighborhood, doing right by your community, doing right by your country, living out our values, living out our dreams, living out our hopes. That's what America was about.

And so when I look out at this crowd, you inspire me. And I have to tell you that the privilege of being your President is something that I thank God for every single day.

I said to you back in 2008 when I was running, I'm not a perfect man – you can ask Michelle about that. (Laughter.) And I told you I wouldn't be a perfect President. But what I did say to you was that I'd always tell you what I thought and I'd always tell you where I stood, and that I would wake up every single morning thinking about you and fighting as hard as I knew how to make your life a little bit better.

And over these last three and a half years, I know times have been tough, and I know change hasn't always come as fast as you'd like. But you know what, I've kept that promise. I thought about you. I fought for you. I believe in you. And if you still believe in me, if you're willing to stand up with me, and campaign with me, and make phone calls for me, and knock on doors with me, I promise you we will finish what we started – and we will restore that basic bargain that built this country, and we'll remind the world just why it is that America is the greatest nation on Earth.

God bless you, and God bless the United States of America.

12

REMARKS TO THE UN GENERAL ASSEMBLY

SEPTEMBER 25, 2012

M r. President, Mr. Secretary General, fellow delegates, ladies and gentleman: I would like to begin today by telling you about an American named Chris Stevens.

Chris was born in a town called Grass Valley, California, the son of a lawyer and a musician. As a young man, Chris joined the Peace Corps, and taught English in Morocco. And he came to love and respect the people of North Africa and the Middle East. He would carry that commitment throughout his life. As a diplomat, he worked from Egypt to Syria, from Saudi Arabia to Libya. He was known for walking the streets of the cities where he worked – tasting the local food, meeting as many people as he could, speaking Arabic, listening with a broad smile.

Chris went to Benghazi in the early days of the Libyan revolution, arriving on a cargo ship. As America's representative, he helped the Libyan people as they coped with violent conflict, cared for the wounded, and crafted a vision for the future in which the rights of all Libyans would be respected. And after the revolution, he supported the birth of a new democracy, as Libyans held elections, and built new institutions, and began to move forward after decades of dictatorship.

Chris Stevens loved his work. He took pride in the country he served, and he saw dignity in the people that he met. And two weeks ago, he traveled to Benghazi to review plans to establish a new cultural center and modernize a hospital. That's when America's compound came under attack. Along with three of his colleagues, Chris was killed in the city that he helped to save. He was 52 years old.

I tell you this story because Chris Stevens embodied the best of America. Like his fellow Foreign Service officers, he built bridges across oceans and cultures, and was deeply invested in the international cooperation that the United Nations represents. He acted with humility, but he also stood up for a set of principles – a belief that individuals should be free to determine their own destiny, and live with liberty, dignity, justice, and opportunity.

The attacks on the civilians in Benghazi were attacks on America. We are grateful for the assistance we received from the Libyan government and from the Libyan people. There should be no doubt that we will be relentless in tracking down the killers and bringing them to justice. And I also appreciate that in recent days, the leaders of other countries in the region – including Egypt, Tunisia and Yemen – have taken steps to secure our diplomatic facilities, and called for calm. And so have religious authorities around the globe.

But understand, the attacks of the last two weeks are not simply an assault on America. They are also an assault on the very ideals upon which the United Nations was founded – the notion that people can resolve their differences peacefully; that diplomacy can take the place of war; that in an interdependent world, all of us have a stake in working towards greater opportunity and security for our citizens.

If we are serious about upholding these ideals, it will not be enough to put more guards in front of an embassy, or to put out statements of regret and wait for the outrage to pass. If we are serious about these ideals, we must speak honestly about the deeper causes of the crisis – because we face a choice between the forces that would drive us apart and the hopes that we hold in common.

Today, we must reaffirm that our future will be determined by people like Chris Stevens – and not by his killers. Today, we must declare that this violence and intolerance has no place among our United Nations.

It has been less than two years since a vendor in Tunisia set himself on fire to protest the oppressive corruption in his country, and sparked what became known as the Arab Spring. And since then, the world has been captivated by the transformation that's taken place, and the United States has supported the forces of change.

We were inspired by the Tunisian protests that toppled a dictator, because we recognized our own beliefs in the aspiration of men and women who took to the streets.

We insisted on change in Egypt, because our support for democracy ultimately put us on the side of the people.

We supported a transition of leadership in Yemen, because the interests of the people were no longer being served by a corrupt status quo.

We intervened in Libya alongside a broad coalition, and with the mandate of the United Nations Security Council, because we had the ability to stop the slaughter of innocents, and because we believed that the aspirations of the people were more powerful than a tyrant.

And as we meet here, we again declare that the regime of Bashar al-Assad must come to an end so that the suffering of the Syrian people can stop and a new dawn can begin.

We have taken these positions because we believe that freedom and self-determination are not unique to one culture. These are not simply American values or Western values – they are universal values. And even as there will be huge challenges to come with a transition to democracy, I am convinced that ultimately government of the people, by the people, and for the people is more likely to bring about the stability, prosperity, and individual opportunity that serve as a basis for peace in our world.

So let us remember that this is a season of progress. For the first time in decades, Tunisians, Egyptians and Libyans voted for new leaders in elections that were credible, competitive, and fair. This democratic spirit has not been restricted to the Arab world. Over the past year, we've seen peaceful transitions of power in Malawi and Senegal, and a new President in Somalia. In Burma, a President has freed political prisoners and opened a closed society, a courageous dissident has been elected to parliament, and people look forward to further reform. Around the globe, people are making their voices heard, insisting on their innate dignity, and the right to determine their future.

And yet the turmoil of recent weeks reminds us that the path to democracy does not end with the casting of a ballot. Nelson Mandela once said: "To be free is not merely to cast off one's chains, but to live in a way that respects and enhances the freedom of others."

True democracy demands that citizens cannot be thrown in jail because of what they believe, and that businesses can be opened without paying a bribe. It depends on the freedom of citizens to speak their minds and assemble without fear, and on the rule of law and due process that guarantees the rights of all people.

In other words, true democracy – real freedom – is hard work. Those in power have to resist the temptation to crack down on dissidents. In hard economic times, countries must be tempted – may be tempted to rally the people around perceived enemies, at home and abroad, rather than focusing on the painstaking work of reform.

Moreover, there will always be those that reject human progress – dictators who cling to power, corrupt interests that depend on the status quo, and extremists who fan the flames of hate and division. From Northern Ireland to South Asia, from Africa to the Americas, from the Balkans to the Pacific Rim, we've witnessed convulsions that can accompany transitions to a new political order.

At time, the conflicts arise along the fault lines of race or tribe. And often they arise from the difficulties of reconciling tradition and faith with the diversity and interdependence of the modern world. In every country, there are those who find different religious beliefs threatening; in every culture, those who love freedom for themselves must ask themselves how much they're willing to tolerate freedom for others.

That is what we saw play out in the last two weeks, as a crude and disgusting video sparked outrage throughout the Muslim world. Now, I have made it clear that the United States government had nothing to do with this video, and I believe its message must be rejected by all who respect our common humanity.

It is an insult not only to Muslims, but to America as well – for as the city outside these walls makes clear, we are a country that has welcomed people of every race and every faith. We are home to Muslims who worship across our country. We not only respect the freedom of religion, we have laws that protect individuals from being harmed because of how they look or what they believe. We understand why people take offense to this video because millions of our citizens are among them.

I know there are some who ask why we don't just ban such a video. And the answer is enshrined in our laws: Our Constitution protects the right to practice free speech.

Here in the United States, countless publications provoke offense. Like me, the majority of Americans are Christian, and yet we do not ban blasphemy against our most sacred beliefs. As President of our country and Commander-in-Chief of our military, I accept that people are going to call me awful things every day – (laughter) – and I will always defend their right to do so.

Americans have fought and died around the globe to protect the right of all people to express their views, even views that we profoundly disagree with. We do not do so because we support hateful speech, but because our founders understood that without such protections, the capacity of each individual to express their own views and practice their own faith may be threatened. We do so because in a diverse society, efforts to restrict speech can quickly become a tool to silence critics and oppress minorities.

We do so because given the power of faith in our lives, and the passion that religious differences can inflame, the strongest weapon against hateful speech is not repression; it is more speech – the voices of tolerance that rally against bigotry and blasphemy, and lift up the values of understanding and mutual respect.

Now, I know that not all countries in this body share this particular understanding of the protection of free speech. We recognize that. But in 2012, at a time when anyone with a cell phone can spread offensive views around the world with the click of a button, the notion that we can control the flow of information is obsolete. The question, then, is how do we respond?

And on this we must agree: There is no speech that justifies mindless violence. There are no words that excuse the killing of innocents. There's no video that justifies an attack on an embassy. There's no slander that provides an excuse for people to burn a restaurant in Lebanon, or destroy a school in Tunis, or cause death and destruction in Pakistan.

In this modern world with modern technologies, for us to respond in that way to hateful speech empowers any individual who engages in such speech to create chaos around the world. We empower the worst of us if that's how we respond.

More broadly, the events of the last two weeks also speak to the need for all of us to honestly address the tensions between the West and the Arab world that is moving towards democracy.

Now, let me be clear: Just as we cannot solve every problem in the world, the United States has not and will not seek to dictate the outcome of democratic transitions abroad. We do not expect other nations to agree with us on every issue, nor do we assume that the violence of the past weeks or the hateful speech by some individuals represent the views of the overwhelming majority of Muslims, any more than the views of the people who produced this video represents those of Americans. However, I do believe that it is the obligation of all leaders in all countries to speak out forcefully against violence and extremism.

It is time to marginalize those who – even when not directly resorting to violence – use hatred of America, or the West, or Israel, as the central organizing principle of politics. For that only gives cover, and sometimes makes an excuse, for those who do resort to violence.

That brand of politics – one that pits East against West, and South against North, Muslims against Christians and Hindu and Jews – can't deliver on the promise of freedom. To the youth, it offers only false hope. Burning an American flag does nothing to provide a child an education. Smashing apart a restaurant does not fill an empty stomach. Attacking an embassy won't create a single job. That brand of politics only makes it harder to achieve what we must do together: educating our children, and creating the opportunities that they deserve; protecting human rights, and extending democracy's promise.

Understand America will never retreat from the world. We will bring justice to those who harm our citizens and our friends, and we will stand with our allies. We are willing to partner with countries around the world to deepen ties of trade and investment, and science and technology, energy and development – all efforts that can spark economic growth for all our people and stabilize democratic change.

But such efforts depend on a spirit of mutual interest and mutual respect. No government or company, no school or NGO will be confident working in a country where its people are endangered. For partnerships to be effective our citizens must be secure and our efforts must be welcomed.

A politics based only on anger – one based on dividing the world between "us" and "them" – not only sets back international cooperation, it ultimately undermines those who tolerate it. All of us have an interest in standing up to these forces.

Let us remember that Muslims have suffered the most at the hands of extremism. On the same day our civilians were killed in Benghazi, a Turkish police officer was murdered in Istanbul only days before his wedding; more than 10 Yemenis were killed in a car bomb in Sana'a; several Afghan children were mourned by their parents just days after they were killed by a suicide bomber in Kabul.

The impulse towards intolerance and violence may initially be focused on the West, but over time it cannot be contained. The same impulses toward extremism are used to justify war between Sunni and Shia, between tribes and clans. It leads not to strength and prosperity but to chaos. In less than two years, we have seen largely peaceful protests bring more change to Muslim-majority countries than a decade of violence. And extremists understand this. Because they have nothing to offer to improve the lives of people, violence is their only way to stay relevant. They don't build; they only destroy.

It is time to leave the call of violence and the politics of division behind. On so many issues, we face a choice between the promise of the future, or the prisons of the past. And we cannot afford to get it wrong. We must seize this moment. And America stands ready to work with all who are willing to embrace a better future.

The future must not belong to those who target Coptic Christians in Egypt – it must be claimed by those in Tahrir Square who chanted, "Muslims, Christians, we are one." The future must not belong to those who bully women – it must be shaped by girls who go to school, and those who stand for a world where our daughters can live their dreams just like our sons.

The future must not belong to those corrupt few who steal a country's resources –

it must be won by the students and entrepreneurs, the workers and business owners who seek a broader prosperity for all people. Those are the women and men that America stands with; theirs is the vision we will support.

The future must not belong to those who slander the prophet of Islam. But to be credible, those who condemn that slander must also condemn the hate we see in the images of Jesus Christ that are desecrated, or churches that are destroyed, or the Holocaust that is denied.

Let us condemn incitement against Sufi Muslims and Shiite pilgrims. It's time to heed the words of Gandhi: "Intolerance is itself a form of violence and an obstacle to the growth of a true democratic spirit." Together, we must work towards a world where we are strengthened by our differences, and not defined by them. That is what America embodies, that's the vision we will support.

Among Israelis and Palestinians, the future must not belong to those who turn their backs on a prospect of peace. Let us leave behind those who thrive on conflict, those who reject the right of Israel to exist. The road is hard, but the destination is clear – a secure, Jewish state of Israel and an independent, prosperous Palestine. Understanding that such a peace must come through a just agreement between the parties, America will walk alongside all who are prepared to make that journey.

In Syria, the future must not belong to a dictator who massacres his people. If there is a cause that cries out for protest in the world today, peaceful protest, it is a regime that tortures children and shoots rockets at apartment buildings. And we must remain engaged to assure that what began with citizens demanding their rights does not end in a cycle of sectarian violence.

Together, we must stand with those Syrians who believe in a different vision – a Syria that is united and inclusive, where children don't need to fear their own government, and all Syrians have a say in how they are governed – Sunnis and Alawites, Kurds and Christians. That's what America stands for. That is the outcome that we will work for – with sanctions and consequences for those who persecute, and assistance and support for those who work for this common good. Because we believe that the Syrians who embrace this vision will have the strength and the legitimacy to lead.

In Iran, we see where the path of a violent and unaccountable ideology leads. The Iranian people have a remarkable and ancient history, and many Iranians wish to enjoy peace and prosperity alongside their neighbors. But just as it restricts the rights of its own people, the Iranian government continues to prop up a dictator in Damascus and supports terrorist groups abroad. Time and again, it has failed to take the opportunity to demonstrate that its nuclear program is peaceful, and to meet its obligations to the United Nations.

So let me be clear. America wants to resolve this issue through diplomacy, and we believe that there is still time and space to do so. But that time is not unlimited. We respect the right of nations to access peaceful nuclear power, but one of the purposes of the United Nations is to see that we harness that power for peace. And make no mistake, a nuclear-armed Iran is not a challenge that can be contained. It would threaten the elimination of Israel, the security of Gulf nations, and the stability of the global economy. It risks triggering a nuclear-arms race in the region, and the unraveling of the non-proliferation treaty. That's why a coalition of countries is holding the Iranian government accountable. And that's why the United States will do what we must to prevent Iran from obtaining a nuclear weapon.

We know from painful experience that the path to security and prosperity does not lie outside the boundaries of international law and respect for human rights. That's why this institution was established from the rubble of conflict. That is why liberty triumphed over tyranny in the Cold War. And that is the lesson of the last two decades as well.

History shows that peace and progress come to those who make the right choices. Nations in every part of the world have traveled this difficult path. Europe, the bloodiest battlefield of the 20th century, is united, free and at peace. From Brazil to South Africa, from Turkey to South Korea, from India to Indonesia, people of different races, religions, and traditions have lifted millions out of poverty, while respecting the rights of their citizens and meeting their responsibilities as nations.

And it is because of the progress that I've witnessed in my own lifetime, the progress that I've witnessed after nearly four years as President, that I remain ever hopeful about the world that we live in. The war in Iraq is over. American troops have come home. We've begun a transition in Afghanistan, and America and our allies will end our war on schedule in 2014. Al Qaeda has been weakened, and Osama bin Laden is no more. Nations have come together to lock down nuclear materials, and America and Russia are reducing our arsenals. We have seen hard choices made – from Naypyidaw to Cairo to Abidjan – to put more power in the hands of citizens.

At a time of economic challenge, the world has come together to broaden prosperity. Through the G20, we have partnered with emerging countries to keep the world on the path of recovery. America has pursued a development agenda that fuels growth and breaks dependency, and worked with African leaders to help them feed their nations. New partnerships have been forged to combat corruption and promote government that is open and transparent, and new commitments have been made through the Equal Futures Partnership to ensure that women and girls can fully participate in politics and pursue opportunity. And later today, I will discuss our efforts to combat the scourge of human trafficking.

All these things give me hope. But what gives me the most hope is not the actions of us, not the actions of leaders – it is the people that I've seen. The American troops who have risked their lives and sacrificed their limbs for strangers half a world away; the students in Jakarta or Seoul who are eager to use their knowledge to benefit mankind; the faces in a square in Prague or a parliament in Ghana who see democracy giving voice to their aspirations; the young people in the favelas of Rio and the schools of Mumbai whose eyes shine with promise. These men, women, and children of every race and every faith remind me that for every angry mob that gets shown on television, there are billions around the world who share similar hopes and dreams. They tell us that there is a common heartbeat to humanity.

So much attention in our world turns to what divides us. That's what we see on the news. That's what consumes our political debates. But when you strip it all away, people everywhere long for the freedom to determine their destiny; the dignity that comes with work; the comfort that comes with faith; and the justice that exists when governments serve their people – and not the other way around.

The United States of America will always stand up for these aspirations, for our own people and for people all across the world. That was our founding purpose. That is what our history shows. That is what Chris Stevens worked for throughout his life.

And I promise you this: Long after the killers are brought to justice, Chris Stevens's legacy will live on in the lives that he touched – in the tens of thousands who marched against violence through the streets of Benghazi; in the Libyans who changed their Facebook photo to one of Chris; in the signs that read, simply, "Chris Stevens was a friend to all Libyans."

They should give us hope. They should remind us that so long as we work for it, justice will be done, that history is on our side, and that a rising tide of liberty will never be reversed.

Thank you very much.

13

STATEMENT ON THE SCHOOL
SHOOTING IN NEWTOWN, CT

DECEMBER 14, 2012

T his afternoon, I spoke with Governor Malloy and FBI Director Mueller. I offered Governor Malloy my condolences on behalf of the nation, and made it clear he will have every single resource that he needs to investigate this heinous crime, care for the victims, counsel their families.

We've endured too many of these tragedies in the past few years. And each time I learn the news I react not as a President, but as anybody else would – as a parent. And that was especially true today. I know there's not a parent in America who doesn't feel the same overwhelming grief that I do.

The majority of those who died today were children – beautiful little kids between the ages of 5 and 10 years old. They had their entire lives ahead of them – birthdays, graduations, weddings, kids of their own. Among the fallen were also teachers – men and women who devoted their lives to helping our children fulfill their dreams.

So our hearts are broken today – for the parents and grandparents, sisters and brothers of these little children, and for the families of the adults who were lost. Our hearts are broken for the parents of the survivors as well, for as blessed as they are to have their children home tonight, they know that their children's innocence has been torn away from them too early, and there are no words that will ease their pain.

As a country, we have been through this too many times. Whether it's an elementary school in Newtown, or a shopping mall in Oregon, or a temple in Wisconsin, or a movie theater in Aurora, or a street corner in Chicago – these neighborhoods are our neighborhoods, and these children are our children. And we're going to have to come together and take meaningful action to prevent more tragedies like this, regardless of the politics.

This evening, Michelle and I will do what I know every parent in America will do, which is hug our children a little tighter and we'll tell them that we love them, and we'll remind each other how deeply we love one another. But there are families in Connecticut who cannot do that tonight. And they need all of us right now. In the hard days to come, that community needs us to be at our best as Americans. And I will do everything in my power as President to help.

Because while nothing can fill the space of a lost child or loved one, all of us can extend a hand to those in need – to remind them that we are there for them, that we are praying for them, that the love they felt for those they lost endures not just in their memories but also in ours.

May God bless the memory of the victims and, in the words of Scripture, heal the brokenhearted and bind up their wounds.

❧ 14 ❧

SECOND INAUGURAL ADDRESS
JANUARY 21, 2013

Vice President Biden, Mr. Chief Justice, members of the United States Congress, distinguished guests, and fellow citizens:

Each time we gather to inaugurate a President we bear witness to the enduring strength of our Constitution. We affirm the promise of our democracy. We recall that what binds this nation together is not the colors of our skin or the tenets of our faith or the origins of our names. What makes us exceptional – what makes us American – is our allegiance to an idea articulated in a declaration made more than two centuries ago: "We hold these truths to be self-evident, that all men are created equal; that they are endowed by their Creator with certain unalienable rights; that among these are life, liberty, and the pursuit of happiness."

Today we continue a never-ending journey to bridge the meaning of those words with the realities of our time. For history tells us that while these truths may be self-evident, they've never been self-executing; that while freedom is a gift from God, it must be secured by His people here on Earth. The patriots of 1776 did not fight to replace the tyranny of a king with the privileges of a few or the rule of a mob. They gave to us a republic, a government of, and by, and for the people, entrusting each generation to keep safe our founding creed.

And for more than two hundred years, we have.

Through blood drawn by lash and blood drawn by sword, we learned that no union founded on the principles of liberty and equality could survive half-slave and half-free. We made ourselves anew, and vowed to move forward together.

Together, we determined that a modern economy requires railroads and highways to speed travel and commerce, schools and colleges to train our workers.

Together, we discovered that a free market only thrives when there are rules to ensure competition and fair play.

Together, we resolved that a great nation must care for the vulnerable, and protect its people from life's worst hazards and misfortune.

Through it all, we have never relinquished our skepticism of central authority, nor have we succumbed to the fiction that all society's ills can be cured through government alone. Our celebration of initiative and enterprise, our insistence on hard work and personal responsibility, these are constants in our character.

But we have always understood that when times change, so must we; that fidelity to our founding principles requires new responses to new challenges; that preserving our individual freedoms ultimately requires collective action. For the American people can no more meet the demands of today's world by acting alone than American soldiers could have met the forces of fascism or communism with muskets and militias. No single person can train all the math and science teachers we'll need to equip our children for the future, or build the roads and networks and research labs that will bring new jobs and businesses to our shores. Now, more than ever, we must do these things together, as one nation and one people.

This generation of Americans has been tested by crises that steeled our resolve and proved our resilience. A decade of war is now ending. An economic recovery has begun. America's possibilities are limitless, for we possess all the qualities that this world without boundaries demands: youth and drive; diversity and openness; an endless capacity for risk and a gift for reinvention. My fellow Americans, we are made for this moment, and we will seize it – so long as we seize it together.

For we, the people, understand that our country cannot succeed when a shrinking few do very well and a growing many barely make it. We believe that America's prosperity must rest upon the broad shoulders of a rising middle class. We know that America thrives when every person can find independence and pride in their work; when the wages of honest labor liberate families from the brink of hardship. We are true to our creed when a little girl born into the bleakest poverty knows that she has the same chance to succeed as anybody else, because she is an American; she is free, and she is equal, not just in the eyes of God but also in our own.

We understand that outworn programs are inadequate to the needs of our time. So we must harness new ideas and technology to remake our government, revamp our tax code, reform our schools, and empower our citizens with the skills they need to work harder, learn more, reach higher. But while the means will change, our purpose endures: a nation that rewards the effort and determination of every single American. That is what this moment requires. That is what will give real meaning to our creed.

We, the people, still believe that every citizen deserves a basic measure of security and dignity. We must make the hard choices to reduce the cost of health care and the size of our deficit. But we reject the belief that America must choose between caring for the generation that built this country and investing in the generation that will build its future. For we remember the lessons of our past, when twilight years were spent in poverty and parents of a child with a disability had nowhere to turn.

We do not believe that in this country freedom is reserved for the lucky, or happiness for the few. We recognize that no matter how responsibly we live our lives, any one of us at any time may face a job loss, or a sudden illness, or a home swept away in a terrible storm. The commitments we make to each other through Medicare and Medicaid and Social Security, these things do not sap our initiative, they strengthen us. They do not make us a nation of takers; they free us to take the risks that make this country great.

We, the people, still believe that our obligations as Americans are not just to ourselves, but to all posterity. We will respond to the threat of climate change, knowing that the failure to do so would betray our children and future generations. Some may still deny the overwhelming judgment of science, but none can avoid the devastating impact of raging fires and crippling drought and more powerful storms.

The path towards sustainable energy sources will be long and sometimes difficult. But America cannot resist this transition, we must lead it. We cannot cede to other nations the technology that will power new jobs and new industries, we must claim its promise. That's how we will maintain our economic vitality and our national treasure – our forests and waterways, our crop lands and snow-capped peaks. That is how we will preserve our planet, commanded to our care by God. That's what will lend meaning to the creed our fathers once declared.

We, the people, still believe that enduring security and lasting peace do not require perpetual war. Our brave men and women in uniform, tempered by the flames of battle, are unmatched in skill and courage. Our citizens, seared by the memory of those we have lost, know too well the price that is paid for liberty. The knowledge of their sacrifice will keep us forever vigilant against those who would do us harm. But we are also heirs to those who won the peace and not just the war; who turned sworn enemies into the surest of friends – and we must carry those lessons into this time as well.

We will defend our people and uphold our values through strength of arms and rule of law. We will show the courage to try and resolve our differences with other nations peacefully — not because we are naïve about the dangers we face, but because engagement can more durably lift suspicion and fear.

America will remain the anchor of strong alliances in every corner of the globe. And we will renew those institutions that extend our capacity to manage crisis abroad, for no one has a greater stake in a peaceful world than its most powerful nation. We will support democracy from Asia to Africa, from the Americas to the Middle East, because our interests and our conscience compel us to act on behalf of those who long for freedom. And we must be a source of hope to the poor, the sick, the marginalized, the victims of prejudice — not out of mere charity, but because peace in our time requires the constant advance of those principles that our common creed describes: tolerance and opportunity, human dignity and justice.

We, the people, declare today that the most evident of truths — that all of us are created equal — is the star that guides us still; just as it guided our forebears through Seneca Falls, and Selma, and Stonewall; just as it guided all those men and women, sung and unsung, who left footprints along this great Mall, to hear a preacher say that we cannot walk alone; to hear a King proclaim that our individual freedom is inextricably bound to the freedom of every soul on Earth.

It is now our generation's task to carry on what those pioneers began. For our journey is not complete until our wives, our mothers and daughters can earn a living equal to their efforts. Our journey is not complete until our gay brothers and sisters are treated like anyone else under the law – for if we are truly created equal, then surely the love we commit to one another must be equal as well. Our journey is not complete until no citizen is forced to wait for hours to exercise the right to vote. Our journey is not complete until we find a better way to welcome the striving, hopeful immigrants who still see America as a land of opportunity – until bright young students and engineers are enlisted in our workforce rather than expelled from our country. Our journey is not complete until all our children, from the streets of Detroit to the hills of Appalachia, to the quiet lanes of Newtown, know that they are cared for and cherished and always safe from harm.

That is our generation's task – to make these words, these rights, these values of life and liberty and the pursuit of happiness real for every American. Being true to our founding documents does not require us to agree on every contour of life. It does not mean we all define liberty in exactly the same way or follow the same precise path to happiness. Progress does not compel us to settle centuries-long debates about the role of government for all time, but it does require us to act in our time.

For now decisions are upon us and we cannot afford delay. We cannot mistake absolutism for principle, or substitute spectacle for politics, or treat name-calling as reasoned debate. We must act, knowing that our work will be imperfect. We must act, knowing that today's victories will be only partial and that it will be up to those who stand here in four years and 40 years and 400 years hence to advance the timeless spirit once conferred to us in a spare Philadelphia hall.

My fellow Americans, the oath I have sworn before you today, like the one recited by others who serve in this Capitol, was an oath to God and country, not party or faction. And we must faithfully execute that pledge during the duration of our service. But the words I spoke today are not so different from the oath that is taken each time a soldier signs up for duty or an immigrant realizes her dream. My oath is not so different from the pledge we all make to the flag that waves above and that fills our hearts with pride.

They are the words of citizens and they represent our greatest hope. You and I, as citizens, have the power to set this country's course. You and I, as citizens, have the obligation to shape the debates of our time – not only with the votes we cast, but with the voices we lift in defense of our most ancient values and enduring ideals.

Let us, each of us, now embrace with solemn duty and awesome joy what is our lasting birthright. With common effort and common purpose, with passion and dedication, let us answer the call of history and carry into an uncertain future that precious light of freedom.

Thank you. God bless you, and may He forever bless these United States of America.

✤ 15 ✤

2013 STATE OF THE UNION ADDRESS
FEBRUARY 12, 2013

P lease, everybody, have a seat. Mr. Speaker, Mr. Vice President, Members of Congress, fellow Americans: Fifty-one years ago, John F. Kennedy declared to this Chamber that "the Constitution makes us not rivals for power, but partners for progress." "It is my task," he said, "to report the state of the Union; to improve it is the task of us all."

Tonight, thanks to the grit and determination of the American people, there is much progress to report. After a decade of grinding war, our brave men and women in uniform are coming home. After years of grueling recession, our businesses have created over 6 million new jobs. We buy more American cars than we have in 5 years and less foreign oil than we have in 20. Our housing market is healing, our stock market is rebounding, and consumers, patients, and homeowners enjoy stronger protections than ever before.

So together, we have cleared away the rubble of crisis, and we can say with renewed confidence that the state of our Union is stronger.

But we gather here knowing that there are millions of Americans whose hard work and dedication have not yet been rewarded. Our economy is adding jobs, but too many people still can't find full-time employment. Corporate profits have skyrocketed to alltime highs, but for more than a decade, wages and incomes have barely budged.

It is our generation's task, then, to reignite the true engine of America's economic growth: a rising, thriving middle class.

It is our unfinished task to restore the basic bargain that built this country: the idea that if you work hard and meet your responsibilities, you can get ahead, no matter where you come from, no matter what you look like or who you love.

It is our unfinished task to make sure that this Government works on behalf of the many, and not just the few; that it encourages free enterprise, rewards individual initiative, and opens the doors of opportunity to every child across this great Nation.

The American people don't expect government to solve every problem. They don't expect those of us in this Chamber to agree on every issue. But they do expect us to put the Nation's interests before party. They do expect us to forge reasonable compromise where we can. For they know that America moves forward only when we do so together and that the responsibility of improving this Union remains the task of us all.

Now, our work must begin by making some basic decisions about our budget, decisions that will have a huge impact on the strength of our recovery.

Over the last few years, both parties have worked together to reduce the deficit by more than $2.5 trillion, mostly through spending cuts, but also by raising tax rates on the wealthiest 1 percent of Americans. As a result, we are more than halfway towards the goal of $4 trillion in deficit reduction that economists say we need to stabilize our finances.

Now we need to finish the job. And the question is, how?

In 2011, Congress passed a law saying that if both parties couldn't agree on a plan to reach our deficit goal, about a trillion dollars' worth of budget cuts would automatically go into effect this year. These sudden, harsh, arbitrary cuts would jeopardize our military readiness. They'd devastate priorities like education and energy and medical research. They would certainly slow our recovery and cost us hundreds of thousands of jobs. And that's why Democrats, Republicans, business leaders, and economists have already said that these cuts– known here in Washington as the sequester–are a really bad idea.

Now, some in Congress have proposed preventing only the defense cuts by making even bigger cuts to things like education and job training, Medicare, and Social Security benefits. That idea is even worse.

Yes, the biggest driver of our long-term debt is the rising cost of health care for an aging population. And those of us who care deeply about programs like Medicare must embrace the need for modest reforms; otherwise, our retirement programs will crowd out the investments we need for our children and jeopardize the promise of a secure retirement for future generations.

But we can't ask senior citizens and working families to shoulder the entire burden of deficit reduction while asking nothing more from the wealthiest and the most powerful. We won't grow the middle class simply by shifting the cost of health care or college onto families that are already struggling or by forcing communities to lay off more teachers and more cops and more firefighters. Most Americans–Democrats, Republicans, and Independents–understand that we can't just cut our way to prosperity. They know that broad-based economic growth requires a balanced approach to deficit reduction, with spending cuts and revenue and with everybody doing their fair share. And that's the approach I offer tonight.

On Medicare, I'm prepared to enact reforms that will achieve the same amount of health care savings by the beginning of the next decade as the reforms proposed by the bipartisan Simpson-Bowles Commission.

Already, the Affordable Care Act is helping to slow the growth of health care costs. And the reforms I'm proposing go even further. We'll reduce taxpayer subsidies to prescription drug companies and ask more from the wealthiest seniors. We'll bring down costs by changing the way our Government pays for Medicare, because our medical bills shouldn't be based on the number of tests ordered or days spent in the hospital; they should be based on the quality of care that our seniors receive. And I am open to additional reforms from both parties, so long as they don't violate the guarantee of a secure retirement. Our Government shouldn't make promises we cannot keep, but we must keep the promises we've already made.

To hit the rest of our deficit reduction target, we should do what leaders in both parties have already suggested and save hundreds of billions of dollars by getting rid of tax loopholes and deductions for the well-off and the well-connected. After all, why would we choose to make deeper cuts to education and Medicare just to protect special interest tax breaks? How is that fair? Why is it that deficit reduction is a big emergency justifying making cuts in Social Security benefits, but not closing some loopholes? How does that promote growth?

Now is our best chance for bipartisan, comprehensive tax reform that encourages job creation and helps bring down the deficit. We can get this done. The American people deserve a Tax Code that helps small businesses spend less time filling out complicated forms and more time expanding and hiring; a Tax Code that ensures billionaires with high- powered accountants can't work the system and pay a lower rate than their hard-working secretaries; a Tax Code that lowers incentives to move jobs overseas and lowers tax rates for businesses and manufacturers that are creating jobs right here in the United States of America. That's what tax reform can deliver. That's what we can do together.

I realize that tax reform and entitlement reform will not be easy. The politics will be hard for both sides. None of us will get a hundred percent of what we want. But the alternative will cost us jobs, hurt our economy, visit hardship on millions of hard-working Americans. So let's set party interests aside and work to pass a budget that replaces reckless cuts with smart savings and wise investments in our future. And let's do it without the brinksmanship that stresses consumers and scares off investors. The greatest nation on Earth cannot keep conducting its business by drifting from one manufactured crisis to the next. We can't do it.

Let's agree right here, right now to keep the people's Government open and pay our bills on time and always uphold the full faith and credit of the United States of America. The American people have worked too hard, for too long, rebuilding from one crisis to see their elected officials cause another.

Now, most of us agree that a plan to reduce the deficit must be part of our agenda. But let's be clear: Deficit reduction alone is not an economic plan. A growing economy that creates good, middle class jobs, that must be the north star that guides our efforts. Every day, we should ask ourselves three questions as a nation: How do we attract more jobs to our shores? How do we equip our people with the skills they need to get those jobs? And how do we make sure that hard work leads to a decent living?

Now, a year and a half ago, I put forward an American Jobs Act that independent economists said would create more than 1 million new jobs. And I thank the last Congress for passing some of that agenda. I urge this Congress to pass the rest. But tonight I'll lay out additional proposals that are fully paid for and fully consistent with the budget framework both parties agreed to just 18 months ago. Let me repeat: Nothing I'm proposing tonight should increase our deficit by a single dime. It is not a bigger Government we need, but a smarter Government that sets priorities and invests in broad-based growth. That's what we should be looking for.

Our first priority is making America a magnet for new jobs and manufacturing. After shedding jobs for more than 10 years, our manufacturers have added about 500,000 jobs over the past 3. Caterpillar is bringing jobs back from Japan. Ford is bringing jobs back from Mexico. And this year, Apple will start making Macs in America again.

There are things we can do right now to accelerate this trend. Last year, we created our first manufacturing innovation institute in Youngstown, Ohio. A once-shuttered warehouse is now a state-of-the-art lab where new workers are mastering the 3-D printing that has the potential to revolutionize the way we make almost everything. There's no reason this can't happen in other towns.

So tonight I'm announcing the launch of three more of these manufacturing hubs, where businesses will partner with the Department of Defense and Energy to turn regions left behind by globalization into global centers of high-tech jobs. And I ask this Congress to help create a network of 15 of these hubs and guarantee that the next revolution in manufacturing is made right here in America. We can get that done.

Now, if we want to make the best products, we also have to invest in the best ideas. Every dollar we invested to map the human genome returned $140 to our economy—every dollar. Today, our scientists are mapping the human brain to unlock the answers to Alzheimer's. They're developing drugs to regenerate damaged organs, devising new materials to make batteries 10 times more powerful. Now is not the time to gut these job-creating investments in science and innovation, now is the time to reach a level of research and development not seen since the height of the space race. We need to make those investments.

Today, no area holds more promise than our investments in American energy. After years of talking about it, we're finally poised to control our own energy future. We produce more oil at home than we have in 15 years. We have doubled the distance our cars will go on a gallon of gas and the amount of renewable energy we generate from sources like wind and solar, with tens of thousands of good American jobs to show for it. We produce more natural gas than ever before, and nearly every-one's energy bill is lower because of it. And over the last 4 years, our emissions of the dangerous carbon pollution that threatens our planet have actually fallen.

But for the sake of our children and our future, we must do more to combat climate change. Now, it's true that no single event makes a trend. But the fact is, the 12 hottest years on record have all come in the last 15. Heat waves, droughts, wild-fires, floods–all are now more frequent and more intense. We can choose to believe that Superstorm Sandy and the most severe drought in decades and the worst wild-fires some States have ever seen were all just a freak coincidence. Or we can choose to believe in the overwhelming judgment of science and act before it's too late.

Now, the good news is we can make meaningful progress on this issue while driving strong economic growth. I urge this Congress to get together, pursue a bipartisan, market-based solution to climate change, like the one John McCain and Joe Lieberman worked on together a few years ago. But if Congress won't act soon to protect future generations, I will. I will direct my Cabinet to come up with executive actions we can take, now and in the future, to reduce pollution, prepare our communities for the consequences of climate change, and speed the transition to more sustainable sources of energy.

And 4 years ago, other countries dominated the clean energy market and the jobs that came with it. And we've begun to change that. Last year, wind energy added nearly half of all new power capacity in America. So let's generate even more. Solar energy gets cheaper by the year; let's drive down costs even further. As long as countries like China keep going all in on clean energy, so must we.

Now, in the meantime, the natural gas boom has led to cleaner power and greater energy independence. We need to encourage that. And that's why my administration will keep cutting redtape and speeding up new oil and gas permits. That's got to be part of an all-of-the-above plan. But I also want to work with this Congress to encourage the research and technology that helps natural gas burn even cleaner and protects our air and our water.

In fact, much of our new-found energy is drawn from lands and waters that we, the public, own together. So tonight I propose we use some of our oil and gas revenues to fund an energy security trust that will drive new research and technology to shift our cars and trucks off oil for good. If a nonpartisan coalition of CEOs and retired generals and admirals can get behind this idea, then so can we. Let's take their advice and free our families and businesses from the painful spikes in gas prices we've put up with for far too long.

I'm also issuing a new goal for America: Let's cut in half the energy wasted by our homes and businesses over the next 20 years. We'll work with the States to do it. Those States with the best ideas to create jobs and lower energy bills by constructing more efficient buildings will receive Federal support to help make that happen.

America's energy sector is just one part of an aging infrastructure badly in need of repair. Ask any CEO where they'd rather locate and hire, a country with deteriorating roads and bridges or one with high- speed rail and Internet, high-tech schools, self-healing power grids. The CEO of Siemens America–a company that brought hundreds of new jobs to North Carolina–said that if we upgrade our infrastructure, they'll bring even more jobs. And that's the attitude of a lot of companies all around the world. And I know you want these job-creating projects in your district. I've seen all those ribbon-cuttings. [Laughter]

So tonight I propose a Fix-It-First program to put people to work as soon as possible on our most urgent repairs, like the nearly 70,000 structurally deficient bridges across the country. And to make sure taxpayers don't shoulder the whole burden, I'm also proposing a partnership to rebuild America that attracts private capital to upgrade what our businesses need most: modern ports to move our goods, modern pipelines to withstand a storm, modern schools worthy of our children. Let's prove there's no better place to do business than here in the United States of America, and let's start right away. We can get this done.

And part of our rebuilding effort must also involve our housing sector. The good news is, our housing market is finally healing from the collapse of 2007. Home prices are rising at the fastest pace in 6 years. Home purchases are up nearly 50 percent, and construction is expanding again.

But even with mortgage rates near a 50-year low, too many families with solid credit who want to buy a home are being rejected. Too many families who never missed a payment and want to refinance are being told no. That's holding our entire economy back. We need to fix it.

Right now there's a bill in this Congress that would give every responsible home-owner in America the chance to save $3,000 a year by refinancing at today's rates. Democrats and Republicans have supported it before, so what are we waiting for? Take a vote and send me that bill. Why are—why would we be against that? Why would that be a partisan issue, helping folks refinance? Right now overlapping regulations keep responsible young families from buying their first home. What's holding us back? Let's streamline the process and help our economy grow.

These initiatives in manufacturing, energy, infrastructure, housing, all these things will help entrepreneurs and small-business owners expand and create new jobs. But none of it will matter unless we also equip our citizens with the skills and training to fill those jobs.

And that has to start at the earliest possible age. Study after study shows that the sooner a child begins learning, the better he or she does down the road. But today, fewer than 3 in 10 4-year-olds are enrolled in a high-quality preschool program. Most middle class parents can't afford a few hundred bucks a week for a private preschool. And for poor kids who need help the most, this lack of access to preschool education can shadow them for the rest of their lives. So tonight I propose working with States to make high-quality preschool available to every single child in America. That's something we should be able to do.

Every dollar we invest in high-quality early childhood education can save more than 7 dollars later on: by boosting graduation rates, reducing teen pregnancy, even reducing violent crime. In States that make it a priority to educate our youngest children, like Georgia or Oklahoma, studies show students grow up more likely to read and do math at grade level, graduate high school, hold a job, form more stable families of their own. We know this works. So let's do what works and make sure none of our children start the race of life already behind. Let's give our kids that chance.

Let's also make sure that a high school diploma puts our kids on a path to a good job. Right now countries like Germany focus on graduating their high school students with the equivalent of a technical degree from one of our community colleges. So those German kids, they're ready for a job when they graduate high school. They've been trained for the jobs that are there. Now at schools like P-TECH in Brooklyn, a collaboration between New York Public Schools and City University of New York and IBM, students will graduate with a high school diploma and an associate's degree in computers or engineering. We need to give every American student opportunities like this.

And 4 years ago, we started Race to the Top, a competition that convinced almost every State to develop smarter curricula and higher standards, all for about 1 percent of what we spend on education each year. Tonight I'm announcing a new challenge to redesign America's high schools so they better equip graduates for the demands of a high-tech economy. And we'll reward schools that develop new partnerships with colleges and employers and create classes that focus on science, technology, engineering, and math: the skills today's employers are looking for to fill the jobs that are there right now and will be there in the future.

Now, even with better high schools, most young people will need some higher education. It's a simple fact: The more education you've got, the more likely you are to have a good job and work your way into the middle class. But today, skyrocketing costs price too many young people out of a higher education or saddle them with unsustainable debt.

Through tax credits, grants, and better loans, we've made college more affordable for millions of students and families over the last few years. But taxpayers can't keep on subsidizing higher and higher and higher costs for higher education. Colleges must do their part to keep costs down, and it's our job to make sure that they do.

So tonight I ask Congress to change the Higher Education Act so that affordability and value are included in determining which colleges receive certain types of Federal aid. And tomorrow my administration will release a new college scorecard that parents and students can use to compare schools based on a simple criterion: where you can get the most bang for your educational buck.

Now, to grow our middle class, our citizens have to have access to the education and training that today's jobs require. But we also have to make sure that America remains a place where everyone who's willing to work–everybody who's willing to work hard–has the chance to get ahead.

Our economy is stronger when we harness the talents and ingenuity of striving, hopeful immigrants. And right now leaders from the business, labor, law enforcement, faith communities, they all agree that the time has come to pass comprehensive immigration reform. Now is the time to do it. Now is the time to get it done. [Applause] Now is the time to get it done.

Real reform means stronger border security, and we can build on the progress my administration has already made: putting more boots on the southern border than at any time in our history and reducing illegal crossings to their lowest levels in 40 years.

Real reform means establishing a responsible pathway to earned citizenship, a path that includes passing a background check, paying taxes and a meaningful penalty, learning English, and going to the back of the line behind the folks trying to come here legally.

And real reform means fixing the legal immigration system to cut waiting periods and attract the highly skilled entrepreneurs and engineers that will help create jobs and grow our economy.

In other words, we know what needs to be done. And as we speak, bipartisan groups in both Chambers are working diligently to draft a bill, and I applaud their efforts. So let's get this done. Send me a comprehensive immigration reform bill in the next few months, and I will sign it right away. And America will be better for it. Let's get it done. [Applause] Let's get it done.

But we can't stop there. We know our economy is stronger when our wives, our mothers, our daughters can live their lives free from discrimination in the workplace and free from the fear of domestic violence. Today the Senate passed the "Violence Against Women's Act" that Joe Biden originally wrote almost 20 years ago. And I now urge the House to do the same. Good job, Joe. And I ask this Congress to declare that women should earn a living equal to their efforts, and finally pass the "Paycheck Fairness Act" this year.

We know our economy is stronger when we reward an honest day's work with honest wages. But today, a full-time worker making the minimum wage earns $14,500 a year. Even with the tax relief we put in place, a family with two kids that earns the minimum wage still lives below the poverty line. That's wrong. That's why, since the last time this Congress raised the minimum wage, 19 States have chosen to bump theirs even higher.

Tonight let's declare that in the wealthiest nation on Earth, no one who works full-time should have to live in poverty and raise the Federal minimum wage to $9 an hour. We should be able to get that done.

This single step would raise the incomes of millions of working families. It could mean the difference between groceries or the food bank, rent or eviction, scraping by or finally getting ahead. For businesses across the country, it would mean customers with more money in their pockets. And a whole lot of folks out there would probably need less help from government. In fact, working folks shouldn't have to wait year after year for the minimum wage to go up while CEO pay has never been higher. So here's an idea that Governor Romney and I actually agreed on last year: Let's tie the minimum wage to the cost of living so that it finally becomes a wage you can live on.

Tonight let's also recognize that there are communities in this country where no matter how hard you work, it is virtually impossible to get ahead: factory towns decimated from years of plants packing up; inescapable pockets of poverty, urban and rural, where young adults are still fighting for their first job. America is not a place where the chance of birth or circumstance should decide our destiny. And that's why we need to build new ladders of opportunity into the middle class for all who are willing to climb them.

Let's offer incentives to companies that hire Americans who've got what it takes to fill that job opening, but have been out of work so long that no one will give them a chance anymore. Let's put people back to work rebuilding vacant homes in rundown neighborhoods. And this year, my administration will begin to partner with 20 of the hardest hit towns in America to get these communities back on their feet. Now, we'll work with local leaders to target resources at public safety and education and housing.

We'll give new tax credits to businesses that hire and invest. And we'll work to strengthen families by removing the financial deterrents to marriage for low-income couples and do more to encourage fatherhood, because what makes you a man isn't the ability to conceive a child, it's having the courage to raise one. And we want to encourage that. We want to help that.

Stronger families. Stronger communities. A stronger America. It is this kind of prosperity–broad, shared, built on a thriving middle class–that has always been the source of our progress at home. It's also the foundation of our power and influence throughout the world.

Tonight we stand united in saluting the troops and civilians who sacrifice every day to protect us. Because of them, we can say with confidence that America will complete its mission in Afghanistan and achieve our objective of defeating the core of Al Qaida.

Already, we have brought home 33,000 of our brave service men and women. This spring, our forces will move into a support role, while Afghan security forces take the lead. Tonight I can announce that over the next year, another 34,000 American troops will come home from Afghanistan. This drawdown will continue, and by the end of next year, our war in Afghanistan will be over.

Beyond 2014, America's commitment to a unified and sovereign Afghanistan will endure, but the nature of our commitment will change. We're negotiating an agreement with the Afghan Government that focuses on two missions: training and equipping Afghan forces so that the country does not again slip into chaos and counterterrorism efforts that allow us to pursue the remnants of Al Qaida and their affiliates.

Today, the organization that attacked us on 9/11 is a shadow of its former self. It's true, different Al Qaida affiliates and extremist groups have emerged, from the Arabian Peninsula to Africa. The threat these groups pose is evolving. But to meet this threat, we don't need to send tens of thousands of our sons and daughters abroad or occupy other nations. Instead, we'll need to help countries like Yemen and Libya and Somalia provide for their own security and help allies who take the fight to terrorists, as we have in Mali. And where necessary, through a range of capabilities, we will continue to take direct action against those terrorists who pose the gravest threat to Americans.

Now, as we do, we must enlist our values in the fight. That's why my administration has worked tirelessly to forge a durable legal and policy framework to guide our counterterrorism efforts. Throughout, we have kept Congress fully informed of our efforts. I recognize that in our democracy, no one should just take my word for it that we're doing things the right way. So, in the months ahead, I will continue to engage Congress to ensure not only that our targeting, detention, and prosecution of terrorists remains consistent with our laws and system of checks and balances, but that our efforts are even more transparent to the American people and to the world.

Of course, our challenges don't end with Al Qaida. America will continue to lead the effort to prevent the spread of the world's most dangerous weapons. The regime in North Korea must know they will only achieve security and prosperity by meeting their international obligations. Provocations of the sort we saw last night will only further isolate them, as we stand by our allies, strengthen our own missile defense, and lead the world in taking firm action in response to these threats.

Likewise, the leaders of Iran must recognize that now is the time for a diplomatic solution, because a coalition stands united in demanding that they meet their obligations, and we will do what is necessary to prevent them from getting a nuclear weapon.

At the same time, we'll engage Russia to seek further reductions in our nuclear arsenals and continue leading the global effort to secure nuclear materials that could fall into the wrong hands, because our ability to influence others depends on our willingness to lead and meet our obligations.

America must also face the rapidly growing threat from cyber attacks. Now, we know hackers steal people's identities and infiltrate private e-mails. We know foreign countries and companies swipe our corporate secrets. Now our enemies are also seeking the ability to sabotage our power grid, our financial institutions, our air traffic control systems. We cannot look back years from now and wonder why we did nothing in the face of real threats to our security and our economy.

And that's why, earlier today, I signed a new Executive order that will strengthen our cyber defenses by increasing information sharing and developing standards to protect our national security, our jobs, and our privacy.

But now Congress must act as well, by passing legislation to give our Government a greater capacity to secure our networks and deter attacks. This is something we should be able to get done on a bipartisan basis.

Now, even as we protect our people, we should remember that today's world presents not just dangers, not just threats, it presents opportunities. To boost American exports, support American jobs and level the playing field in the growing markets of Asia, we intend to complete negotiations on a Trans-Pacific Partnership. And tonight I'm announcing that we will launch talks on a comprehensive transatlantic trade and investment partnership with the European Union, because trade that is fair and free across the Atlantic supports millions of good- paying American jobs.

We also know that progress in the most impoverished parts of our world enriches us all, not only because it creates new markets, more stable order in certain regions of the world, but also because it's the right thing to do. In many places, people live on little more than a dollar a day. So the United States will join with our allies to eradicate such extreme poverty in the next two decades by connecting more people to the global economy, by empowering women, by giving our young and brightest minds new opportunities to serve and helping communities to feed and power and educate themselves, by saving the world's children from preventable deaths, and by realizing the promise of an AIDS-free generation, which is within our reach.

You see, America must remain a beacon to all who seek freedom during this period of historic change. I saw the power of hope last year in Rangoon, in Burma, when Aung San Suu Kyi welcomed an American President into the home where she had been imprisoned for years; when thousands of Burmese lined the streets, waving American flags, including a man who said: "There is justice and law in the United States. I want our country to be like that."

In defense of freedom, we'll remain the anchor of strong alliances from the Americas to Africa, from Europe to Asia. In the Middle East, we will stand with citizens as they demand their universal rights and support stable transitions to democracy.

We know the process will be messy, and we cannot presume to dictate the course of change in countries like Egypt, but we can and will insist on respect for the fundamental rights of all people. We'll keep the pressure on a Syrian regime that has murdered its own people and support opposition leaders that respect the rights of every Syrian. And we will stand steadfast with Israel in pursuit of security and a lasting peace.

These are the messages I'll deliver when I travel to the Middle East next month. And all this work depends on the courage and sacrifice of those who serve in dangerous places at great personal risk: our diplomats, our intelligence officers, and the men and women of the United States Armed Forces. As long as I'm Commander in Chief, we will do whatever we must to protect those who serve their country abroad, and we will maintain the best military the world has ever known.

We'll invest in new capabilities, even as we reduce waste and wartime spending. We will ensure equal treatment for all servicemembers and equal benefits for their families, gay and straight. We will draw upon the courage and skills of our sisters and daughters and moms, because women have proven under fire that they are ready for combat.

We will keep faith with our veterans, investing in world-class care– including mental health care–for our wounded warriors, supporting our military families, giving our veterans the benefits and education and job opportunities that they have earned. And I want to thank my wife Michelle and Dr. Jill Biden for their continued dedication to serving our military families as well as they have served us. Thank you, honey. Thank you, Jill.

Defending our freedom, though, is not just the job of our military alone. We must all do our part to make sure our God-given rights are protected here at home. That includes one of the most fundamental rights of a democracy: the right to vote. Now, when any American, no matter where they live or what their party, are denied that right because they can't afford to wait for 5 or 6 or 7 hours just to cast their ballot, we are betraying our ideals.

So tonight I'm announcing a nonpartisan commission to improve the voting experience in America. And it definitely needs improvement. I'm asking two long-time experts in the field–who, by the way, recently served as the top attorneys for my campaign and for Governor Romney's campaign–to lead it. We can fix this, and we will. The American people demand it, and so does our democracy.

Of course, what I've said tonight matters little if we don't come together to protect our most precious resource: our children. It has been 2 months since Newtown. I know this is not the first time this country has debated how to reduce gun violence. But this time is different. Overwhelming majorities of Americans–Americans who believe in the Second Amendment–have come together around commonsense reform, like background checks that will make it harder for criminals to get their hands on a gun. Senators of both parties are working together on tough new laws to prevent anyone from buying guns for resale to criminals. Police chiefs are asking our help to get weapons of war and massive ammunition magazines off our streets, because these police chiefs, they're tired of seeing their guys and gals being outgunned.

Each of these proposals deserves a vote in Congress. Now, if you want to vote no, that's your choice. But these proposals deserve a vote. Because in the 2 months since Newtown, more than a thousand birthdays, graduations, anniversaries have been stolen from our lives by a bullet from a gun–more than a thousand.

One of those we lost was a young girl named Hadiya Pendleton. She was 15 years old. She loved Fig Newtons and lip gloss. She was a majorette. She was so good to her friends, they all thought they were her best friend. Just 3 weeks ago, she was here, in Washington, with her classmates, performing for her country at my Inauguration. And a week later, she was shot and killed in a Chicago park after school, just a mile away from my house.

Hadiya's parents, Nate and Cleo, are in this Chamber tonight, along with more than two dozen Americans whose lives have been torn apart by gun violence. They deserve a vote. They deserve a vote. [Applause] They deserve a vote. Gabby Giffords deserves a vote. The families of Newtown deserve a vote. The families of Aurora deserve a vote. The families of Oak Creek and Tucson and Blacksburg, and the countless other communities ripped open by gun violence, they deserve a simple vote. They deserve a simple vote.

Our actions will not prevent every senseless act of violence in this country. In fact, no laws, no initiatives, no administrative acts will perfectly solve all the challenges I've outlined tonight. But we were never sent here to be perfect. We were sent here to make what difference we can, to secure this Nation, expand opportunity, uphold our ideals through the hard, often frustrating, but absolutely necessary work of self-government.

We were sent here to look out for our fellow Americans the same way they look out for one another, every single day, usually without fanfare, all across this country. We should follow their example.

We should follow the example of a New York City nurse named Menchu Sanchez. When Hurricane Sandy plunged her hospital into darkness, she wasn't thinking about how her own home was faring. Her mind was on the 20 precious newborns in her care and the rescue plan she devised that kept them all safe.

We should follow the example of a North Miami woman named Desiline Victor. When Desiline arrived at her polling place, she was told the wait to vote might be 6 hours. And as time ticked by, her concern was not with her tired body or aching feet, but whether folks like her would get to have their say. And hour after hour, a throng of people stayed in line to support her, because Desiline is 102 years old. And they erupted in cheers when she finally put on a sticker that read, "I voted." [Applause] There's Desiline.

We should follow the example of a police officer named Brian Murphy. When a gunman opened fire on a Sikh temple in Wisconsin and Brian was the first to arrive—and he did not consider his own safety. He fought back until help arrived and ordered his fellow officers to protect the safety of the Americans worshiping inside, even as he lay bleeding from 12 bullet wounds. And when asked how he did that, Brian said, "That's just the way we're made."

That's just the way we're made. We may do different jobs and wear different uniforms and hold different views than the person beside us. But as Americans, we all share the same proud title: We are citizens. It's a word that doesn't just describe our nationality or legal status. It describes the way we're made. It describes what we believe. It captures the enduring idea that this country only works when we accept certain obligations to one another and to future generations; that our rights are wrapped up in the rights of others; and that well into our third century as a nation, it remains the task of us all, as citizens of these United States, to be the authors of the next great chapter of our American story.

Thank you. God bless you, and God bless these United States of America.

16

REMARKS AT AN INTERFAITH SERVICE IN BOSTON, MA, ON THE BOSTON MARATHON BOMBINGS

APRIL 18, 2013

Hello, Boston!

Scripture tells us to "run with endurance the race that is set before us." Run with endurance the race that is set before us.

On Monday morning, the sun rose over Boston. The sunlight glistened off the Statehouse dome. In the Common and the Public Garden, spring was in bloom. On this Patriot's Day, like so many before, fans jumped onto the T to see the Sox at Fenway. In Hopkinton, runners laced up their shoes and set out on a 26.2-mile test of dedication and grit and the human spirit. And across this city, hundreds of thousands of Bostonians lined the streets – to hand the runners cups of water and to cheer them on.

It was a beautiful day to be in Boston – a day that explains why a poet once wrote that this town is not just a capital, not just a place. Boston, he said, "is the perfect state of grace."

And then, in an instant, the day's beauty was shattered. A celebration became a tragedy. And so we come together to pray, and mourn, and measure our loss. But we also come together today to reclaim that state of grace – to reaffirm that the spirit of this city is undaunted, and the spirit of this country shall remain undimmed.

To Governor Patrick; Mayor Menino; Cardinal O'Malley and all the faith leaders who are here; Governors Romney, Swift, Weld and Dukakis; members of Congress; and most of all, the people of Boston and the families who've lost a piece of your heart. We thank you for your leadership. We thank you for your courage. We thank you for your grace.

I'm here today on behalf of the American people with a simple message: Every one of us has been touched by this attack on your beloved city. Every one of us stands with you.

Because, after all, it's our beloved city, too. Boston may be your hometown, but we claim it, too. It's one of America's iconic cities. It's one of the world's great cities.

And one of the reasons the world knows Boston so well is that Boston opens its heart to the world.

Over successive generations, you've welcomed again and again new arrivals to our shores – immigrants who constantly reinvigorated this city and this common-wealth and our nation. Every fall, you welcome students from all across America and all across the globe, and every spring you graduate them back into the world – a Boston diaspora that excels in every field of human endeavor. Year after year, you welcome the greatest talents in the arts and science, research – you welcome them to your concert halls and your hospitals and your laboratories to exchange ideas and insights that draw this world together.

And every third Monday in April, you welcome people from all around the world to the Hub for friendship and fellowship and healthy competition – a gathering of men and women of every race and every religion, every shape and every size; a multitude represented by all those flags that flew over the finish line.

So whether folks come here to Boston for just a day, or they stay here for years, they leave with a piece of this town tucked firmly into their hearts. So Boston is your hometown, but we claim it a little bit, too.

I know this because there's a piece of Boston in me. You welcomed me as a young law student across the river; welcomed Michelle, too. You welcomed me during a convention when I was still a state senator and very few people could pronounce my name right. (Laughter.)

Like you, Michelle and I have walked these streets. Like you, we know these neighborhoods. And like you, in this moment of grief, we join you in saying – "Boston, you're my home." For millions of us, what happened on Monday is personal. It's personal.

Today our prayers are with the Campbell family of Medford. They're here today. Their daughter, Krystle, was always smiling. Those who knew her said that with her red hair and her freckles and her ever-eager willingness to speak her mind, she was beautiful, sometimes she could be a little noisy, and everybody loved her for it. She would have turned 30 next month. As her mother said through her tears, "This doesn't make any sense."

Our prayers are with the Lu family of China, who sent their daughter, Lingzi, to BU so that she could experience all this city has to offer. She was a 23-year-old student, far from home. And in the heartache of her family and friends on both sides of a great ocean, we're reminded of the humanity that we all share.

Our prayers are with the Richard family of Dorchester – to Denise and their young daughter, Jane, as they fight to recover. And our hearts are broken for 8-year-old Martin – with his big smile and bright eyes. His last hours were as perfect as an 8-year-old boy could hope for – with his family, eating ice cream at a sporting event. And we're left with two enduring images of this little boy – forever smiling for his beloved Bruins, and forever expressing a wish he made on a blue poster board: "No more hurting people. Peace."

No more hurting people. Peace.

Our prayers are with the injured —— so many wounded, some gravely. From their beds, some are surely watching us gather here today. And if you are, know this: As you begin this long journey of recovery, your city is with you. Your commonwealth is with you. Your country is with you. We will all be with you as you learn to stand and walk and, yes, run again. Of that I have no doubt. You will run again. You will run again.

Because that's what the people of Boston are made of. Your resolve is the greatest rebuke to whoever committed this heinous act. If they sought to intimidate us, to terrorize us, to shake us from those values that Deval described, the values that make us who we are, as Americans – well, it should be pretty clear by now that they picked the wrong city to do it. Not here in Boston. Not here in Boston.

You've shown us, Boston, that in the face of evil, Americans will lift up what's good. In the face of cruelty, we will choose compassion. In the face of those who would visit death upon innocents, we will choose to save and to comfort and to heal. We'll choose friendship. We'll choose love.

Scripture teaches us, "God has not given us a spirit of fear and timidity, but of power, love, and self-discipline." And that's the spirit you've displayed in recent days.

When doctors and nurses, police and firefighters and EMTs and Guardsmen run towards explosions to treat the wounded – that's discipline.

When exhausted runners, including our troops and veterans – who never expected to see such carnage on the streets back home – become first responders themselves, tending to the injured – that's real power.

When Bostonians carry victims in their arms, deliver water and blankets, line up to give blood, open their homes to total strangers, give them rides back to reunite with their families – that's love.

That's the message we send to those who carried this out and anyone who would do harm to our people. Yes, we will find you. And, yes, you will face justice. We will find you. We will hold you accountable. But more than that; our fidelity to our way of life – to our free and open society – will only grow stronger. For God has not given us a spirit of fear and timidity, but one of power and love and self-discipline.

Like Bill Iffrig, 78 years old – the runner in the orange tank top who we all saw get knocked down by the blast – we may be momentarily knocked off our feet, but we'll pick ourselves up. We'll keep going. We will finish the race. In the words of Dick Hoyt, who's pushed his disabled son, Rick, in 31 Boston Marathons – "We can't let something like this stop us." This doesn't stop us.

And that's what you've taught us, Boston. That's what you've reminded us – to push on. To persevere. To not grow weary. To not get faint. Even when it hurts. Even when our heart aches. We summon the strength that maybe we didn't even know we had, and we carry on. We finish the race. We finish the race.

And we do that because of who we are. And we do that because we know that somewhere around the bend a stranger has a cup of water. Around the bend, somebody is there to boost our spirits. On that toughest mile, just when we think that we've hit a wall, someone will be there to cheer us on and pick us up if we fall. We know that.

And that's what the perpetrators of such senseless violence – these small, stunted individuals who would destroy instead of build, and think somehow that makes them important – that's what they don't understand. Our faith in each other, our love for each other, our love for country, our common creed that cuts across whatever superficial differences there may be – that is our power. That's our strength.

That's why a bomb can't beat us. That's why we don't hunker down. That's why we don't cower in fear. We carry on. We race. We strive. We build, and we work, and we love – and we raise our kids to do the same. And we come together to celebrate life, and to walk our cities, and to cheer for our teams. When the Sox and Celtics and Patriots or Bruins are champions again – to the chagrin of New York and Chicago fans – the crowds will gather and watch a parade go down Boylston Street.

And this time next year, on the third Monday in April, the world will return to this great American city to run harder than ever, and to cheer even louder, for the 118th Boston Marathon. Bet on it.

Tomorrow, the sun will rise over Boston. Tomorrow, the sun will rise over this country that we love. This special place. This state of grace.

Scripture tells us to "run with endurance the race that is set before us." As we do, may God hold close those who've been taken from us too soon. May He comfort their families. And may He continue to watch over these United States of America.

17

SPEECH AT THE BRANDENBURG GATE, BERLIN, GERMANY

JUNE 19, 2013

Hello, Berlin! Thank you, Chancellor Merkel, for your leadership, your friendship, and the example of your life – from a child of the East to the leader of a free and united Germany.

As I've said, Angela and I don't exactly look like previous German and American leaders. But the fact that we can stand here today, along the fault line where a city was divided, speaks to an eternal truth: No wall can stand against the yearning of justice, the yearnings for freedom, the yearnings for peace that burns in the human heart.

Mayor Wowereit, distinguished guests, and especially the people of Berlin and of Germany – thank you for this extraordinarily warm welcome. In fact, it's so warm and I feel so good that I'm actually going to take off my jacket, and anybody else who wants to, feel free to. We can be a little more informal among friends.

As your Chancellor mentioned, five years ago I had the privilege to address this city as senator. Today, I'm proud to return as President of the United States. And I bring with me the enduring friendship of the American people, as well as my wife, Michelle, and Malia and Sasha. You may notice that they're not here. The last thing they want to do is to listen to another speech from me. So they're out experiencing the beauty and the history of Berlin. And this history speaks to us today.

Here, for thousands of years, the people of this land have journeyed from tribe to principality to nation-state; through Reformation and Enlightenment, renowned as a "land of poets and thinkers," among them Immanuel Kant, who taught us that freedom is the "unoriginated birthright of man, and it belongs to him by force of his humanity."

Here, for two centuries, this gate stood tall as the world around it convulsed – through the rise and fall of empires; through revolutions and republics; art and music and science that reflected the height of human endeavor, but also war and carnage that exposed the depths of man's cruelty to man.

It was here that Berliners carved out an island of democracy against the greatest of odds. As has already been mentioned, they were supported by an airlift of hope, and we are so honored to be joined by Colonel Halvorsen, 92 years old – the original "candy bomber." We could not be prouder of him. I hope I look that good, by the way, when I'm 92.

During that time, a Marshall Plan seeded a miracle, and a North Atlantic Alliance protected our people. And those in the neighborhoods and nations to the East drew strength from the knowledge that freedom was possible here, in Berlin – that the waves of crackdowns and suppressions might therefore someday be overcome.

Today, 60 years after they rose up against oppression, we remember the East German heroes of June 17th. When the wall finally came down, it was their dreams that were fulfilled. Their strength and their passion, their enduring example remind us that for all the power of militaries, for all the authority of governments, it is citizens who choose whether to be defined by a wall, or whether to tear it down.

And we're now surrounded by the symbols of a Germany reborn. A rebuilt Reichstag and its glistening glass dome. An American embassy back at its historic home on Pariser Platz. And this square itself, once a desolate no man's land, is now open to all. So while I am not the first American President to come to this gate, I am proud to stand on its Eastern side to pay tribute to the past.

For throughout all this history, the fate of this city came down to a simple question: Will we live free or in chains? Under governments that uphold our universal rights, or regimes that suppress them? In open societies that respect the sanctity of the individual and our free will, or in closed societies that suffocate the soul?

As free peoples, we stated our convictions long ago. As Americans, we believe that "all men are created equal" with the right to life and liberty, and the pursuit of happiness. And as Germans, you declared in your Basic Law that "the dignity of man is inviolable." Around the world, nations have pledged themselves to a Universal Declaration of Human Rights, which recognizes the inherent dignity and rights of all members of our human family.

And this is what was at stake here in Berlin all those years. And because courageous crowds climbed atop that wall, because corrupt dictatorships gave way to new democracies, because millions across this continent now breathe the fresh air of freedom, we can say, here in Berlin, here in Europe – our values won. Openness won. Tolerance won. And freedom won here in Berlin.

And yet, more than two decades after that triumph, we must acknowledge that there can, at times, be a complacency among our Western democracies. Today, people often come together in places like this to remember history – not to make it. After all, we face no concrete walls, no barbed wire. There are no tanks poised across a border. There are no visits to fallout shelters. And so sometimes there can be a sense that the great challenges have somehow passed. And that brings with it a temptation to turn inward – to think of our own pursuits, and not the sweep of history; to believe that we've settled history's accounts, that we can simply enjoy the fruits won by our forebears.

But I come here today, Berlin, to say complacency is not the character of great nations. Today's threats are not as stark as they were half a century ago, but the struggle for freedom and security and human dignity – that struggle goes on. And I've come here, to this city of hope, because the tests of our time demand the same fighting spirit that defined Berlin a half-century ago.

Chancellor Merkel mentioned that we mark the anniversary of President John F. Kennedy's stirring defense of freedom, embodied in the people of this great city. His pledge of solidarity – "Ich bin ein Berliner" – echoes through the ages. But that's not all that he said that day. Less remembered is the challenge that he issued to the crowd before him: "Let me ask you," he said to those Berliners, "let me ask you to lift your eyes beyond the dangers of today" and "beyond the freedom of merely this city." Look, he said, "to the day of peace with justice, beyond yourselves and ourselves to all mankind."

President Kennedy was taken from us less than six months after he spoke those words. And like so many who died in those decades of division, he did not live to see Berlin united and free. Instead, he lives forever as a young man in our memory. But his words are timeless because they call upon us to care more about things than just our own self-comfort, about our own city, about our own country. They demand that we embrace the common endeavor of all humanity.

And if we lift our eyes, as President Kennedy called us to do, then we'll recognize that our work is not yet done. For we are not only citizens of America or Germany – we are also citizens of the world. And our fates and fortunes are linked like never before.

We may no longer live in fear of global annihilation, but so long as nuclear weapons exist, we are not truly safe. We may strike blows against terrorist networks, but if we ignore the instability and intolerance that fuels extremism, our own freedom will eventually be endangered. We may enjoy a standard of living that is the envy of the world, but so long as hundreds of millions endure the agony of an empty stomach or the anguish of unemployment, we're not truly prosperous.

I say all this here, in the heart of Europe, because our shared past shows that none of these challenges can be met unless we see ourselves as part of something bigger than our own experience. Our alliance is the foundation of global security. Our trade and our commerce is the engine of our global economy. Our values call upon us to care about the lives of people we will never meet. When Europe and America lead with our hopes instead of our fears, we do things that no other nations can do, no other nations will do. So we have to lift up our eyes today and consider the day of peace with justice that our generation wants for this world.

I'd suggest that peace with justice begins with the example we set here at home, for we know from our own histories that intolerance breeds injustice. Whether it's based on race, or religion, gender or sexual orientation, we are stronger when all our people – no matter who they are or what they look like – are granted opportunity, and when our wives and our daughters have the same opportunities as our husbands and our sons.

When we respect the faiths practiced in our churches and synagogues, our mosques and our temples, we're more secure. When we welcome the immigrant with his talents or her dreams, we are renewed. When we stand up for our gay and lesbian brothers and sisters and treat their love and their rights equally under the law, we defend our own liberty as well. We are more free when all people can pursue their own happiness. And as long as walls exist in our hearts to separate us from those who don't look like us, or think like us, or worship as we do, then we're going to have to work harder, together, to bring those walls of division down.

Peace with justice means free enterprise that unleashes the talents and creativity that reside in each of us; in other models, direct economic growth from the top down or relies solely on the resources extracted from the earth. But we believe that real prosperity comes from our most precious resource – our people. And that's why we choose to invest in education, and science and research.

And now, as we emerge from recession, we must not avert our eyes from the insult of widening inequality, or the pain of youth who are unemployed. We have to build new ladders of opportunity in our own societies that – even as we pursue new trade and investment that fuels growth across the Atlantic.

America will stand with Europe as you strengthen your union. And we want to work with you to make sure that every person can enjoy the dignity that comes from work – whether they live in Chicago or Cleveland or Belfast or Berlin, in Athens or Madrid, everybody deserves opportunity. We have to have economies that are working for all people, not just those at the very top.

Peace with justice means extending a hand to those who reach for freedom, wherever they live. Different peoples and cultures will follow their own path, but we must reject the lie that those who live in distant places don't yearn for freedom and self-determination just like we do; that they don't somehow yearn for dignity and rule of law just like we do. We cannot dictate the pace of change in places like the Arab world, but we must reject the excuse that we can do nothing to support it.

We cannot shrink from our role of advancing the values we believe in – whether it's supporting Afghans as they take responsibility for their future, or working for an Israeli-Palestinian peace – or engaging as we've done in Burma to help create space for brave people to emerge from decades of dictatorship. In this century, these are the citizens who long to join the free world. They are who you were. They deserve our support, for they too, in their own way, are citizens of Berlin. And we have to help them every day.

Peace with justice means pursuing the security of a world without nuclear weapons – no matter how distant that dream may be. And so, as President, I've strengthened our efforts to stop the spread of nuclear weapons, and reduced the number and role of America's nuclear weapons. Because of the New START Treaty, we're on track to cut American and Russian deployed nuclear warheads to their lowest levels since the 1950s.

But we have more work to do. So today, I'm announcing additional steps forward. After a comprehensive review, I've determined that we can ensure the security of America and our allies, and maintain a strong and credible strategic deterrent, while reducing our deployed strategic nuclear weapons by up to one-third. And I intend to seek negotiated cuts with Russia to move beyond Cold War nuclear postures.

At the same time, we'll work with our NATO allies to seek bold reductions in U.S. and Russian tactical weapons in Europe. And we can forge a new international framework for peaceful nuclear power, and reject the nuclear weaponization that North Korea and Iran may be seeking.

America will host a summit in 2016 to continue our efforts to secure nuclear materials around the world, and we will work to build support in the United States to ratify the Comprehensive Nuclear Test Ban Treaty, and call on all nations to begin negotiations on a treaty that ends the production of fissile materials for nuclear weapons. These are steps we can take to create a world of peace with justice.

Peace with justice means refusing to condemn our children to a harsher, less hospitable planet. The effort to slow climate change requires bold action. And on this, Germany and Europe have led.

In the United States, we have recently doubled our renewable energy from clean sources like wind and solar power. We're doubling fuel efficiency on our cars. Our dangerous carbon emissions have come down. But we know we have to do more – and we will do more.

With a global middle class consuming more energy every day, this must now be an effort of all nations, not just some. For the grim alternative affects all nations – more severe storms, more famine and floods, new waves of refugees, coastlines that vanish, oceans that rise. This is the future we must avert. This is the global threat of our time. And for the sake of future generations, our generation must move toward a global compact to confront a changing climate before it is too late. That is our job. That is our task. We have to get to work.

Peace with justice means meeting our moral obligations. And we have a moral obligation and a profound interest in helping lift the impoverished corners of the world. By promoting growth so we spare a child born today a lifetime of extreme poverty. By investing in agriculture, so we aren't just sending food, but also teaching farmers to grow food. By strengthening public health, so we're not just sending medicine, but training doctors and nurses who will help end the outrage of children dying from preventable diseases. Making sure that we do everything we can to realize the promise – an achievable promise – of the first AIDS-free generation. That is something that is possible if we feel a sufficient sense of urgency.

Our efforts have to be about more than just charity. They're about new models of empowering people – to build institutions; to abandon the rot of corruption; to create ties of trade, not just aid, both with the West and among the nations they're seeking to rise and increase their capacity. Because when they succeed, we will be more successful as well. Our fates are linked, and we cannot ignore those who are yearning not only for freedom but also prosperity.

And finally, let's remember that peace with justice depends on our ability to sustain both the security of our societies and the openness that defines them. Threats to freedom don't merely come from the outside. They can emerge from within – from our own fears, from the disengagement of our citizens.

For over a decade, America has been at war. Yet much has now changed over the five years since I last spoke here in Berlin. The Iraq war is now over. The Afghan war is coming to an end. Osama bin Laden is no more. Our efforts against al Qaeda are evolving.

And given these changes, last month, I spoke about America's efforts against terrorism. And I drew inspiration from one of our founding fathers, James Madison, who wrote, "No nation could preserve its freedom in the midst of continual warfare." James Madison is right – which is why, even as we remain vigilant about the threat of terrorism, we must move beyond a mindset of perpetual war. And in America, that means redoubling our efforts to close the prison at Guantanamo. It means tightly controlling our use of new technologies like drones. It means balancing the pursuit of security with the protection of privacy.

And I'm confident that that balance can be struck. I'm confident of that, and I'm confident that working with Germany, we can keep each other safe while at the same time maintaining those essential values for which we fought for.

Our current programs are bound by the rule of law, and they're focused on threats to our security – not the communications of ordinary persons. They help confront real dangers, and they keep people safe here in the United States and here in Europe. But we must accept the challenge that all of us in democratic governments face: to listen to the voices who disagree with us; to have an open debate about how we use our powers and how we must constrain them; and to always remember that government exists to serve the power of the individual, and not the other way around. That's what makes us who we are, and that's what makes us different from those on the other side of the wall.

That is how we'll stay true to our better history while reaching for the day of peace and justice that is to come. These are the beliefs that guide us, the values that inspire us, the principles that bind us together as free peoples who still believe the words of Dr. Martin Luther King Jr. – that "injustice anywhere is a threat to justice everywhere."

And we should ask, should anyone ask if our generation has the courage to meet these tests? If anybody asks if President Kennedy's words ring true today, let them come to Berlin, for here they will find the people who emerged from the ruins of war to reap the blessings of peace; from the pain of division to the joy of reunification. And here, they will recall how people trapped behind a wall braved bullets, and jumped barbed wire, and dashed across minefields, and dug through tunnels, and leapt from buildings, and swam across the Spree to claim their most basic right of freedom.

The wall belongs to history. But we have history to make as well. And the heroes that came before us now call to us to live up to those highest ideals – to care for the young people who can't find a job in our own countries, and the girls who aren't allowed to go to school overseas; to be vigilant in safeguarding our own freedoms, but also to extend a hand to those who are reaching for freedom abroad.

This is the lesson of the ages. This is the spirit of Berlin. And the greatest tribute that we can pay to those who came before us is by carrying on their work to pursue peace and justice not only in our countries but for all mankind.

Vielen Dank. God bless you. God bless the peoples of Germany. And God bless the United States of America. Thank you very much.

18

SPEECH AT THE LINCOLN MEMORIAL COMMEMORATING THE 50TH ANNIVERSARY OF THE MARCH ON WASHINGTON

AUGUST 28, 2013

To the King family, who have sacrificed and inspired so much; to President Clinton; President Carter; Vice President Biden and Jill; fellow Americans.

Five decades ago today, Americans came to this honored place to lay claim to a promise made at our founding: "We hold these truths to be self-evident, that all men are created equal, that they are endowed by their Creator with certain unalienable rights, that among these are Life, Liberty and the pursuit of Happiness."

In 1963, almost 200 years after those words were set to paper, a full century after a great war was fought and emancipation proclaimed, that promise – those truths – remained unmet. And so they came by the thousands from every corner of our country, men and women, young and old, blacks who longed for freedom and whites who could no longer accept freedom for themselves while witnessing the subjugation of others.

Across the land, congregations sent them off with food and with prayer. In the middle of the night, entire blocks of Harlem came out to wish them well. With the few dollars they scrimped from their labor, some bought tickets and boarded buses, even if they couldn't always sit where they wanted to sit. Those with less money hitchhiked or walked. They were seamstresses and steelworkers, students and teachers, maids and Pullman porters. They shared simple meals and bunked together on floors. And then, on a hot summer day, they assembled here, in our nation's capital, under the shadow of the Great Emancipator – to offer testimony of injustice, to petition their government for redress, and to awaken America's long-slumbering conscience.

We rightly and best remember Dr. King's soaring oratory that day, how he gave mighty voice to the quiet hopes of millions; how he offered a salvation path for oppressed and oppressors alike. His words belong to the ages, possessing a power and prophecy unmatched in our time.

But we would do well to recall that day itself also belonged to those ordinary

137

people whose names never appeared in the history books, never got on TV. Many had gone to segregated schools and sat at segregated lunch counters. They lived in towns where they couldn't vote and cities where their votes didn't matter. They were couples in love who couldn't marry, soldiers who fought for freedom abroad that they found denied to them at home. They had seen loved ones beaten, and children fire-hosed, and they had every reason to lash out in anger, or resign themselves to a bitter fate.

And yet they chose a different path. In the face of hatred, they prayed for their tormentors. In the face of violence, they stood up and sat in, with the moral force of nonviolence. Willingly, they went to jail to protest unjust laws, their cells swelling with the sound of freedom songs. A lifetime of indignities had taught them that no man can take away the dignity and grace that God grants us. They had learned through hard experience what Frederick Douglass once taught – that freedom is not given, it must be won, through struggle and discipline, persistence and faith.

That was the spirit they brought here that day. That was the spirit young people like John Lewis brought to that day. That was the spirit that they carried with them, like a torch, back to their cities and their neighborhoods. That steady flame of conscience and courage that would sustain them through the campaigns to come – through boycotts and voter registration drives and smaller marches far from the spotlight; through the loss of four little girls in Birmingham, and the carnage of the Edmund Pettus Bridge, and the agony of Dallas and California and Memphis. Through setbacks and heartbreaks and gnawing doubt, that flame of justice flickered; it never died.

And because they kept marching, America changed. Because they marched, a Civil Rights law was passed. Because they marched, a Voting Rights law was signed. Because they marched, doors of opportunity and education swung open so their daughters and sons could finally imagine a life for themselves beyond washing somebody else's laundry or shining somebody else's shoes. Because they marched, city councils changed and state legislatures changed, and Congress changed, and, yes, eventually, the White House changed.

Because they marched, America became more free and more fair – not just for African Americans, but for women and Latinos, Asians and Native Americans; for Catholics, Jews, and Muslims; for gays, for Americans with a disability. America changed for you and for me. and the entire world drew strength from that example, whether the young people who watched from the other side of an Iron Curtain and would eventually tear down that wall, or the young people inside South Africa who would eventually end the scourge of apartheid.

Those are the victories they won, with iron wills and hope in their hearts. That is the transformation that they wrought, with each step of their well-worn shoes. That's the debt that I and millions of Americans owe those maids, those laborers, those porters, those secretaries; folks who could have run a company maybe if they had ever had a chance; those white students who put themselves in harm's way, even though they didn't have; those Japanese Americans who recalled their own internment; those Jewish Americans who had survived the Holocaust; people who could have given up and given in, but kept on keeping on, knowing that "weeping may endure for a night, but joy cometh in the morning."

On the battlefield of justice, men and women without rank or wealth or title or fame would liberate us all in ways that our children now take for granted, as people of all colors and creeds live together and learn together and walk together, and fight alongside one another, and love one another, and judge one another by the content of our character in this greatest nation on Earth.

To dismiss the magnitude of this progress – to suggest, as some sometimes do, that little has changed – that dishonors the courage and the sacrifice of those who paid the price to march in those years. Medgar Evers, James Chaney, Andrew Goodman, Michael Schwerner, Martin Luther King Jr. – they did not die in vain. Their victory was great.

But we would dishonor those heroes as well to suggest that the work of this nation is somehow complete. The arc of the moral universe may bend towards justice, but it doesn't bend on its own. To secure the gains this country has made requires constant vigilance, not complacency. Whether by challenging those who erect new barriers to the vote, or ensuring that the scales of justice work equally for all, and the criminal justice system is not simply a pipeline from underfunded schools to overcrowded jails, it requires vigilance.

And we'll suffer the occasional setback. But we will win these fights. This country has changed too much. People of goodwill, regardless of party, are too plentiful for those with ill will to change history's currents.

In some ways, though, the securing of civil rights, voting rights, the eradication of legalized discrimination – the very significance of these victories may have obscured a second goal of the March. For the men and women who gathered 50 years ago were not there in search of some abstract ideal. They were there seeking jobs as well as justice – not just the absence of oppression but the presence of economic opportunity.

For what does it profit a man, Dr. King would ask, to sit at an integrated lunch counter if he can't afford the meal? This idea – that one's liberty is linked to one's livelihood; that the pursuit of happiness requires the dignity of work, the skills to find work, decent pay, some measure of material security – this idea was not new. Lincoln himself understood the Declaration of Independence in such terms – as a promise that in due time, "the weights should be lifted from the shoulders of all men, and that all should have an equal chance."

And Dr. King explained that the goals of African Americans were identical to working people of all races: "Decent wages, fair working conditions, livable housing, old-age security, health and welfare measures, conditions in which families can grow, have education for their children, and respect in the community."

What King was describing has been the dream of every American. It's what's lured for centuries new arrivals to our shores. And it's along this second dimension – of economic opportunity, the chance through honest toil to advance one's station in life – where the goals of 50 years ago have fallen most short.

Yes, there have been examples of success within black America that would have been unimaginable a half century ago. But as has already been noted, black unemployment has remained almost twice as high as white unemployment, Latino unemployment close behind. The gap in wealth between races has not lessened, it's grown. And as President Clinton indicated, the position of all working Americans, regardless of color, has eroded, making the dream Dr. King described even more elusive.

For over a decade, working Americans of all races have seen their wages and incomes stagnate, even as corporate profits soar, even as the pay of a fortunate few explodes. Inequality has steadily risen over the decades. Upward mobility has become harder. In too many communities across this country, in cities and suburbs and rural hamlets, the shadow of poverty casts a pall over our youth, their lives a fortress of substandard schools and diminished prospects, inadequate health care and perennial violence.

And so as we mark this anniversary, we must remind ourselves that the measure of progress for those who marched 50 years ago was not merely how many blacks could join the ranks of millionaires. It was whether this country would admit all people who are willing to work hard regardless of race into the ranks of a middle-class life.

The test was not, and never has been, whether the doors of opportunity are cracked a bit wider for a few. It was whether our economic system provides a fair shot for the many – for the black custodian and the white steelworker, the immigrant dishwasher and the Native American veteran. To win that battle, to answer that call – this remains our great unfinished business.

We shouldn't fool ourselves. The task will not be easy. Since 1963, the economy has changed. The twin forces of technology and global competition have subtracted those jobs that once provided a foothold into the middle class – reduced the bargaining power of American workers. And our politics has suffered. Entrenched interests, those who benefit from an unjust status quo, resisted any government efforts to give working families a fair deal – marshaling an army of lobbyists and opinion makers to argue that minimum wage increases or stronger labor laws or taxes on the wealthy who could afford it just to fund crumbling schools, that all these things violated sound economic principles. We'd be told that growing inequality was a price for a growing economy, a measure of this free market; that greed was good and compassion ineffective, and those without jobs or health care had only themselves to blame.

And then, there were those elected officials who found it useful to practice the old politics of division, doing their best to convince middle-class Americans of a great untruth – that government was somehow itself to blame for their growing economic insecurity; that distant bureaucrats were taking their hard-earned dollars to benefit the welfare cheat or the illegal immigrant.

And then, if we're honest with ourselves, we'll admit that during the course of 50 years, there were times when some of us claiming to push for change lost our way. The anguish of assassinations set off self-defeating riots. Legitimate grievances against police brutality tipped into excuse-making for criminal behavior. Racial politics could cut both ways, as the transformative message of unity and brotherhood was drowned out by the language of recrimination. And what had once been a call for equality of opportunity, the chance for all Americans to work hard and get ahead was too often framed as a mere desire for government support – as if we had no agency in our own liberation, as if poverty was an excuse for not raising your child, and the bigotry of others was reason to give up on yourself.

All of that history is how progress stalled. That's how hope was diverted. It's how our country remained divided. But the good news is, just as was true in 1963, we now have a choice. We can continue down our current path, in which the gears of this great democracy grind to a halt and our children accept a life of lower expectations; where politics is a zero-sum game where a few do very well while struggling families of every race fight over a shrinking economic pie – that's one path. Or we can have the courage to change.

The March on Washington teaches us that we are not trapped by the mistakes of history; that we are masters of our fate. But it also teaches us that the promise of this nation will only be kept when we work together. We'll have to reignite the embers of empathy and fellow feeling, the coalition of conscience that found expression in this place 50 years ago.

And I believe that spirit is there, that truth force inside each of us. I see it when a white mother recognizes her own daughter in the face of a poor black child. I see it when the black youth thinks of his own grandfather in the dignified steps of an elderly white man. It's there when the native-born recognizing that striving spirit of the new immigrant; when the interracial couple connects the pain of a gay couple who are discriminated against and understands it as their own.

That's where courage comes from – when we turn not from each other, or on each other, but towards one another, and we find that we do not walk alone. That's where courage comes from.

And with that courage, we can stand together for good jobs and just wages. With that courage, we can stand together for the right to health care in the richest nation on Earth for every person. With that courage, we can stand together for the right of every child, from the corners of Anacostia to the hills of Appalachia, to get an education that stirs the mind and captures the spirit, and prepares them for the world that awaits them.

With that courage, we can feed the hungry, and house the homeless, and transform bleak wastelands of poverty into fields of commerce and promise.

America, I know the road will be long, but I know we can get there. Yes, we will stumble, but I know we'll get back up. That's how a movement happens. That's how history bends. That's how when somebody is faint of heart, somebody else brings them along and says, come on, we're marching.

There's a reason why so many who marched that day, and in the days to come, were young – for the young are unconstrained by habits of fear, unconstrained by the conventions of what is. They dared to dream differently, to imagine something better. And I am convinced that same imagination, the same hunger of purpose stirs in this generation.

We might not face the same dangers of 1963, but the fierce urgency of now remains. We may never duplicate the swelling crowds and dazzling procession of that day so long ago – no one can match King's brilliance – but the same flame that lit the heart of all who are willing to take a first step for justice, I know that flame remains.

That tireless teacher who gets to class early and stays late and dips into her own pocket to buy supplies because she believes that every child is her charge – she's marching.

That successful businessman who doesn't have to but pays his workers a fair wage and then offers a shot to a man, maybe an ex-con who is down on his luck – he's marching.

The mother who pours her love into her daughter so that she grows up with the confidence to walk through the same door as anybody's son – she's marching.

The father who realizes the most important job he'll ever have is raising his boy right, even if he didn't have a father – especially if he didn't have a father at home – he's marching.

The battle-scarred veterans who devote themselves not only to helping their fellow warriors stand again, and walk again, and run again, but to keep serving their country when they come home – they are marching.

Everyone who realizes what those glorious patriots knew on that day – that change does not come from Washington, but to Washington; that change has always been built on our willingness, We The People, to take on the mantle of citizenship – you are marching.

And that's the lesson of our past. That's the promise of tomorrow – that in the face of impossible odds, people who love their country can change it. That when millions of Americans of every race and every region, every faith and every station, can join together in a spirit of brotherhood, then those mountains will be made low, and those rough places will be made plain, and those crooked places, they straighten out towards grace, and we will vindicate the faith of those who sacrificed so much and live up to the true meaning of our creed, as one nation, under God, indivisible, with liberty and justice for all.

❦ 19 ❦

REMARKS ON TRAYVON MARTIN

JULY 19, 2013

I wanted to come out here, first of all, to tell you that Jay is prepared for all your questions and is very much looking forward to the session. The second thing is I want to let you know that over the next couple of weeks, there's going to obviously be a whole range of issues – immigration, economics, et cetera – we'll try to arrange a fuller press conference to address your questions.

The reason I actually wanted to come out today is not to take questions, but to speak to an issue that obviously has gotten a lot of attention over the course of the last week – the issue of the Trayvon Martin ruling. I gave a preliminary statement right after the ruling on Sunday. But watching the debate over the course of the last week, I thought it might be useful for me to expand on my thoughts a little bit.

First of all, I want to make sure that, once again, I send my thoughts and prayers, as well as Michelle's, to the family of Trayvon Martin, and to remark on the incredible grace and dignity with which they've dealt with the entire situation. I can only imagine what they're going through, and it's remarkable how they've handled it.

The second thing I want to say is to reiterate what I said on Sunday, which is there's going to be a lot of arguments about the legal issues in the case – I'll let all the legal analysts and talking heads address those issues. The judge conducted the trial in a professional manner. The prosecution and the defense made their arguments. The juries were properly instructed that in a case such as this reasonable doubt was relevant, and they rendered a verdict. And once the jury has spoken, that's how our system works. But I did want to just talk a little bit about context and how people have responded to it and how people are feeling.

You know, when Trayvon Martin was first shot I said that this could have been my son. Another way of saying that is Trayvon Martin could have been me 35 years ago. And when you think about why, in the African American community at least, there's a lot of pain around what happened here, I think it's important to recognize that the

African American community is looking at this issue through a set of experiences and a history that doesn't go away.

There are very few African American men in this country who haven't had the experience of being followed when they were shopping in a department store. That includes me. There are very few African American men who haven't had the experience of walking across the street and hearing the locks click on the doors of cars. That happens to me – at least before I was a senator. There are very few African Americans who haven't had the experience of getting on an elevator and a woman clutching her purse nervously and holding her breath until she had a chance to get off. That happens often.

And I don't want to exaggerate this, but those sets of experiences inform how the African American community interprets what happened one night in Florida. And it's inescapable for people to bring those experiences to bear. The African American community is also knowledgeable that there is a history of racial disparities in the application of our criminal laws – everything from the death penalty to enforcement of our drug laws. And that ends up having an impact in terms of how people interpret the case.

Now, this isn't to say that the African American community is naïve about the fact that African American young men are disproportionately involved in the criminal justice system; that they're disproportionately both victims and perpetrators of violence. It's not to make excuses for that fact – although black folks do interpret the reasons for that in a historical context. They understand that some of the violence that takes place in poor black neighborhoods around the country is born out of a very violent past in this country, and that the poverty and dysfunction that we see in those communities can be traced to a very difficult history.

And so the fact that sometimes that's unacknowledged adds to the frustration. And the fact that a lot of African American boys are painted with a broad brush and the excuse is given, well, there are these statistics out there that show that African American boys are more violent – using that as an excuse to then see sons treated differently causes pain.

I think the African American community is also not naïve in understanding that, statistically, somebody like Trayvon Martin was statistically more likely to be shot by a peer than he was by somebody else. So folks understand the challenges that exist for African American boys. But they get frustrated, I think, if they feel that there's no context for it and that context is being denied. And that all contributes I think to a sense that if a white male teen was involved in the same kind of scenario, that, from top to bottom, both the outcome and the aftermath might have been different.

Now, the question for me at least, and I think for a lot of folks, is where do we take this? How do we learn some lessons from this and move in a positive direction? I think it's understandable that there have been demonstrations and vigils and protests, and some of that stuff is just going to have to work its way through, as long as it remains nonviolent. If I see any violence, then I will remind folks that that dishonors what happened to Trayvon Martin and his family. But beyond protests or vigils, the question is, are there some concrete things that we might be able to do.

I know that Eric Holder is reviewing what happened down there, but I think it's important for people to have some clear expectations here. Traditionally, these are issues of state and local government, the criminal code. And law enforcement is traditionally done at the state and local levels, not at the federal levels.

That doesn't mean, though, that as a nation we can't do some things that I think would be productive. So let me just give a couple of specifics that I'm still bouncing around with my staff, so we're not rolling out some five-point plan, but some areas where I think all of us could potentially focus.

Number one, precisely because law enforcement is often determined at the state and local level, I think it would be productive for the Justice Department, governors, mayors to work with law enforcement about training at the state and local levels in order to reduce the kind of mistrust in the system that sometimes currently exists.

When I was in Illinois, I passed racial profiling legislation, and it actually did just two simple things. One, it collected data on traffic stops and the race of the person who was stopped. But the other thing was it resourced us training police departments across the state on how to think about potential racial bias and ways to further professionalize what they were doing.

And initially, the police departments across the state were resistant, but actually they came to recognize that if it was done in a fair, straightforward way that it would allow them to do their jobs better and communities would have more confidence in them and, in turn, be more helpful in applying the law. And obviously, law enforcement has got a very tough job.

So that's one area where I think there are a lot of resources and best practices that could be brought to bear if state and local governments are receptive. And I think a lot of them would be. And let's figure out are there ways for us to push out that kind of training.

Along the same lines, I think it would be useful for us to examine some state and local laws to see if it – if they are designed in such a way that they may encourage the kinds of altercations and confrontations and tragedies that we saw in the Florida case, rather than diffuse potential altercations.

I know that there's been commentary about the fact that the "stand your ground" laws in Florida were not used as a defense in the case. On the other hand, if we're sending a message as a society in our communities that someone who is armed potentially has the right to use those firearms even if there's a way for them to exit from a situation, is that really going to be contributing to the kind of peace and security and order that we'd like to see?

And for those who resist that idea that we should think about something like these "stand your ground" laws, I'd just ask people to consider, if Trayvon Martin was of age and armed, could he have stood his ground on that sidewalk? And do we actually think that he would have been justified in shooting Mr. Zimmerman who had followed him in a car because he felt threatened? And if the answer to that question is at least ambiguous, then it seems to me that we might want to examine those kinds of laws.

Number three – and this is a long-term project – we need to spend some time in thinking about how do we bolster and reinforce our African American boys. And this is something that Michelle and I talk a lot about. There are a lot of kids out there who need help who are getting a lot of negative reinforcement. And is there more that we can do to give them the sense that their country cares about them and values them and is willing to invest in them?

I'm not naïve about the prospects of some grand, new federal program. I'm not sure that that's what we're talking about here. But I do recognize that as President, I've got some convening power, and there are a lot of good programs that are being done across the country on this front. And for us to be able to gather together business leaders and local elected officials and clergy and celebrities and athletes, and figure out how are we doing a better job helping young African American men feel that they're a full part of this society and that they've got pathways and avenues to succeed – I think that would be a pretty good outcome from what was obviously a tragic situation. And we're going to spend some time working on that and thinking about that.

And then, finally, I think it's going to be important for all of us to do some soul-searching. There has been talk about should we convene a conversation on race. I haven't seen that be particularly productive when politicians try to organize conversations. They end up being stilted and politicized, and folks are locked into the positions they already have. On the other hand, in families and churches and workplaces, there's the possibility that people are a little bit more honest, and at least you ask yourself your own questions about, am I wringing as much bias out of myself as I can? Am I judging people as much as I can, based on not the color of their skin, but the content of their character? That would, I think, be an appropriate exercise in the wake of this tragedy.

And let me just leave you with a final thought that, as difficult and challenging as this whole episode has been for a lot of people, I don't want us to lose sight that things are getting better. Each successive generation seems to be making progress in changing attitudes when it comes to race. It doesn't mean we're in a post-racial society. It doesn't mean that racism is eliminated. But when I talk to Malia and Sasha, and I listen to their friends and I seem them interact, they're better than we are – they're better than we were – on these issues. And that's true in every community that I've visited all across the country.

And so we have to be vigilant and we have to work on these issues. And those of us in authority should be doing everything we can to encourage the better angels of our nature, as opposed to using these episodes to heighten divisions. But we should also have confidence that kids these days, I think, have more sense than we did back then, and certainly more than our parents did or our grandparents did; and that along this long, difficult journey, we're becoming a more perfect union – not a perfect union, but a more perfect union.

Thank you, guys.

2014 STATE OF THE UNION ADDRESS

JANUARY 28, 2014

Mr. Speaker, Mr. Vice President, Members of Congress, my fellow Americans: Today in America, a teacher spent extra time with a student who needed it and did her part to lift America's graduation rate to its highest levels in more than three decades. An entrepreneur flipped on the lights in her tech startup and did her part to add to the more than 8 million new jobs our businesses have created over the past 4 years. An autoworker fine-tuned some of the best, most fuel- efficient cars in the world and did his part to help America wean itself off foreign oil.

A farmer prepared for the spring after the strongest 5-year stretch of farm exports in our history. A rural doctor gave a young child the first prescription to treat asthma that his mother could afford. A man took the bus home from the graveyard shift, bone-tired, but dreaming big dreams for his son. And in tight-knit communities all across America, fathers and mothers will tuck in their kids, put an arm around their spouse, remember fallen comrades, and give thanks for being home from a war that after 12 long years is finally coming to an end.

Tonight this Chamber speaks with one voice to the people we represent: It is you, our citizens, who make the state of our Union strong.

And here are the results of your efforts: the lowest unemployment rate in over 5 years; a rebounding housing market; a manufacturing sector that's adding jobs for the first time since the 1990s; more oil produced at home than we buy from the rest of the world, the first time that's happened in nearly 20 years; our deficits cut by more than half. And for the first time in over a decade, business leaders around the world have declared that China is no longer the world's number-one place to invest, America is.

That's why I believe this can be a breakthrough year for America. After 5 years of grit and determined effort, the United States is better positioned for the 21st century than any other nation on Earth.

The question for everyone in this Chamber, running through every decision we make this year, is whether we are going to help or hinder this progress. For several years now, this town has been consumed by a rancorous argument over the proper size of the Federal Government. It's an important debate, one that dates back to our very founding. But when that debate prevents us from carrying out even the most basic functions of our democracy—when our differences shut down Government or threaten the full faith and credit of the United States—then we are not doing right by the American people.

Now, as President, I'm committed to making Washington work better and rebuilding the trust of the people who sent us here. And I believe most of you are too. Last month, thanks to the work of Democrats and Republicans, Congress finally produced a budget that undoes some of last year's severe cuts to priorities like education. Nobody got everything they wanted, and we can still do more to invest in this country's future while bringing down our deficit in a balanced way, but the budget compromise should leave us freer to focus on creating new jobs, not creating new crises.

And in the coming months, let's see where else we can make progress together. Let's make this a year of action. That's what most Americans want: for all of us in this Chamber to focus on their lives, their hopes, their aspirations. And what I believe unites the people of this Nation—regardless of race or region or party, young or old, rich or poor—is the simple, profound belief in opportunity for all: the notion that if you work hard and take responsibility, you can get ahead in America.

Now, let's face it, that belief has suffered some serious blows. Over more than three decades, even before the great recession hit, massive shifts in technology and global competition had eliminated a lot of good, middle class jobs and weakened the economic foundations that families depend on.

Today, after 4 years of economic growth, corporate profits and stock prices have rarely been higher, and those at the top have never done better. But average wages have barely budged. Inequality has deepened. Upward mobility has stalled. The cold, hard fact is that even in the midst of recovery, too many Americans are working more than ever just to get by, let alone to get ahead. And too many still aren't working at all.

So our job is to reverse these trends. It won't happen right away, and we won't agree on everything. But what I offer tonight is a set of concrete, practical proposals to speed up growth, strengthen the middle class, and build new ladders of opportunity into the middle class. Some require congressional action, and I am eager to work with all of you. But America does not stand still, and neither will I. So wherever and whenever I can take steps without legislation to expand opportunity for more American families, that's what I'm going to do.

As usual, our First Lady sets a good example. [Applause] Well– [applause]. Michelle's "Let's Move!" partnership with schools, businesses, local leaders has helped bring down childhood obesity rates for the first time in 30 years. And that's an achievement that will improve lives and reduce health care costs for decades to come. The Joining Forces alliance that Michelle and Jill Biden launched has already encouraged employers to hire or train nearly 400,000 veterans and military spouses.

Taking a page from that playbook, the White House just organized a College Opportunity Summit, where already, 150 universities, businesses, nonprofits have made concrete commitments to reduce inequality in access to higher education and to help every hard-working kid go to college and succeed when they get to campus. And across the country, we're partnering with mayors, Governors, and State legislatures on issues from homelessness to marriage equality.

The point is, there are millions of Americans outside of Washington who are tired of stale political arguments and are moving this country forward. They believe–and I believe–that here in America, our success should depend not on accident of birth, but the strength of our work ethic and the scope of our dreams. That's what drew our forebears here. That's how the daughter of a factory worker is CEO of America's largest automaker; how the son of a barkeep is Speaker of the House; how the son of a single mom can be President of the greatest nation on Earth.

Opportunity is who we are. And the defining project of our generation must be to restore that promise. We know where to start: The best measure of opportunity is access to a good job. With the economy picking up speed, companies say they intend to hire more people this year. And over half of big manufacturers say they're thinking of insourcing jobs from abroad.

So let's make that decision easier for more companies. Both Democrats and Republicans have argued that our Tax Code is riddled with wasteful, complicated loopholes that punish businesses investing here and reward companies that keep profits abroad. Let's flip that equation. Let's work together to close those loopholes, end those incentives to ship jobs overseas, and lower tax rates for businesses that create jobs right here at home.

Moreover, we can take the money we save from this transition to tax reform to create jobs rebuilding our roads, upgrading our ports, unclogging our commutes, because in today's global economy, first-class jobs gravitate to first-class infrastructure. We'll need Congress to protect more than 3 million jobs by finishing transportation and waterways bills this summer. That can happen. But I'll act on my own to slash bureaucracy and streamline the permitting process for key projects so we can get more construction workers on the job as fast as possible.

We also have the chance, right now, to beat other countries in the race for the next wave of high-tech manufacturing jobs. My administration has launched two hubs for high-tech manufacturing in Raleigh, North Carolina, and Youngstown, Ohio, where we've connected businesses to research universities that can help America lead the world in advanced technologies. Tonight I'm announcing, we'll launch six more this year. Bipartisan bills in both Houses could double the number of these hubs and the jobs they create. So get those bills to my desk. Put more Americans back to work.

Let's do more to help the entrepreneurs and small-business owners who create most new jobs in America. Over the past 5 years, my administration has made more loans to small-business owners than any other. And when 98 percent of our exporters are small businesses, new trade partnerships with Europe and Asia–the Asia-Pacific will help them create more jobs. We need to work together on tools like bipartisan trade promotion authority to protect our workers, protect our environment, and open new markets to new goods stamped "Made in the U.S.A."

Listen, China and Europe aren't standing on the sidelines, and neither should we. We know that the nation that goes all-in on innovation today will own the global economy tomorrow. This is an edge America cannot surrender. Federally funded research helped lead to the ideas and inventions behind Google and smartphones. And that's why Congress should undo the damage done by last year's cuts to basic research so we can unleash the next great American discovery. There are entire industries to be built based on vaccines that stay ahead of drug-resistant bacteria or paper-thin material that's stronger than steel. And let's pass a patent reform bill that allows our businesses to stay focused on innovation, not costly and needless litigation.

Now, one of the biggest factors in bringing more jobs back is our commitment to American energy. The all-of-the-above energy strategy I announced a few years ago is working, and today, America is closer to energy independence than we have been in decades.

One of the reasons why is natural gas. If extracted safely, it's the bridge fuel that can power our economy with less of the carbon pollution that causes climate change. Businesses plan to invest almost $100 billion in new factories that use natural gas. I'll cut redtape to help States get those factories built and put folks to work, and this Congress can help by putting people to work building fueling stations that shift more cars and trucks from foreign oil to American natural gas.

Meanwhile, my administration will keep working with the industry to sustain production and jobs growth while strengthening protection of our air, our water, our communities. And while we're at it, I'll use my authority to protect more of our pristine Federal lands for future generations.

Well, it's not just oil and natural gas production that's booming, we're becoming a global leader in solar too. Every 4 minutes, another American home or business goes solar, every panel pounded into place by a worker whose job cannot be outsourced. Let's continue that progress with a smarter tax policy that stops giving $4 billion a year to fossil fuel industries that don't need it so we can invest more in fuels of the future that do.

And even as we've increased energy production, we've partnered with businesses, builders, and local communities to reduce the energy we consume. When we rescued our automakers, for example, we worked with them to set higher fuel efficiency standards for our cars. In the coming months, I'll build on that success by setting new standards for our trucks so we can keep driving down oil imports and what we pay at the pump.

And taken together, our energy policy is creating jobs and leading to a cleaner, safer planet. Over the past 8 years, the United States has reduced our total carbon pollution more than any other nation on Earth. But we have to act with more urgency, because a changing climate is already harming Western communities struggling with drought and coastal cities dealing with floods. That's why I directed my administration to work with States, utilities, and others to set new standards on the amount of carbon pollution our power plants are allowed to dump into the air.

The shift to a cleaner energy economy won't happen overnight, and it will require some tough choices along the way. But the debate is settled. Climate change is a fact. And when our children's children look us in the eye and ask if we did all we could to leave them a safer, more stable world, with new sources of energy, I want us to be able to say, yes, we did.

Finally, if we're serious about economic growth, it is time to heed the call of business leaders, labor leaders, faith leaders, law enforcement and fix our broken immigration system. Republicans and Democrats in the Senate have acted, and I know that members of both parties in the House want to do the same. Independent economists say immigration reform will grow our economy and shrink our deficits by almost $1 trillion in the next two decades. And for good reason: When people come here to fulfill their dreams–to study, invent, contribute to our culture–they make our country a more attractive place for businesses to locate and create jobs for everybody. So let's get immigration reform done this year. [Applause] Let's get it done. It's time.

The ideas I've outlined so far can speed up growth and create more jobs. But in this rapidly changing economy, we have to make sure that every American has the skills to fill those jobs. The good news is, we know how to do it.

Two years ago, as the auto industry came roaring back, Andra Rush opened up a manufacturing firm in Detroit. She knew that Ford needed parts for the best selling truck in America, and she knew how to make those parts. She just needed the workforce. So she dialed up what we call an American Job Center, places where folks can walk in to get the help or training they need to find a new job or a better job. She was flooded with new workers. And today, Detroit Manufacturing Systems has more than 700 employees. And what Andra and her employees experienced is how it should be for every employer and every job seeker.

So tonight I've asked Vice President Biden to lead an across-the-board reform of America's training programs to make sure they have one mission: train Americans with the skills employers need and match them to good jobs that need to be filled right now. That means more on-the- job training and more apprenticeships that set a young worker on an upward trajectory for life. It means connecting companies to community colleges that can help design training to fill their specific needs. And if Congress wants to help, you can concentrate funding on proven programs that connect more ready-to-work Americans with ready-to-be- filled jobs.

I'm also convinced we can help Americans return to the workforce faster by reforming unemployment insurance so that it's more effective in today's economy. But first, this Congress needs to restore the unemployment insurance you just let expire for 1.6 million people.

Let me tell you why. Misty DeMars is a mother of two young boys. She'd been steadily employed since she was a teenager, put herself through college. She'd never collected unemployment benefits, but she'd been paying taxes. In May, she and her husband used their life savings to buy their first home. A week later, budget cuts claimed the job she loved. Last month, when their unemployment insurance was cut off, she sat down and wrote me a letter, the kind I get every day. "We are the face of the unemployment crisis," she wrote. "I'm not dependent on the government. Our country depends on people like us who build careers, contribute to society, care about our neighbors. I'm confident that in time, I will find a job, I will pay my taxes, and we will raise our children in their own home in the community we love. Please give us this chance."

Congress, give these hard-working, responsible Americans that chance. Give them that chance. [Applause] Give them the chance. They need our help right now. But more important, this country needs them in the game. That's why I've been asking CEOs to give more long-term unemployed workers a fair shot at new jobs, a new chance to support their families. And in fact, this week, many will come to the White House to make that commitment real. Tonight I ask every business leader in America to join us and to do the same, because we are stronger when America fields a full team.

Of course, it's not enough to train today's workforce. We also have to prepare tomorrow's workforce, by guaranteeing every child access to a world-class education. Estiven Rodriguez couldn't speak a word of English when he moved to New York City at age 9. But last month, thanks to the support of great teachers and an innovative tutoring program, he led a march of his classmates through a crowd of cheering parents and neighbors from their high school to the post office, where they mailed off their college applications. And this son of a factory worker just found out, he's going to college this fall.

Five years ago, we set out to change the odds for all our kids. We worked with lenders to reform student loans, and today, more young people are earning college degrees than ever before. Race to the Top, with the help of Governors from both parties, has helped States raise expectations and performance. Teachers and principals in schools from Tennessee to Washington, DC, are making big strides in preparing students with the skills for the new economy: problem solving, critical thinking, science, technology, engineering, math.

Now, some of this change is hard. It requires everything from more challenging curriculums and more demanding parents to better support for teachers and new ways to measure how well our kids think, not how well they can fill in a bubble on a test. But it is worth it, and it is working. The problem is, we're still not reaching enough kids, and we're not reaching them in time. And that has to change.

Research shows that one of the best investments we can make in a child's life is high-quality early education. Last year, I asked this Congress to help States make high-quality pre-K available to every 4- year-old. And as a parent as well as a President, I repeat that request tonight. But in the meantime, 30 States have raised pre-K funding on their own. They know we can't wait. So just as we worked with States to reform our schools, this year, we'll invest in new partnerships with States and communities across the country in a Race to the Top for our youngest children. And as Congress decides what it's going to do, I'm going to pull together a coalition of elected officials, business leaders, and philanthropists willing to help more kids access the high- quality pre-K that they need. It is right for America. We need to get this done.

Last year, I also pledged to connect 99 percent of our students to high-speed broadband over the next 4 years. Tonight I can announce that with the support of the FCC and companies like Apple, Microsoft, Sprint, and Verizon, we've got a down payment to start connecting more than 15,000 schools and 20 million students over the next 2 years, without adding a dime to the deficit.

We're working to redesign high schools and partner them with colleges and employers that offer the real-world education and hands-on training that can lead directly to a job and career. We're shaking up our system of higher education to give parents more information and colleges more incentive to offer better value so that no middle class kid is priced out of a college education.

We're offering millions the opportunity to cap their monthly student loan payments to 10 percent of their income, and I want to work with Congress to see how we can help even more Americans who feel trapped by student loan debt. And I'm reaching out to some of America's leading foundations and corporations on a new initiative to help more young men of color facing especially tough odds to stay on track and reach their full potential.

The bottom line is, Michelle and I want every child to have the same chance this country gave us. But we know our opportunity agenda won't be complete, and too many young people entering the workforce today will see the American Dream as an empty promise, unless we also do more to make sure our economy honors the dignity of work and hard work pays off for every single American.

Today, women make up about half our workforce, but they still make 77 cents for every dollar a man earns. That is wrong, and in 2014, it's an embarrassment. Women deserve equal pay for equal work. She deserves to have a baby without sacrificing her job. A mother deserves a day off to care for a sick child or a sick parent without running into hardship. And you know what, a father does too. It is time to do away with workplace policies that belong in a "Mad Men" episode. [Laughter] This year, let's all come together–Congress, the White House, businesses from Wall Street to Main Street–to give every woman the opportunity she deserves. Because I believe when women succeed, America succeeds.

Now, women hold a majority of lower wage jobs, but they're not the only ones stifled by stagnant wages. Americans understand that some people will earn more money than others, and we don't resent those who, by virtue of their efforts, achieve incredible success. That's what America is all about. But Americans overwhelmingly agree that no one who works full-time should ever have to raise a family in poverty.

In the year since I asked this Congress to raise the minimum wage, five States have passed laws to raise theirs. Many businesses have done it on their own. Nick Chute is here today with his boss, John Soranno. John's an owner of Punch Pizza in Minneapolis, and Nick helps make the dough. [Laughter] Only now he makes more of it. [Laughter] John just gave his employees a raise to 10 bucks an hour, and that's a decision that has eased their financial stress and boosted their morale.

Tonight I ask more of America's business leaders to follow John's lead: Do what you can to raise your employees' wages. It's good for the economy. It's good for America. To every mayor, Governor, State legislator in America, I say: You don't have to wait for Congress to act; Americans will support you if you take this on.

And as a chief executive, I intend to lead by example. Profitable corporations like Costco see higher wages as the smart way to boost productivity and reduce turnover. We should too. In the coming weeks, I will issue an Executive order requiring Federal contractors to pay their federally funded employees a fair wage of at least 10 dollars and 10 cents an hour. Because if you cook our troops' meals or wash their dishes, you should not have to live in poverty.

Of course, to reach millions more, Congress does need to get on board. Today, the Federal minimum wage is worth about 20 percent less than it was when Ronald Reagan first stood here. And Tom Harkin and George Miller have a bill to fix that by lifting the minimum wage to 10 dollars and 10 cents. It's easy to remember: 10-10. This will help families. It will give businesses customers with more money to spend. It does not involve any new bureaucratic program. So join the rest of the country. Say yes. Give America a raise. Give them a raise.

There are other steps we can take to help families make ends meet, and few are more effective at reducing inequality and helping families pull themselves up through hard work than the earned-income tax credit. Right now it helps about half of all parents at some point. Think about that: It helps about half of all parents in America at some point in their lives. But I agree with Republicans like Senator Rubio that it doesn't do enough for single workers who don't have kids. So let's work together to strengthen the credit, reward work, help more Americans get ahead.

Let's do more to help Americans save for retirement. Today, most workers don't have a pension. A Social Security check often isn't enough on its own. And while the stock market has doubled over the last 5 years, that doesn't help folks who don't have 401(k)s. That's why, tomorrow, I will direct the Treasury to create a new way for working Americans to start their own retirement savings: MyI–MyRA.

It's a new savings bond that encourages folks to build a nest egg. MyRA guarantees a decent return with no risk of losing what you put in. And if this Congress wants to help, work with me to fix an upside-down Tax Code that gives big tax breaks to help the wealthy save, but does little or nothing for middle class Americans. Offer every American access to an automatic IRA on the job so they can save at work just like everybody in this Chamber can.

And since the most important investment many families make is their home, send me legislation that protects taxpayers from footing the bill for a housing crisis ever again and keeps the dream of homeownership alive for future generations.

One last point on financial security: For decades, few things exposed hardworking families to economic hardship more than a broken health care system. And in case you haven't heard, we're in the process of fixing that. Now, a preexisting condition used to mean that someone like Amanda Shelley, a physician's assistant and single mom from Arizona, couldn't get health insurance. But on January 1, she got covered. On January 3, she felt a sharp pain. On January 6, she had emergency surgery. Just one week earlier, Amanda said, and that surgery would have meant bankruptcy.

That's what health insurance reform is all about: the peace of mind that if misfortune strikes, you don't have to lose everything. Already, because of the Affordable Care Act, more than 3 million Americans under age 26 have gained coverage under their parent's plan. More than 9 million Americans have signed up for private health insurance or Medicaid coverage. Nine million.

And here's another number: zero. Because of this law, no American–none, zero–can ever again be dropped or denied coverage for a preexisting condition like asthma or back pain or cancer. No woman can ever be charged more just because she's a woman. And we did all this while adding years to Medicare's finances, keeping Medicare premiums flat, and lowering prescription costs for millions of seniors.

Now, I do not expect to convince my Republican friends on the merits of this law. [Laughter] But I know that the American people are not interested in refighting old battles. So again, if you have specific plans to cut costs, cover more people, increase choice, tell America what you'd do differently. Let's see if the numbers add up. But let's not have another 40-something votes to repeal a law that's already helping millions of Americans like Amanda. The first 40 were plenty. [Laughter]

We all owe it to the American people to say what we're for, not just what we're against. And if you want to know the real impact this law is having, just talk to Governor Steve Beshear of Kentucky, who's here tonight. Now, Kentucky is not the most liberal part of the country. That's not where I got my highest vote totals. [Laughter] But he's like a man possessed when it comes to covering his Commonwealth's families. They're our neighbors and our friends, he said: "They're people we shop and go to church with, farmers out on the tractor, grocery clerks. They're people who go to work every morning praying they don't get sick. No one deserves to live that way."

Steve's right. That's why tonight I ask every American who knows someone without health insurance to help them get covered by March 31. [Applause] Help them get covered. Moms, get on your kids to sign up. Kids, call your mom and walk her through the application. It will give her some peace of mind, and plus, she'll appreciate hearing from you. [Laughter]

After all, that's the spirit that has always moved this Nation forward. It's the spirit of citizenship, the recognition that through hard work and responsibility, we can pursue our individual dreams, but still come together as one American family to make sure the next generation can pursue its dreams as well.

Citizenship means standing up for everyone's right to vote. Last year, part of the Voting Rights Act was weakened, but conservative Republicans and liberal Democrats are working together to strengthen it. And the bipartisan Commission I appointed, chaired by my campaign lawyer and Governor Romney's campaign lawyer, came together and have offered reforms so that no one has to wait more than a half hour to vote. Let's support these efforts. It should be the power of our vote, not the size of our bank accounts, that drives our democracy.

Citizenship means standing up for the lives that gun violence steals from us each day. I've seen the courage of parents, students, pastors, police officers all over this country who say, "We are not afraid." And I intend to keep trying, with or without Congress, to help stop more tragedies from visiting innocent Americans in our movie theaters, in our shopping malls, or schools like Sandy Hook.

Citizenship demands a sense of common purpose, participation in the hard work of self-government, an obligation to serve our communities. And I know this Chamber agrees that few Americans give more to their country than our diplomats and the men and women of the United States Armed Forces. Thank you. Tonight, because of the extraordinary troops and civilians who risk and lay down their lives to keep us free, the United States is more secure. When I took office, nearly 180,000 Americans were serving in Iraq and Afghanistan. Today, all our troops are out of Iraq.

More than 60,000 of our troops have already come home from Afghanistan. With Afghan forces now in the lead for their own security, our troops have moved to a support role. Together with our allies, we will complete our mission there by the end of this year, and America's longest war will finally be over.

After 2014, we will support a unified Afghanistan as it takes responsibility for its own future. If the Afghan Government signs a security agreement that we have negotiated, a small force of Americans could remain in Afghanistan with NATO allies to carry out two narrow missions: training and assisting Afghan forces and counterterrorism operations to pursue any remnants of Al Qaida. For while our relationship with Afghanistan will change, one thing will not: our resolve that terrorists do not launch attacks against our country.

The fact is, that danger remains. While we've put Al Qaida's core leadership on a path to defeat, the threat has evolved as Al Qaida affiliates and other extremists take root in different parts of the world. In Yemen, Somalia, Iraq, Mali, we have to keep working with partners to disrupt and disable those networks. In Syria, we'll support the opposition that rejects the agenda of terrorist networks. Here at home, we'll keep strengthening our defenses and combat new threats like cyber attacks. And as we reform our defense budget, we will have to keep faith with our men and women in uniform and invest in the capabilities they need to succeed in future missions.

We have to remain vigilant. But I strongly believe our leadership and our security cannot depend on our outstanding military alone. As Commander in Chief, I have used force when needed to protect the American people, and I will never hesitate to do so as long as I hold this office. But I will not send our troops into harm's way unless it is truly necessary, nor will I allow our sons and daughters to be mired in open-ended conflicts. We must fight the battles that need to be fought, not those that terrorists prefer from us: large-scale deployments that drain our strength and may ultimately feed extremism.

So even as we actively and aggressively pursue terrorist networks through more targeted efforts and by building the capacity of our foreign partners, America must move off a permanent war footing. That's why I've imposed prudent limits on the use of drones. For we will not be safer if people abroad believe we strike within their countries without regard for the consequence.

That's why, working with this Congress, I will reform our surveillance programs, because the vital work of our intelligence community depends on public confidence, here and abroad, that privacy of ordinary people is not being violated.

And with the Afghan war ending, this needs to be the year Congress lifts the remaining restrictions on detainee transfers and we close the prison at Guantanamo Bay. Because we counter terrorism not just through intelligence and military actions, but by remaining true to our constitutional ideals and setting an example for the rest of the world.

You see, in a world of complex threats, our security, our leadership, depends on all elements of our power, including strong and principled diplomacy. American diplomacy has rallied more than 50 countries to prevent nuclear materials from falling into the wrong hands and allowed us to reduce our own reliance on cold war stockpiles. American diplomacy, backed by the threat of force, is why Syria's chemical weapons are being eliminated.

And we will continue to work with the international community to usher in the future the Syrian people deserve, a future free of dictatorship, terror, and fear. As we speak, American diplomacy is supporting Israelis and Palestinians as they engage in the difficult but necessary talks to end the conflict there, to achieve dignity and an independent state for Palestinians and lasting peace and security for the State of Israel, a Jewish state that knows America will always be at their side.

And it is American diplomacy, backed by pressure, that has halted the progress of Iran's nuclear program and rolled back parts of that program for the very first time in a decade. As we gather here tonight, Iran has begun to eliminate its stockpile of higher levels of enriched uranium. It's not installing advanced centrifuges. Unprecedented inspections help the world verify every day that Iran is not building a bomb. And with our allies and partners, we're engaged in negotiations to see if we can peacefully achieve a goal we all share: preventing Iran from obtaining a nuclear weapon.

These negotiations will be difficult. They may not succeed. We are clear eyed about Iran's support for terrorist organizations like Hizballah, which threatens our allies. And we're clear about the mistrust between our nations, mistrust that cannot be wished away. But these negotiations don't rely on trust. Any long-term deal we agree to must be based on verifiable action that convinces us and the international community that Iran is not building a nuclear bomb. If John F. Kennedy and Ronald Reagan could negotiate with the Soviet Union, then surely a strong and confident America can negotiate with less powerful adversaries today.

The sanctions that we put in place helped make this opportunity possible. But let me be clear: If this Congress sends me a new sanctions bill now that threatens to derail these talks, I will veto it. For the sake of our national security, we must give diplomacy a chance to succeed. If Iran's leaders do not seize this opportunity, then I will be the first to call for more sanctions and stand ready to exercise all options to make sure Iran does not build a nuclear weapon. But if Iran's leaders do seize the chance–and we'll know soon enough– then Iran could take an important step to rejoin the community of nations, and we will have resolved one of the leading security challenges of our time without the risks of war.

Now, finally, let's remember that our leadership is defined not just by our defense against threats, but by the enormous opportunities to do good and promote understanding around the globe: to forge greater cooperation, to expand new markets, to free people from fear and want. And no one is better positioned to take advantage of those opportunities than America.

Our alliance with Europe remains the strongest the world has ever known. From Tunisia to Burma, we're supporting those who are willing to do the hard work of building democracy. In Ukraine, we stand for the principle that all people have the right to express themselves freely and peacefully and to have a say in their country's future. Across Africa, we're bringing together businesses and governments to double access to electricity and help end extreme poverty. In the Americas, we're building new ties of commerce, but we're also expanding cultural and educational exchanges among young people. And we will continue to focus on the Asia-Pacific, where we support our allies, shape a future of greater security and prosperity, and extend a hand to those devastated by disaster, as we did in the Philippines, when our Marines and civilians rushed to aid those battered by a typhoon, and who were greeted with words like, "We will never forget your kindness" and "God bless America."

We do these things because they help promote our long-term security, and we do them because we believe in the inherent dignity and equality of every human being, regardless of race or religion, creed or sexual orientation. And next week, the world will see one expression of that commitment, when Team U.S.A. marches the red, white, and blue into the Olympic Stadium and brings home the gold. [Laughter]

Audience members. U.S.A.! U.S.A.! U.S.A.!

The President. My fellow Americans, no other country in the world does what we do. On every issue, the world turns to us, not simply because of the size of our economy or our military might, but because of the ideals we stand for and the burdens we bear to advance them. No one knows this better than those who serve in uniform.

As this time of war draws to a close, a new generation of heroes returns to civilian life. We'll keep slashing that backlog so our veterans receive the benefits they've earned and our wounded warriors receive the health care–including the mental health care–that they need. We'll keep working to help all our veterans translate their skills and leadership into jobs here at home. And we will all continue to join forces to honor and support our remarkable military families.

Let me tell you about one of those families I've come to know. I first met Cory Remsburg, a proud Army Ranger, at Omaha Beach on the 65th anniversary of D-day. Along with some of his fellow Rangers, he walked me through the program and the ceremony. He was a strong, impressive young man, had an easy manner, he was sharp as a tack. And we joked around and took pictures, and I told him to stay in touch.

A few months later, on his 10th deployment, Cory was nearly killed by a massive roadside bomb in Afghanistan. His comrades found him in a canal, face down, underwater, shrapnel in his brain. For months, he lay in a coma. And the next time I met him, in the hospital, he couldn't speak, could barely move. Over the years, he's endured dozens of surgeries and procedures, hours of grueling rehab every day.

Even now, Cory is still blind in one eye, still struggles on his left side. But slowly, steadily, with the support of caregivers like his dad Craig and the community around him, Cory has grown stronger. And day by day, he's learned to speak again and stand again and walk again. And he's working toward the day when he can serve his country again. "My recovery has not been easy," he says. "Nothing in life that's worth anything is easy." Cory is here tonight. And like the Army he loves, like the America he serves, Sergeant First Class Cory Remsburg never gives up, and he does not quit. Cory.

My fellow Americans, men and women like Cory remind us that America has never come easy. Our freedom, our democracy, has never been easy. Sometimes, we stumble, we make mistakes; we get frustrated or discouraged. But for more than 200 years, we have put those things aside and placed our collective shoulder to the wheel of progress: to create and build and expand the possibilities of individual achievement, to free other nations from tyranny and fear, to promote justice and fairness and equality under the law so that the words set to paper by our Founders are made real for every citizen. The America we want for our kids–a rising America where honest work is plentiful and communities are strong, where prosperity is widely shared and opportunity for all lets us go as far as our dreams and toil will take us–none of it is easy. But if we work together–if we summon what is best in us, the way Cory summoned what is best in him–with our feet planted firmly in today, but our eyes cast toward tomorrow, I know it is within our reach. Believe it.

God bless you, and God bless the United States of America.

❧ 21 ❧

2015 STATE OF THE UNION ADDRESS
JANUARY 20, 2015

M r. Speaker, Mr. Vice President, Members of Congress, my fellow Americans: We are 15 years into this new century. Fifteen years that dawned with terror touching our shores, that unfolded with a new generation fighting two long and costly wars, that saw a vicious recession spread across our Nation and the world. It has been and still is a hard time for many.

But tonight we turn the page. Tonight, after a breakthrough year for America, our economy is growing and creating jobs at the fastest pace since 1999. Our unemployment rate is now lower than it was before the financial crisis. More of our kids are graduating than ever before. More of our people are insured than ever before. And we are as free from the grip of foreign oil as we've been in almost 30 years.

Tonight, for the first time since 9/11, our combat mission in Afghanistan is over. Six years ago, nearly 180,000 American troops served in Iraq and Afghanistan. Today, fewer than 15,000 remain. And we salute the courage and sacrifice of every man and woman in this 9/11 generation who has served to keep us safe. We are humbled and grateful for your service.

America, for all that we have endured, for all the grit and hard work required to come back, for all the tasks that lie ahead, know this: The shadow of crisis has passed, and the State of the Union is strong.

At this moment–with a growing economy, shrinking deficits, bustling industry, booming energy production–we have risen from recession freer to write our own future than any other nation on Earth. It's now up to us to choose who we want to be over the next 15 years and for decades to come.

Will we accept an economy where only a few of us do spectacularly well? Or will we commit ourselves to an economy that generates rising incomes and chances for everyone who makes the effort?

Will we approach the world fearful and reactive, dragged into costly conflicts that

160

strain our military and set back our standing? Or will we lead wisely, using all elements of our power to defeat new threats and protect our planet?

Will we allow ourselves to be sorted into factions and turned against one another? Or will we recapture the sense of common purpose that has always propelled America forward?

In 2 weeks, I will send this Congress a budget filled with ideas that are practical, not partisan. And in the months ahead, I'll crisscross the country making a case for those ideas. So tonight I want to focus less on a checklist of proposals and focus more on the values at stake in the choices before us.

It begins with our economy. Seven years ago, Rebekah and Ben Erler of Minneapolis were newlyweds. [Laughter] She waited tables. He worked construction. Their first child Jack was on the way. They were young and in love in America. And it doesn't get much better than that. "If only we had known," Rebekah wrote to me last spring, "what was about to happen to the housing and construction market." As the crisis worsened, Ben's business dried up, so he took what jobs he could find, even if they kept him on the road for long stretches of time. Rebekah took out student loans and enrolled in community college and retrained for a new career. They sacrificed for each other. And slowly, it paid off. They bought their first home. They had a second son Henry. Rebekah got a better job and then a raise. Ben is back in construction and home for dinner every night.

"It is amazing," Rebekah wrote, "what you can bounce back from when you have to. . . . We are a strong, tight-knit family who has made it through some very, very hard times." We are a strong, tight-knit family who has made it through some very, very hard times.

America, Rebekah and Ben's story is our story. They represent the millions who have worked hard and scrimped and sacrificed and retooled. You are the reason that I ran for this office. You are the people I was thinking of 6 years ago today, in the darkest months of the crisis, when I stood on the steps of this Capitol and promised we would rebuild our economy on a new foundation. And it has been your resilience, your effort that has made it possible for our country to emerge stronger.

We believed we could reverse the tide of outsourcing and draw new jobs to our shores. And over the past 5 years, our businesses have created more than 11 million new jobs.

We believed we could reduce our dependence on foreign oil and protect our planet. And today, America is number one in oil and gas. America is number one in wind power. Every 3 weeks, we bring online as much solar power as we did in all of 2008. And thanks to lower gas prices and higher fuel standards, the typical family this year should save about $750 at the pump.

We believed we could prepare our kids for a more competitive world. And today, our younger students have earned the highest math and reading scores on record. Our high school graduation rate has hit an alltime high. More Americans finish college than ever before.

We believed that sensible regulations could prevent another crisis, shield families from ruin, and encourage fair competition. Today, we have new tools to stop taxpayer-funded bailouts and a new consumer watchdog to protect us from predatory lending and abusive credit card practices. And in the past year alone, about 10 million uninsured Americans finally gained the security of health coverage.

At every step, we were told our goals were misguided or too ambitious, that we would crush jobs and explode deficits. Instead, we've seen the fastest economic growth in over a decade, our deficits cut by two- thirds, a stock market that has doubled, and health care inflation at its lowest rate in 50 years. This is good news, people. [Laughter]

So the verdict is clear. Middle class economics works. Expanding opportunity works. And these policies will continue to work as long as politics don't get in the way. We can't slow down businesses or put our economy at risk with Government shutdowns or fiscal showdowns. We can't put the security of families at risk by taking away their health insurance or unraveling the new rules on Wall Street or refighting past battles on immigration when we've got to fix a broken system. And if a bill comes to my desk that tries to do any of these things, I will veto it. It will have earned my veto.

Today, thanks to a growing economy, the recovery is touching more and more lives. Wages are finally starting to rise again. We know that more small-business owners plan to raise their employees' pay than at any time since 2007. But here's the thing: Those of us here tonight, we need to set our sights higher than just making sure Government doesn't screw things up–[laughter]–that Government doesn't halt the progress we're making. We need to do more than just do no harm. Tonight, together, let's do more to restore the link between hard work and growing opportunity for every American.

Because families like Rebekah's still need our help. She and Ben are working as hard as ever, but they've had to forego vacations and a new car so that they can pay off student loans and save for retirement. Friday night pizza, that's a big splurge. Basic childcare for Jack and Henry costs more than their mortgage and almost as much as a year at the University of Minnesota. Like millions of hard-working Americans, Rebekah isn't asking for a handout, but she is asking that we look for more ways to help families get ahead.

And in fact, at every moment of economic change throughout our history, this country has taken bold action to adapt to new circumstances and to make sure everyone gets a fair shot. We set up worker protections, Social Security, Medicare, Medicaid to protect ourselves from the harshest adversity. We gave our citizens schools and colleges, infrastructure and the Internet, tools they needed to go as far as their efforts and their dreams will take them.

That's what middle class economics is: the idea that this country does best when everyone gets their fair shot, everyone does their fair share, everyone plays by the same set of rules. We don't just want everyone to share in America's success, we want everyone to contribute to our success.

So what does middle class economics require in our time? First, middle class economics means helping working families feel more secure in a world of constant change. That means helping folks afford childcare, college, health care, a home, retirement. And my budget will address each of these issues, lowering the taxes of working families and putting thousands of dollars back into their pockets each year.

Here's one example. During World War II, when men like my grandfather went off to war, having women like my grandmother in the workforce was a national security priority, so this country provided universal childcare. In today's economy, when having both parents in the workforce is an economic necessity for many families, we need affordable, high-quality childcare more than ever.

It's not a nice-to-have, it's a must-have. So it's time we stop treating childcare as a side issue, or as a women's issue, and treat it like the national economic priority that it is for all of us. And that's why my plan will make quality childcare more available and more affordable for every middle class and low-income family with young children in America, by creating more slots and a new tax cut of up to $3,000 per child, per year.

Here's another example. Today, we are the only advanced country on Earth that doesn't guarantee paid sick leave or paid maternity leave to our workers. Forty-three million workers have no paid sick leave–43 million. Think about that. And that forces too many parents to make the gut-wrenching choice between a paycheck and a sick kid at home. So I'll be taking new action to help States adopt paid leave laws of their own. And since paid sick leave won where it was on the ballot last November, let's put it to a vote right here in Washington. Send me a bill that gives every worker in America the opportunity to earn 7 days of paid sick leave. It's the right thing to do. [Applause] It's the right thing to do.

Of course, nothing helps families make ends meet like higher wages. That's why this Congress still needs to pass a law that makes sure a woman is paid the same as a man for doing the same work. I mean, it's 2015. [Laughter] It's time. We still need to make sure employees get the overtime they've earned. And to everyone in this Congress who still refuses to raise the minimum wage, I say this: If you truly believe you could work full time and support a family on less than $15,000 a year, try it. If not, vote to give millions of the hardest working people in America a raise.

Now, these ideas won't make everybody rich, won't relieve every hardship. That's not the job of government. To give working families a fair shot, we still need more employers to see beyond next quarter's earnings and recognize that investing in their workforce is in their company's long-term interest. We still need laws that strengthen rather than weaken unions, and give American workers a voice.

But you know, things like childcare and sick leave and equal pay, things like lower mortgage premiums and a higher minimum wage–these ideas will make a meaningful difference in the lives of millions of families. That's a fact. And that's what all of us, Republicans and Democrats alike, were sent here to do.

Now, second, to make sure folks keep earning higher wages down the road, we have to do more to help Americans upgrade their skills. America thrived in the 20th century because we made high school free, sent a generation of GIs to college, trained the best workforce in the world. We were ahead of the curve. But other countries caught on. And in a 21st-century economy that rewards knowledge like never before, we need to up our game. We need to do more.

By the end of this decade, two in three job openings will require some higher education–two in three. And yet we still live in a country where too many bright, striving Americans are priced out of the education they need. It's not fair to them, and it's sure not smart for our future. And that's why I'm sending this Congress a bold new plan to lower the cost of community college to zero.

Keep in mind, 40 percent of our college students choose community college. Some are young and starting out. Some are older and looking for a better job. Some are veterans and single parents trying to transition back into the job market. Whoever you are, this plan is your chance to graduate ready for the new economy without a load of debt. Understand, you've got to earn it. You've got to keep your grades up and graduate on time.

Tennessee, a State with Republican leadership, and Chicago, a city with Democratic leadership, are showing that free community college is possible. I want to spread that idea all across America so that 2 years of college becomes as free and universal in America as high school is today. Let's stay ahead of the curve. And I want to work with this Congress to make sure those already burdened with student loans can reduce their monthly payments so that student debt doesn't derail anyone's dreams.

Thanks to Vice President Biden's great work to update our job training system, we're connecting community colleges with local employers to train workers to fill high-paying jobs like coding and nursing and robotics. Tonight I'm also asking more businesses to follow the lead of companies like CVS and UPS and offer more educational benefits and paid apprenticeships, opportunities that give workers the chance to earn higher paying jobs even if they don't have a higher education.

And as a new generation of veterans comes home, we owe them every opportunity to live the American Dream they helped defend. Already, we've made strides towards ensuring that every veteran has access to the highest quality care. We're slashing the backlog that had too many veterans waiting years to get the benefits they need. And we're making it easier for vets to translate their training and experience into civilian jobs. And Joining Forces, the national campaign launched by Michelle and Jill Biden–[applause]–thank you, Michelle; thank you, Jill–has helped nearly 700,000 veterans and military spouses get a new job. So to every CEO in America, let me repeat: If you want somebody who's going to get the job done and done right, hire a veteran.

Finally, as we better train our workers, we need the new economy to keep churning out high-wage jobs for our workers to fill. Since 2010, America has put more people back to work than Europe, Japan, and all advanced economies combined.

Our manufacturers have added almost 800,000 new jobs. Some of our bedrock sectors, like our auto industry, are booming. But there are also millions of Americans who work in jobs that didn't even exist 10 or 20 years ago, jobs at companies like Google and eBay and Tesla.

So no one knows for certain which industries will generate the jobs of the future. But we do know we want them here in America. We know that. And that's why the third part of middle class economics is all about building the most competitive economy anywhere, the place where businesses want to locate and hire.

Twenty-first century businesses need 21st-century infrastructure: modern ports and stronger bridges, faster trains and the fastest Internet. Democrats and Republicans used to agree on this. So let's set our sights higher than a single oil pipeline. Let's pass a bipartisan infrastructure plan that could create more than 30 times as many jobs per year and make this country stronger for decades to come. Let's do it. Let's get it done. [Applause] Let's get it done.

Twenty-first century businesses, including small businesses, need to sell more American products overseas. Today, our businesses export more than ever, and exporters tend to pay their workers higher wages. But as we speak, China wants to write the rules for the world's fastest growing region. That would put our workers and our businesses at a disadvantage. Why would we let that happen? We should write those rules. We should level the playing field. And that's why I'm asking both parties to give me trade promotion authority to protect American workers, with strong new trade deals from Asia to Europe that aren't just free, but are also fair. It's the right thing to do.

Look, I'm the first one to admit that past trade deals haven't always lived up to the hype, and that's why we've gone after countries that break the rules at our expense. But 95 percent of the world's customers live outside our borders. We can't close ourselves off from those opportunities. More than half of manufacturing executives have said they're actively looking to bring jobs back from China. So let's give them one more reason to get it done.

Twenty-first century businesses will rely on American science and technology, research and development. I want the country that eliminated polio and mapped the human genome to lead a new era of medicine, one that delivers the right treatment at the right time.

In some patients with cystic fibrosis, this approach has reversed a disease once thought unstoppable. So tonight I'm launching a new precision medicine initiative to bring us closer to curing diseases like cancer and diabetes and to give all of us access to the personalized information we need to keep ourselves and our families healthier. We can do this.

I intend to protect a free and open Internet, extend its reach to every classroom and every community and help folks build the fastest networks so that the next generation of digital innovators and entrepreneurs have the platform to keep reshaping our world. I want Americans to win the race for the kinds of discoveries that unleash new jobs: converting sunlight into liquid fuel; creating revolutionary prosthetics so that a veteran who gave his arms for his country can play catch with his kids again; pushing out into the solar system not just to visit, but to stay. Last month, we launched a new spacecraft as part of a reenergized space program that will send American astronauts to Mars. And in 2 months, to prepare us for those missions, Scott Kelly will begin a year-long stay in space. So good luck, Captain. Make sure to Instagram it. We're proud of you.

Now, the truth is, when it comes to issues like infrastructure and basic research, I know there's bipartisan support in this Chamber. Members of both parties have told me so. Where we too often run onto the rocks is how to pay for these investments. As Americans, we don't mind paying our fair share of taxes as long as everybody else does too. But for far too long, lobbyists have rigged the Tax Code with loopholes that let some corporations pay nothing while others pay full freight. They've riddled it with giveaways that the super-rich don't need, while denying a break to middle class families who do.

This year, we have an opportunity to change that. Let's close loopholes so we stop rewarding companies that keep profits abroad and reward those that invest here in America. Let's use those savings to rebuild our infrastructure and to make it more attractive for companies to bring jobs home. Let's simplify the system and let a small-business owner file based on her actual bank statement, instead of the number of accountants she can afford. And let's close the loopholes that lead to inequality by allowing the top 1 percent to avoid paying taxes on their accumulated wealth. We can use that money to help more families pay for childcare and send their kids to college. We need a Tax Code that truly helps working Americans trying to get a leg up in the new economy, and we can achieve that together. [Applause] We can achieve it together.

Helping hard-working families make ends meet, giving them the tools they need for good-paying jobs in this new economy, maintaining the conditions of growth and competitiveness–this is where America needs to go. I believe it's where the American people want to go. It will make our economy stronger a year from now, 15 years from now, and deep into the century ahead.

Of course, if there's one thing this new century has taught us, it's that we cannot separate our work here at home from challenges beyond our shores. My first duty as Commander in Chief is to defend the United States of America. In doing so, the question is not whether America leads in the world, but how. When we make rash decisions, reacting to the headlines instead of using our heads, when the first response to a challenge is to send in our military, then we risk getting drawn into unnecessary conflicts and neglect the broader strategy we need for a safer, more prosperous world. That's what our enemies want us to do.

I believe in a smarter kind of American leadership. We lead best when we combine military power with strong diplomacy, when we leverage our power with coalition building, when we don't let our fears blind us to the opportunities that this new century presents. That's exactly what we're doing right now. And around the globe, it is making a difference.

First, we stand united with people around the world who have been targeted by terrorists, from a school in Pakistan to the streets of Paris. We will continue to hunt down terrorists and dismantle their networks, and we reserve the right to act unilaterally, as we have done relentlessly since I took office, to take out terrorists who pose a direct threat to us and our allies. At the same time, we've learned some costly lessons over the last 13 years. Instead of Americans patrolling the valleys of Afghanistan, we've trained their security forces, who have now taken the lead, and we've honored our troops' sacrifice by supporting that country's first democratic transition. Instead of sending large ground forces overseas, we're partnering with nations from South Asia to North Africa to deny safe haven to terrorists who threaten America.

In Iraq and Syria, American leadership–including our military power–is stopping ISIL's advance. Instead of getting dragged into another ground war in the Middle East, we are leading a broad coalition, including Arab nations, to degrade and ultimately destroy this terrorist group. We're also supporting a moderate opposition in Syria that can help us in this effort and assisting people everywhere who stand up to the bankrupt ideology of violent extremism.

Now, this effort will take time. It will require focus. But we will succeed. And tonight I call on this Congress to show the world that we are united in this mission by passing a resolution to authorize the use of force against ISIL. We need that authority.

Second, we're demonstrating the power of American strength and diplomacy. We're upholding the principle that bigger nations can't bully the small, by opposing Russian aggression and supporting Ukraine's democracy and reassuring our NATO allies.

Last year, as we were doing the hard work of imposing sanctions along with our allies, as we were reinforcing our presence with frontline states, Mr. Putin's aggression, it was suggested, was a masterful display of strategy and strength. That's what I heard from some folks. [Laughter] Well, today, it is America that stands strong and united with our allies, while Russia is isolated with its economy in tatters. That's how America leads: not with bluster, but with persistent, steady resolve.

In Cuba, we are ending a policy that was long past its expiration date. When what you're doing doesn't work for 50 years, it's time to try something new. [Laughter] And our shift in Cuba policy has the potential to end a legacy of mistrust in our hemisphere. It removes a phony excuse for restrictions in Cuba. It stands up for democratic values and extends the hand of friendship to the Cuban people. And this year, Congress should begin the work of ending the embargo.

As His Holiness Pope Francis has said, diplomacy is the work of "small steps." And these small steps have added up to new hope for the future in Cuba. And after years in prison, we are overjoyed that Alan Gross is back where he belongs. Welcome home, Alan. We're glad you're here.

Our diplomacy is at work with respect to Iran, where, for the first time in a decade, we've halted the progress of its nuclear program and reduced its stockpile of nuclear material. Between now and this spring, we have a chance to negotiate a comprehensive agreement that prevents a nuclear-armed Iran, secures America and our allies, including Israel, while avoiding yet another Middle East conflict. There are no guarantees that negotiations will succeed, and I keep all options on the table to prevent a nuclear Iran.

But new sanctions passed by this Congress, at this moment in time, will all but guarantee that diplomacy fails: alienating America from its allies, making it harder to maintain sanctions, and ensuring that Iran starts up its nuclear program again. It doesn't make sense. And that's why I will veto any new sanctions bill that threatens to undo this progress. The American people expect us only to go to war as a last resort, and I intend to stay true to that wisdom. Third, we're looking beyond the issues that have consumed us in the past to shape the coming century. No foreign nation, no hacker, should be able to shut down our networks, steal our trade secrets, or invade the privacy of American families, especially our kids. So we're making sure our Government integrates intelligence to combat cyber threats, just as we have done to combat terrorism.

And tonight I urge this Congress to finally pass the legislation we need to better meet the evolving threat of cyber attacks, combat identity theft, and protect our children's information. That should be a bipartisan effort. If we don't act, we'll leave our Nation and our economy vulnerable. If we do, we can continue to protect the technologies that have unleashed untold opportunities for people around the globe.

In West Africa, our troops, our scientists, our doctors, our nurses, our health care workers are rolling back Ebola, saving countless lives and stopping the spread of disease. I could not be prouder of them, and I thank this Congress for your bipartisan support of their efforts. But the job is not yet done, and the world needs to use this lesson to build a more effective global effort to prevent the spread of future pandemics, invest in smart development, and eradicate extreme poverty.

In the Asia-Pacific, we are modernizing alliances while making sure that other nations play by the rules: in how they trade, how they resolve maritime disputes, how they participate in meeting common international challenges like nonproliferation and disaster relief. And no challenge—no challenge—poses a greater threat to future generations than climate change.

Two thousand fourteen was the planet's warmest year on record. Now, 1 year doesn't make a trend, but this does: 14 of the 15 warmest years on record have all fallen in the first 15 years of this century.

Now, I've heard some folks try to dodge the evidence by saying they're not scientists, that we don't have enough information to act. Well, I'm not a scientist, either. But you know what, I know a lot of really good scientists—[laughter]—at NASA and at NOAA and at our major universities. And the best scientists in the world are all telling us that our activities are changing the climate, and if we don't act forcefully, we'll continue to see rising oceans, longer, hotter heat waves, dangerous droughts and floods, and massive disruptions that can trigger greater migration and conflict and hunger around the globe. The Pentagon says that climate change poses immediate risks to our national security. We should act like it.

And that's why, over the past 6 years, we've done more than ever to combat climate change, from the way we produce energy to the way we use it. That's why we've set aside more public lands and waters than any administration in history. And that's why I will not let this Congress endanger the health of our children by turning back the clock on our efforts. I am determined to make sure that American leadership drives international action.

In Beijing, we made a historic announcement: The United States will double the pace at which we cut carbon pollution. And China committed, for the first time, to limiting their emissions. And because the world's two largest economies came together, other nations are now stepping up and offering hope that this year the world will finally reach an agreement to protect the one planet we've got.

And there's one last pillar of our leadership, and that's the example of our values. As Americans, we respect human dignity, even when we're threatened, which is why I have prohibited torture and worked to make sure our use of new technology like drones is properly constrained. It's why we speak out against the deplorable anti-Semitism that has resurfaced in certain parts of the world. It's why we continue to reject offensive stereotypes of Muslims, the vast majority of whom share our commitment to peace. That's why we defend free speech and advocate for political prisoners and condemn the persecution of women or religious minorities or people who are lesbian, gay, bisexual, or transgender. We do these things not only because they are the right thing to do, but because ultimately, they will make us safer.

As Americans, we have a profound commitment to justice. So it makes no sense to spend $3 million per prisoner to keep open a prison that the world condemns and terrorists use to recruit. Since I've been President, we've worked responsibly to cut the population of Gitmo in half. Now it is time to finish the job. And I will not relent in my determination to shut it down. It is not who we are. It's time to close Gitmo.

As Americans, we cherish our civil liberties, and we need to uphold that commitment if we want maximum cooperation from other countries and industry in our fight against terrorist networks. So while some have moved on from the debates over our surveillance programs, I have not. As promised, our intelligence agencies have worked hard, with the recommendations of privacy advocates, to increase transparency and build more safeguards against potential abuse. And next month, we'll issue a report on how we're keeping our promise to keep our country safe while strengthening privacy.

Looking to the future instead of the past, making sure we match our power with diplomacy and use force wisely, building coalitions to meet new challenges and opportunities, leading always with the example of our values—that's what makes us exceptional. That's what keeps us strong. That's why we have to keep striving to hold ourselves to the highest of standards: our own.

You know, just over a decade ago, I gave a speech in Boston where I said there wasn't a liberal America or a conservative America, a Black America or a White America, but a United States of America. I said this because I had seen it in my own life, in a nation that gave someone like me a chance; because I grew up in Hawaii, a melting pot of races and customs; because I made Illinois my home, a State of small towns, rich farmland, one of the world's great cities, a microcosm of the country where Democrats and Republicans and Independents, good people of every ethnicity and every faith, share certain bedrock values.

Over the past 6 years, the pundits have pointed out more than once that my Presidency hasn't delivered on this vision. How ironic, they say, that our politics seems more divided than ever. It's held up as proof not just of my own flaws—of which there are many—but also as proof that the vision itself is misguided, naive, that there are too many people in this town who actually benefit from partisanship and gridlock for us to ever do anything about it.

I know how tempting such cynicism may be. But I still think the cynics are wrong. I still believe that we are one people. I still believe that together, we can do great things, even when the odds are long.

I believe this because over and over in my 6 years in office, I have seen America at its best. I've seen the hopeful faces of young graduates from New York to California and our newest officers at West Point, Annapolis, Colorado Springs, New London. I've mourned with grieving families in Tucson and Newtown, in Boston, in West, Texas, and West Virginia. I've watched Americans beat back adversity from the Gulf Coast to the Great Plains, from Midwest assembly lines to the Mid- Atlantic seaboard. I've seen something like gay marriage go from a wedge issue used to drive us apart to a story of freedom across our country, a civil right now legal in States that 7 in 10 Americans call home. So I know the good and optimistic and big-hearted generosity of the American people who every day live the idea that we are our brother's keeper and our sister's keeper. And I know they expect those of us who serve here to set a better example.

So the question for those of us here tonight is how we, all of us, can better reflect America's hopes. I've served in Congress with many of you. I know many of you well. There are a lot of good people here on both sides of the aisle. And many of you have told me that this isn't what you signed up for: arguing past each other on cable shows, the constant fundraising, always looking over your shoulder at how the base will react to every decision.

Imagine if we broke out of these tired old patterns. Imagine if we did something different. Understand, a better politics isn't one where Democrats abandon their agenda or Republicans simply embrace mine. A better politics is one where we appeal to each other's basic decency instead of our basest fears. A better politics is one where we debate without demonizing each other, where we talk issues and values and principles and facts rather than "gotcha" moments or trivial gaffes or fake controversies that have nothing to do with people's daily lives.

A politics–a better politics is one where we spend less time drowning in dark money for ads that pull us into the gutter and spend more time lifting young people up with a sense of purpose and possibility, asking them to join in the great mission of building America.

If we're going to have arguments, let's have arguments, but let's make them debates worthy of this body and worthy of this country. We still may not agree on a woman's right to choose, but surely we can agree it's a good thing that teen pregnancies and abortions are nearing alltime lows and that every woman should have access to the health care that she needs.

Yes, passions still fly on immigration, but surely we can all see something of ourselves in the striving young student and agree that no one benefits when a hardworking mom is snatched from her child and that it's possible to shape a law that upholds our tradition as a nation of laws and a nation of immigrants. I've talked to Republicans and Democrats about that. That's something that we can share.

We may go at it in campaign season, but surely we can agree that the right to vote is sacred, that it's being denied to too many, and that on this 50th anniversary of the great march from Selma to Montgomery and the passage of the Voting Rights Act, we can come together, Democrats and Republicans, to make voting easier for every single American.

We may have different takes on the events of Ferguson and New York. But surely we can understand a father who fears his son can't walk home without being harassed. And surely we can understand the wife who won't rest until the police officer she married walks through the front door at the end of his shift. And surely we can agree that it's a good thing that for the first time in 40 years, the crime rate and the incarceration rate have come down together, and use that as a starting point for Democrats and Republicans, community leaders and law enforcement, to reform America's criminal justice system so that it protects and serves all of us.

That's a better politics. That's how we start rebuilding trust. That's how we move this country forward. That's what the American people want. And that's what they deserve.

I have no more campaigns to run.

[At this point, some audience members applauded.]

My only agenda–[laughter]. Audience member. [Inaudible]

The President. I know because I won both of them. [Laughter] My only agenda for the next 2 years is the same as the one I've had since the day I swore an oath on the steps of this Capitol: to do what I believe is best for America. If you share the broad vision I outlined tonight, I ask you to join me in the work at hand. If you disagree with parts of it, I hope you'll at least work with me where you do agree. And I commit to every Republican here tonight that I will not only seek out your ideas, I will seek to work with you to make this country stronger.

Because I want this Chamber, I want this city to reflect the truth: that for all our blind spots and shortcomings, we are a people with the strength and generosity of spirit to bridge divides, to unite in common effort, to help our neighbors, whether down the street or on the other side of the world.

I want our actions to tell every child in every neighborhood, your life matters, and we are committed to improving your life chances, as committed as we are to working on behalf of our own kids. I want future generations to know that we are a people who see our differences as a great gift, that we're a people who value the dignity and worth of every citizen: man and woman, young and old, Black and White, Latino, Asian, immigrant, Native American, gay, straight, Americans with mental illness or physical disability. Everybody matters. I want them to grow up in a country that shows the world what we still know to be true: that we are still more than a collection of red States and blue States, that we are the United States of America.

I want them to grow up in a country where a young mom can sit down and write a letter to her President with a story that sums up these past 6 years: "It's amazing what you can bounce back from when you have to. . . . We are a strong, tight-knit family who's made it through some very, very hard times."

My fellow Americans, we too are a strong, tight-knit family. We too have made it through some hard times. Fifteen years into this new century, we have picked ourselves up, dusted ourselves off, and begun again the work of remaking America. We have laid a new foundation. A brighter future is ours to write. Let's begin this new chapter together, and let's start the work right now.

Thank you. God bless you. God bless this country we love. Thank you.

❧ 22 ❧

REMARKS AT THE EDMUND PETTUS
BRIDGE THE 50TH ANNIVERSARY OF
THE SELMA TO MONTGOMERY
MARCHES

MARCH 7, 2015

I t is a rare honor in this life to follow one of your heroes. And John Lewis is one
of my heroes.

Now, I have to imagine that when a younger John Lewis woke up that
morning 50 years ago and made his way to Brown Chapel, heroics were not on his
mind. A day like this was not on his mind. Young folks with bedrolls and backpacks
were milling about. Veterans of the movement trained newcomers in the tactics of
non-violence; the right way to protect yourself when attacked. A doctor described
what tear gas does to the body, while marchers scribbled down instructions for
contacting their loved ones. The air was thick with doubt, anticipation and fear. And
they comforted themselves with the final verse of the final hymn they sung:

"No matter what may be the test, God will take care of you;

Lean, weary one, upon His breast, God will take care of you."

And then, his knapsack stocked with an apple, a toothbrush, and a book on
government – all you need for a night behind bars – John Lewis led them out of the
church on a mission to change America.

President and Mrs. Bush, Governor Bentley, Mayor Evans, Sewell, Reverend
Strong, members of Congress, elected officials, foot soldiers, friends, fellow
Americans:

As John noted, there are places and moments in America where this nation's
destiny has been decided. Many are sites of war – Concord and Lexington, Appomat-
tox, Gettysburg. Others are sites that symbolize the daring of America's character –
Independence Hall and Seneca Falls, Kitty Hawk and Cape Canaveral.

Selma is such a place. In one afternoon 50 years ago, so much of our turbulent
history – the stain of slavery and anguish of civil war; the yoke of segregation and
tyranny of Jim Crow; the death of four little girls in Birmingham; and the dream of a
Baptist preacher – all that history met on this bridge.

It was not a clash of armies, but a clash of wills; a contest to determine the true

172

meaning of America. And because of men and women like John Lewis, Joseph Lowery, Hosea Williams, Amelia Boynton, Diane Nash, Ralph Abernathy, C.T. Vivian, Andrew Young, Fred Shuttlesworth, Dr. Martin Luther King, Jr., and so many others, the idea of a just America and a fair America, an inclusive America, and a generous America – that idea ultimately triumphed.

As is true across the landscape of American history, we cannot examine this moment in isolation. The march on Selma was part of a broader campaign that spanned generations; the leaders that day part of a long line of heroes.

We gather here to celebrate them. We gather here to honor the courage of ordinary Americans willing to endure billy clubs and the chastening rod; tear gas and the trampling hoof; men and women who despite the gush of blood and splintered bone would stay true to their North Star and keep marching towards justice.

They did as Scripture instructed: "Rejoice in hope, be patient in tribulation, be constant in prayer." And in the days to come, they went back again and again. When the trumpet call sounded for more to join, the people came — black and white, young and old, Christian and Jew, waving the American flag and singing the same anthems full of faith and hope. A white newsman, Bill Plante, who covered the marches then and who is with us here today, quipped that the growing number of white people lowered the quality of the singing. To those who marched, though, those old gospel songs must have never sounded so sweet.

In time, their chorus would well up and reach President Johnson. And he would send them protection, and speak to the nation, echoing their call for America and the world to hear: "We shall overcome." What enormous faith these men and women had. Faith in God, but also faith in America.

The Americans who crossed this bridge, they were not physically imposing. But they gave courage to millions. They held no elected office. But they led a nation. They marched as Americans who had endured hundreds of years of brutal violence, count-less daily indignities — but they didn't seek special treatment, just the equal treat-ment promised to them almost a century before.

What they did here will reverberate through the ages. Not because the change they won was preordained; not because their victory was complete; but because they proved that nonviolent change is possible, that love and hope can conquer hate.

As we commemorate their achievement, we are well-served to remember that at the time of the marches, many in power condemned rather than praised them. Back then, they were called Communists, or half-breeds, or outside agitators, sexual and moral degenerates, and worse — they were called everything but the name their parents gave them. Their faith was questioned. Their lives were threatened. Their patriotism challenged.

And yet, what could be more American than what happened in this place? What could more profoundly vindicate the idea of America than plain and humble people — unsung, the downtrodden, the dreamers not of high station, not born to wealth or privilege, not of one religious tradition but many, coming together to shape their country's course?

What greater expression of faith in the American experiment than this, what greater form of patriotism is there than the belief that America is not yet finished, that we are strong enough to be self-critical, that each successive generation can look upon our imperfections and decide that it is in our power to remake this nation to more closely align with our highest ideals?

That's why Selma is not some outlier in the American experience. That's why it's not a museum or a static monument to behold from a distance. It is instead the manifestation of a creed written into our founding documents: "We the People...in order to form a more perfect union." "We hold these truths to be self-evident, that all men are created equal."

These are not just words. They're a living thing, a call to action, a roadmap for citizenship and an insistence in the capacity of free men and women to shape our own destiny. For founders like Franklin and Jefferson, for leaders like Lincoln and FDR, the success of our experiment in self-government rested on engaging all of our citizens in this work. And that's what we celebrate here in Selma. That's what this movement was all about, one leg in our long journey toward freedom.

The American instinct that led these young men and women to pick up the torch and cross this bridge, that's the same instinct that moved patriots to choose revolution over tyranny. It's the same instinct that drew immigrants from across oceans and the Rio Grande; the same instinct that led women to reach for the ballot, workers to organize against an unjust status quo; the same instinct that led us to plant a flag at Iwo Jima and on the surface of the Moon.

It's the idea held by generations of citizens who believed that America is a constant work in progress; who believed that loving this country requires more than singing its praises or avoiding uncomfortable truths. It requires the occasional disruption, the willingness to speak out for what is right, to shake up the status quo. That's America.

That's what makes us unique. That's what cements our reputation as a beacon of opportunity. Young people behind the Iron Curtain would see Selma and eventually tear down that wall. Young people in Soweto would hear Bobby Kennedy talk about ripples of hope and eventually banish the scourge of apartheid. Young people in Burma went to prison rather than submit to military rule. They saw what John Lewis had done. From the streets of Tunis to the Maidan in Ukraine, this generation of young people can draw strength from this place, where the powerless could change the world's greatest power and push their leaders to expand the boundaries of freedom.

They saw that idea made real right here in Selma, Alabama. They saw that idea manifest itself here in America.

Because of campaigns like this, a Voting Rights Act was passed. Political and economic and social barriers came down. And the change these men and women wrought is visible here today in the presence of African Americans who run boardrooms, who sit on the bench, who serve in elected office from small towns to big cities; from the Congressional Black Caucus all the way to the Oval Office.

Because of what they did, the doors of opportunity swung open not just for black folks, but for every American. Women marched through those doors. Latinos marched through those doors. Asian Americans, gay Americans, Americans with disabilities – they all came through those doors. Their endeavors gave the entire

South the chance to rise again, not by reasserting the past, but by transcending the past.

What a glorious thing, Dr. King might say. And what a solemn debt we owe. Which leads us to ask, just how might we repay that debt?

First and foremost, we have to recognize that one day's commemoration, no matter how special, is not enough. If Selma taught us anything, it's that our work is never done. The American experiment in self-government gives work and purpose to each generation.

Selma teaches us, as well, that action requires that we shed our cynicism. For when it comes to the pursuit of justice, we can afford neither complacency nor despair.

Just this week, I was asked whether I thought the Department of Justice's Ferguson report shows that, with respect to race, little has changed in this country. And I understood the question; the report's narrative was sadly familiar. It evoked the kind of abuse and disregard for citizens that spawned the Civil Rights Movement. But I rejected the notion that nothing's changed. What happened in Ferguson may not be unique, but it's no longer endemic. It's no longer sanctioned by law or by custom. And before the Civil Rights Movement, it most surely was.

We do a disservice to the cause of justice by intimating that bias and discrimination are immutable, that racial division is inherent to America. If you think nothing's changed in the past 50 years, ask somebody who lived through the Selma or Chicago or Los Angeles of the 1950s. Ask the female CEO who once might have been assigned to the secretarial pool if nothing's changed. Ask your gay friend if it's easier to be out and proud in America now than it was thirty years ago. To deny this progress, this hard-won progress -- our progress -- would be to rob us of our own agency, our own capacity, our responsibility to do what we can to make America better.

Of course, a more common mistake is to suggest that Ferguson is an isolated incident; that racism is banished; that the work that drew men and women to Selma is now complete, and that whatever racial tensions remain are a consequence of those seeking to play the "race card" for their own purposes. We don't need the Ferguson report to know that's not true. We just need to open our eyes, and our ears, and our hearts to know that this nation's racial history still casts its long shadow upon us.

We know the march is not yet over. We know the race is not yet won. We know that reaching that blessed destination where we are judged, all of us, by the content of our character requires admitting as much, facing up to the truth. "We are capable of bearing a great burden," James Baldwin once wrote, "once we discover that the burden is reality and arrive where reality is."

There's nothing America can't handle if we actually look squarely at the problem. And this is work for all Americans, not just some. Not just whites. Not just blacks. If we want to honor the courage of those who marched that day, then all of us are called to possess their moral imagination. All of us will need to feel as they did the fierce urgency of now. All of us need to recognize as they did that change depends on our actions, on our attitudes, the things we teach our children. And if we make such an effort, no matter how hard it may sometimes seem, laws can be passed, and consciences can be stirred, and consensus can be built.

With such an effort, we can make sure our criminal justice system serves all and not just some. Together, we can raise the level of mutual trust that policing is built on — the idea that police officers are members of the community they risk their lives to protect, and citizens in Ferguson and New York and Cleveland, they just want the same thing young people here marched for 50 years ago — the protection of the law. Together, we can address unfair sentencing and overcrowded prisons, and the stunted circumstances that rob too many boys of the chance to become men, and rob the nation of too many men who could be good dads, and good workers, and good neighbors.

With effort, we can roll back poverty and the roadblocks to opportunity. Americans don't accept a free ride for anybody, nor do we believe in equality of outcomes. But we do expect equal opportunity. And if we really mean it, if we're not just giving lip service to it, but if we really mean it and are willing to sacrifice for it, then, yes, we can make sure every child gets an education suitable to this new century, one that expands imaginations and lifts sights and gives those children the skills they need. We can make sure every person willing to work has the dignity of a job, and a fair wage, and a real voice, and sturdier rungs on that ladder into the middle class.

And with effort, we can protect the foundation stone of our democracy for which so many marched across this bridge — and that is the right to vote. Right now, in 2015, 50 years after Selma, there are laws across this country designed to make it harder for people to vote. As we speak, more of such laws are being proposed. Meanwhile, the Voting Rights Act, the culmination of so much blood, so much sweat and tears, the product of so much sacrifice in the face of wanton violence, the Voting Rights Act stands weakened, its future subject to political rancor.

How can that be? The Voting Rights Act was one of the crowning achievements of our democracy, the result of Republican and Democratic efforts. President Reagan signed its renewal when he was in office. President George W. Bush signed its renewal when he was in office. One hundred members of Congress have come here today to honor people who were willing to die for the right to protect it. If we want to honor this day, let that hundred go back to Washington and gather four hundred more, and together, pledge to make it their mission to restore that law this year. That's how we honor those on this bridge.

Of course, our democracy is not the task of Congress alone, or the courts alone, or even the President alone. If every new voter-suppression law was struck down today, we would still have, here in America, one of the lowest voting rates among free peoples. Fifty years ago, registering to vote here in Selma and much of the South meant guessing the number of jellybeans in a jar, the number of bubbles on a bar of soap. It meant risking your dignity, and sometimes, your life.

What's our excuse today for not voting? How do we so casually discard the right for which so many fought? How do we so fully give away our power, our voice, in shaping America's future? Why are we pointing to somebody else when we could take the time just to go to the polling places? We give away our power.

Fellow marchers, so much has changed in 50 years. We have endured war and we've fashioned peace. We've seen technological wonders that touch every aspect of our lives. We take for granted conveniences that our parents could have scarcely imagined. But what has not changed is the imperative of citizenship; that willingness of a 26-year-old deacon, or a Unitarian minister, or a young mother of five to decide they loved this country so much that they'd risk everything to realize its promise.

That's what it means to love America. That's what it means to believe in America. That's what it means when we say America is exceptional.

For we were born of change. We broke the old aristocracies, declaring ourselves entitled not by bloodline, but endowed by our Creator with certain inalienable rights. We secure our rights and responsibilities through a system of self-government, of and by and for the people. That's why we argue and fight with so much passion and conviction – because we know our efforts matter. We know America is what we make of it.

Look at our history. We are Lewis and Clark and Sacajawea, pioneers who braved the unfamiliar, followed by a stampede of farmers and miners, and entrepreneurs and hucksters. That's our spirit. That's who we are.

We are Sojourner Truth and Fannie Lou Hamer, women who could do as much as any man and then some. And we're Susan B. Anthony, who shook the system until the law reflected that truth. That is our character.

We're the immigrants who stowed away on ships to reach these shores, the huddled masses yearning to breathe free — Holocaust survivors, Soviet defectors, the Lost Boys of Sudan. We're the hopeful strivers who cross the Rio Grande because we want our kids to know a better life. That's how we came to be.

We're the slaves who built the White House and the economy of the South. We're the ranch hands and cowboys who opened up the West, and countless laborers who laid rail, and raised skyscrapers, and organized for workers' rights.

We're the fresh-faced GIs who fought to liberate a continent. And we're the Tuskegee Airmen, and the Navajo code-talkers, and the Japanese Americans who fought for this country even as their own liberty had been denied.

We're the firefighters who rushed into those buildings on 9/11, the volunteers who signed up to fight in Afghanistan and Iraq. We're the gay Americans whose blood ran in the streets of San Francisco and New York, just as blood ran down this bridge.

We are storytellers, writers, poets, artists who abhor unfairness, and despise hypocrisy, and give voice to the voiceless, and tell truths that need to be told.

We're the inventors of gospel and jazz and blues, bluegrass and country, and hip-hop and rock and roll, and our very own sound with all the sweet sorrow and reckless joy of freedom.

We are Jackie Robinson, enduring scorn and spiked cleats and pitches coming straight to his head, and stealing home in the World Series anyway.

We are the people Langston Hughes wrote of who "build our temples for tomorrow, strong as we know how." We are the people Emerson wrote of, "who for truth and honor's sake stand fast and suffer long;" who are "never tired, so long as we can see far enough."

That's what America is. Not stock photos or airbrushed history, or feeble attempts to define some of us as more American than others. We respect the past, but we don't pine for the past. We don't fear the future; we grab for it. America is not some fragile thing. We are large, in the words of Whitman, containing multitudes. We are boisterous and diverse and full of energy, perpetually young in spirit. That's why someone like John Lewis at the ripe old age of 25 could lead a mighty march.

And that's what the young people here today and listening all across the country must take away from this day. You are America. Unconstrained by habit and convention. Unencumbered by what is, because you're ready to seize what ought to be.

For everywhere in this country, there are first steps to be taken, there's new ground to cover, there are more bridges to be crossed. And it is you, the young and fearless at heart, the most diverse and educated generation in our history, who the nation is waiting to follow.

Because Selma shows us that America is not the project of any one person. Because the single-most powerful word in our democracy is the word "We." "We The People." "We Shall Overcome." "Yes We Can." That word is owned by no one. It belongs to everyone. Oh, what a glorious task we are given, to continually try to improve this great nation of ours.

Fifty years from Bloody Sunday, our march is not yet finished, but we're getting closer. Two hundred and thirty-nine years after this nation's founding our union is not yet perfect, but we are getting closer. Our job's easier because somebody already got us through that first mile. Somebody already got us over that bridge. When it feels the road is too hard, when the torch we've been passed feels too heavy, we will remember these early travelers, and draw strength from their example, and hold firmly the words of the prophet Isaiah: "Those who hope in the Lord will renew their strength. They will soar on [the] wings like eagles. They will run and not grow weary. They will walk and not be faint."

We honor those who walked so we could run. We must run so our children soar. And we will not grow weary. For we believe in the power of an awesome God, and we believe in this country's sacred promise.

May He bless those warriors of justice no longer with us, and bless the United States of America. Thank you, everybody.

❧ 23 ❧

EULOGY FOR CLEMENTA PINCKNEY, CHARLESTON, SOUTH CAROLINA

JUNE 26, 2015

Giving all praise and honor to God.

The Bible calls us to hope. To persevere, and have faith in things not seen.

"They were still living by faith when they died," Scripture tells us. "They did not receive the things promised; they only saw them and welcomed them from a distance, admitting that they were foreigners and strangers on Earth."

We are here today to remember a man of God who lived by faith. A man who believed in things not seen. A man who believed there were better days ahead, off in the distance. A man of service who persevered, knowing full well he would not receive all those things he was promised, because he believed his efforts would deliver a better life for those who followed.

To Jennifer, his beloved wife; to Eliana and Malana, his beautiful, wonderful daughters; to the Mother Emanuel family and the people of Charleston, the people of South Carolina.

I cannot claim to have the good fortune to know Reverend Pinckney well. But I did have the pleasure of knowing him and meeting him here in South Carolina, back when we were both a little bit younger. Back when I didn't have visible grey hair. The first thing I noticed was his graciousness, his smile, his reassuring baritone, his deceptive sense of humor – all qualities that helped him wear so effortlessly a heavy burden of expectation.

Friends of his remarked this week that when Clementa Pinckney entered a room, it was like the future arrived; that even from a young age, folks knew he was special. Anointed. He was the progeny of a long line of the faithful – a family of preachers who spread God's word, a family of protesters who sowed change to expand voting rights and desegregate the South. Clem heard their instruction, and he did not forsake their teaching.

He was in the pulpit by 13, pastor by 18, public servant by 23. He did not exhibit any of the cockiness of youth, nor youth's insecurities; instead, he set an example worthy of his position, wise beyond his years, in his speech, in his conduct, in his love, faith, and purity.

As a senator, he represented a sprawling swath of the Lowcountry, a place that has long been one of the most neglected in America. A place still wracked by poverty and inadequate schools; a place where children can still go hungry and the sick can go without treatment. A place that needed somebody like Clem.

His position in the minority party meant the odds of winning more resources for his constituents were often long. His calls for greater equity were too often unheeded, the votes he cast were sometimes lonely. But he never gave up. He stayed true to his convictions. He would not grow discouraged. After a full day at the capitol, he'd climb into his car and head to the church to draw sustenance from his family, from his ministry, from the community that loved and needed him. There he would fortify his faith, and imagine what might be.

Reverend Pinckney embodied a politics that was neither mean, nor small. He conducted himself quietly, and kindly, and diligently. He encouraged progress not by pushing his ideas alone, but by seeking out your ideas, partnering with you to make things happen. He was full of empathy and fellow feeling, able to walk in somebody else's shoes and see through their eyes. No wonder one of his senate colleagues remembered Senator Pinckney as "the most gentle of the 46 of us – the best of the 46 of us."

Clem was often asked why he chose to be a pastor and a public servant. But the person who asked probably didn't know the history of the AME church. As our brothers and sisters in the AME church know, we don't make those distinctions. "Our calling," Clem once said, "is not just within the walls of the congregation, but...the life and community in which our congregation resides."

He embodied the idea that our Christian faith demands deeds and not just words; that the "sweet hour of prayer" actually lasts the whole week long – that to put our faith in action is more than individual salvation, it's about our collective salvation; that to feed the hungry and clothe the naked and house the homeless is not just a call for isolated charity but the imperative of a just society.

What a good man. Sometimes I think that's the best thing to hope for when you're eulogized – after all the words and recitations and resumes are read, to just say someone was a good man.

You don't have to be of high station to be a good man. Preacher by 13. Pastor by 18. Public servant by 23. What a life Clementa Pinckney lived. What an example he set. What a model for his faith. And then to lose him at 41 – slain in his sanctuary with eight wonderful members of his flock, each at different stages in life but bound together by a common commitment to God.

Cynthia Hurd. Susie Jackson. Ethel Lance. DePayne Middleton-Doctor. Tywanza Sanders. Daniel L. Simmons. Sharonda Coleman-Singleton. Myra Thompson. Good people. Decent people. God-fearing people. People so full of life and so full of kindness. People who ran the race, who persevered. People of great faith.

To the families of the fallen, the nation shares in your grief. Our pain cuts that much deeper because it happened in a church. The church is and always has been the center of African-American life – a place to call our own in a too often hostile world, a sanctuary from so many hardships.

Over the course of centuries, black churches served as "hush harbors" where slaves could worship in safety; praise houses where their free descendants could gather and shout hallelujah – rest stops for the weary along the Underground Railroad; bunkers for the foot soldiers of the Civil Rights Movement. They have been, and continue to be, community centers where we organize for jobs and justice; places of scholarship and network; places where children are loved and fed and kept out of harm's way, and told that they are beautiful and smart – and taught that they matter. That's what happens in church.

That's what the black church means. Our beating heart. The place where our dignity as a people is inviolate. When there's no better example of this tradition than Mother Emanuel – a church built by blacks seeking liberty, burned to the ground because its founder sought to end slavery, only to rise up again, a Phoenix from these ashes.

When there were laws banning all-black church gatherings, services happened here anyway, in defiance of unjust laws. When there was a righteous movement to dismantle Jim Crow, Dr. Martin Luther King, Jr. preached from its pulpit, and marches began from its steps. A sacred place, this church. Not just for blacks, not just for Christians, but for every American who cares about the steady expansion – of human rights and human dignity in this country; a foundation stone for liberty and justice for all. That's what the church meant.

We do not know whether the killer of Reverend Pinckney and eight others knew all of this history. But he surely sensed the meaning of his violent act. It was an act that drew on a long history of bombs and arson and shots fired at churches, not random, but as a means of control, a way to terrorize and oppress. An act that he imagined would incite fear and recrimination; violence and suspicion. An act that he presumed would deepen divisions that trace back to our nation's original sin.

Oh, but God works in mysterious ways. God has different ideas.

He didn't know he was being used by God. Blinded by hatred, the alleged killer could not see the grace surrounding Reverend Pinckney and that Bible study group – the light of love that shone as they opened the church doors and invited a stranger to join in their prayer circle. The alleged killer could have never anticipated the way the families of the fallen would respond when they saw him in court – in the midst of unspeakable grief, with words of forgiveness. He couldn't imagine that.

The alleged killer could not imagine how the city of Charleston, under the good and wise leadership of Mayor Riley – how the state of South Carolina, how the United States of America would respond – not merely with revulsion at his evil act, but with big-hearted generosity and, more importantly, with a thoughtful introspection and self-examination that we so rarely see in public life.

Blinded by hatred, he failed to comprehend what Reverend Pinckney so well understood – the power of God's grace.

This whole week, I've been reflecting on this idea of grace. The grace of the families who lost loved ones. The grace that Reverend Pinckney would preach about in his sermons. The grace described in one of my favorite hymnals – the one we all know: Amazing grace, how sweet the sound that saved a wretch like me. I once was lost, but now I'm found; was blind but now I see.

According to the Christian tradition, grace is not earned. Grace is not merited. It's not something we deserve. Rather, grace is the free and benevolent favor of God – as manifested in the salvation of sinners and the bestowal of blessings. Grace.

As a nation, out of this terrible tragedy, God has visited grace upon us, for he has allowed us to see where we've been blind. He has given us the chance, where we've been lost, to find our best selves. We may not have earned it, this grace, with our rancor and complacency, and short-sightedness and fear of each other – but we got it all the same. He gave it to us anyway. He's once more given us grace. But it is up to us now to make the most of it, to receive it with gratitude, and to prove ourselves worthy of this gift.

For too long, we were blind to the pain that the Confederate flag stirred in too many of our citizens. It's true, a flag did not cause these murders. But as people from all walks of life, Republicans and Democrats, now acknowledge – including Governor Haley, whose recent eloquence on the subject is worthy of praise – as we all have to acknowledge, the flag has always represented more than just ancestral pride. For many, black and white, that flag was a reminder of systemic oppression and racial subjugation. We see that now.

Removing the flag from this state's capitol would not be an act of political correctness; it would not be an insult to the valor of Confederate soldiers. It would simply be an acknowledgment that the cause for which they fought – the cause of slavery – was wrong – the imposition of Jim Crow after the Civil War, the resistance to civil rights for all people was wrong. It would be one step in an honest accounting of America's history; a modest but meaningful balm for so many unhealed wounds. It would be an expression of the amazing changes that have transformed this state and this country for the better, because of the work of so many people of goodwill, people of all races striving to form a more perfect union. By taking down that flag, we express God's grace.

But I don't think God wants us to stop there. For too long, we've been blind to the way past injustices continue to shape the present. Perhaps we see that now. Perhaps this tragedy causes us to ask some tough questions about how we can permit so many of our children to languish in poverty, or attend dilapidated schools, or grow up without prospects for a job or for a career.

Perhaps it causes us to examine what we're doing to cause some of our children to hate. Perhaps it softens hearts towards those lost young men, tens and tens of thousands caught up in the criminal justice system – and leads us to make sure that that system is not infected with bias; that we embrace changes in how we train and equip our police so that the bonds of trust between law enforcement and the communities they serve make us all safer and more secure.

Maybe we now realize the way racial bias can infect us even when we don't realize it, so that we're guarding against not just racial slurs, but we're also guarding against the subtle impulse to call Johnny back for a job interview but not Jamal. So that we search our hearts when we consider laws to make it harder for some of our fellow citizens to vote. By recognizing our common humanity by treating every child as important, regardless of the color of their skin or the station into which they were born, and to do what's necessary to make opportunity real for every American – by doing that, we express God's grace.

For too long –

AUDIENCE: For too long!

THE PRESIDENT: For too long, we've been blind to the unique mayhem that gun violence inflicts upon this nation. Sporadically, our eyes are open: When eight of our brothers and sisters are cut down in a church basement, 12 in a movie theater, 26 in an elementary school. But I hope we also see the 30 precious lives cut short by gun violence in this country every single day; the countless more whose lives are forever changed – the survivors crippled, the children traumatized and fearful every day as they walk to school, the husband who will never feel his wife's warm touch, the entire communities whose grief overflows every time they have to watch what happened to them happen to some other place.

The vast majority of Americans – the majority of gun owners – want to do something about this. We see that now. And I'm convinced that by acknowledging the pain and loss of others, even as we respect the traditions and ways of life that make up this beloved country – by making the moral choice to change, we express God's grace.

We don't earn grace. We're all sinners. We don't deserve it. But God gives it to us anyway. And we choose how to receive it. It's our decision how to honor it.

None of us can or should expect a transformation in race relations overnight. Every time something like this happens, somebody says we have to have a conversation about race. We talk a lot about race. There's no shortcut. And we don't need more talk. None of us should believe that a handful of gun safety measures will prevent every tragedy. It will not. People of goodwill will continue to debate the merits of various policies, as our democracy requires – this is a big, raucous place, America is. And there are good people on both sides of these debates. Whatever solutions we find will necessarily be incomplete.

But it would be a betrayal of everything Reverend Pinckney stood for, I believe, if we allowed ourselves to slip into a comfortable silence again. Once the eulogies have been delivered, once the TV cameras move on, to go back to business as usual – that's what we so often do to avoid uncomfortable truths about the prejudice that still infects our society. To settle for symbolic gestures without following up with the hard work of more lasting change – that's how we lose our way again.

It would be a refutation of the forgiveness expressed by those families if we merely slipped into old habits, whereby those who disagree with us are not merely wrong but bad; where we shout instead of listen; where we barricade ourselves behind preconceived notions or well-practiced cynicism.

Reverend Pinckney once said, "Across the South, we have a deep appreciation of history – we haven't always had a deep appreciation of each other's history." What is true in the South is true for America. Clem understood that justice grows out of recognition of ourselves in each other. That my liberty depends on you being free, too. That history can't be a sword to justify injustice, or a shield against progress, but must be a manual for how to avoid repeating the mistakes of the past – how to break the cycle. A roadway toward a better world. He knew that the path of grace involves an open mind – but, more importantly, an open heart.

That's what I've felt this week – an open heart. That, more than any particular policy or analysis, is what's called upon right now, I think – what a friend of mine, the writer Marilyn Robinson, calls "that reservoir of goodness, beyond, and of another kind, that we are able to do each other in the ordinary cause of things."

That reservoir of goodness. If we can find that grace, anything is possible. If we can tap that grace, everything can change.

Amazing grace. Amazing grace.

(Begins to sing) – Amazing grace – how sweet the sound, that saved a wretch like me; I once was lost, but now I'm found; was blind but now I see.

Clementa Pinckney found that grace.

Cynthia Hurd found that grace.

Susie Jackson found that grace.

Ethel Lance found that grace.

DePayne Middleton-Doctor found that grace.

Tywanza Sanders found that grace.

Daniel L. Simmons, Sr. found that grace.

Sharonda Coleman-Singleton found that grace.

Myra Thompson found that grace.

Through the example of their lives, they've now passed it on to us. May we find ourselves worthy of that precious and extraordinary gift, as long as our lives endure. May grace now lead them home. May God continue to shed His grace on the United States of America.

ADDRESS TO THE NATION AFTER THE SAN BERNARDINO ATTACK

DECEMBER 6, 2015

G ood evening. On Wednesday, 14 Americans were killed as they came together to celebrate the holidays. They were taken from family and friends who loved them deeply. They were white and black; Latino and Asian; immigrants and American-born; moms and dads; daughters and sons. Each of them served their fellow citizens and all of them were part of our American family.

Tonight, I want to talk with you about this tragedy, the broader threat of terrorism, and how we can keep our country safe.

The FBI is still gathering the facts about what happened in San Bernardino, but here is what we know. The victims were brutally murdered and injured by one of their coworkers and his wife. So far, we have no evidence that the killers were directed by a terrorist organization overseas, or that they were part of a broader conspiracy here at home. But it is clear that the two of them had gone down the dark path of radicalization, embracing a perverted interpretation of Islam that calls for war against America and the West. They had stockpiled assault weapons, ammunition, and pipe bombs. So this was an act of terrorism, designed to kill innocent people.

Our nation has been at war with terrorists since al Qaeda killed nearly 3,000 Americans on 9/11. In the process, we've hardened our defenses – from airports to financial centers, to other critical infrastructure. Intelligence and law enforcement agencies have disrupted countless plots here and overseas, and worked around the clock to keep us safe. Our military and counterterrorism professionals have relentlessly pursued terrorist networks overseas – disrupting safe havens in several different countries, killing Osama bin Laden, and decimating al Qaeda's leadership.

Over the last few years, however, the terrorist threat has evolved into a new phase. As we've become better at preventing complex, multifaceted attacks like 9/11, terrorists turned to less complicated acts of violence like the mass shootings that are all too common in our society. It is this type of attack that we saw at Fort Hood in 2009; in Chattanooga earlier this year; and now in San Bernardino. And as groups like ISIL grew stronger amidst the chaos of war in Iraq and then Syria, and as the Internet erases the distance between countries, we see growing efforts by terrorists to poison the minds of people like the Boston Marathon bombers and the San Bernardino killers.

For seven years, I've confronted this evolving threat each morning in my intelligence briefing. And since the day I took this office, I've authorized U.S. forces to take out terrorists abroad precisely because I know how real the danger is. As Commander-in-Chief, I have no greater responsibility than the security of the American people. As a father to two young daughters who are the most precious part of my life, I know that we see ourselves with friends and coworkers at a holiday party like the one in San Bernardino. I know we see our kids in the faces of the young people killed in Paris. And I know that after so much war, many Americans are asking whether we are confronted by a cancer that has no immediate cure.

Well, here's what I want you to know: The threat from terrorism is real, but we will overcome it. We will destroy ISIL and any other organization that tries to harm us. Our success won't depend on tough talk, or abandoning our values, or giving into fear. That's what groups like ISIL are hoping for. Instead, we will prevail by being strong and smart, resilient and relentless, and by drawing upon every aspect of American power.

Here's how. First, our military will continue to hunt down terrorist plotters in any country where it is necessary. In Iraq and Syria, airstrikes are taking out ISIL leaders, heavy weapons, oil tankers, infrastructure. And since the attacks in Paris, our closest allies – including France, Germany, and the United Kingdom – have ramped up their contributions to our military campaign, which will help us accelerate our effort to destroy ISIL.

Second, we will continue to provide training and equipment to tens of thousands of Iraqi and Syrian forces fighting ISIL on the ground so that we take away their safe havens. In both countries, we're deploying Special Operations Forces who can accelerate that offensive. We've stepped up this effort since the attacks in Paris, and we'll continue to invest more in approaches that are working on the ground.

Third, we're working with friends and allies to stop ISIL's operations – to disrupt plots, cut off their financing, and prevent them from recruiting more fighters. Since the attacks in Paris, we've surged intelligence-sharing with our European allies. We're working with Turkey to seal its border with Syria. And we are cooperating with Muslim-majority countries – and with our Muslim communities here at home – to counter the vicious ideology that ISIL promotes online.

Fourth, with American leadership, the international community has begun to establish a process – and timeline – to pursue ceasefires and a political resolution to the Syrian war. Doing so will allow the Syrian people and every country, including our allies, but also countries like Russia, to focus on the common goal of destroying ISIL – a group that threatens us all.

This is our strategy to destroy ISIL. It is designed and supported by our military commanders and counterterrorism experts, together with 65 countries that have joined an American-led coalition. And we constantly examine our strategy to determine when additional steps are needed to get the job done. That's why I've ordered the Departments of State and Homeland Security to review the visa waiver program under which the female terrorist in San Bernardino originally came to this country. And that's why I will urge high-tech and law enforcement leaders to make it harder for terrorists to use technology to escape from justice.

Now, here at home, we have to work together to address the challenge. There are several steps that Congress should take right away.

To begin with, Congress should act to make sure no one on a no-fly list is able to buy a gun. What could possibly be the argument for allowing a terrorist suspect to buy a semi-automatic weapon? This is a matter of national security.

We also need to make it harder for people to buy powerful assault weapons like the ones that were used in San Bernardino. I know there are some who reject any gun safety measures. But the fact is that our intelligence and law enforcement agencies – no matter how effective they are – cannot identify every would-be mass shooter, whether that individual is motivated by ISIL or some other hateful ideology. What we can do – and must do – is make it harder for them to kill.

Next, we should put in place stronger screening for those who come to America without a visa so that we can take a hard look at whether they've traveled to warzones. And we're working with members of both parties in Congress to do exactly that.

Finally, if Congress believes, as I do, that we are at war with ISIL, it should go ahead and vote to authorize the continued use of military force against these terrorists. For over a year, I have ordered our military to take thousands of airstrikes against ISIL targets. I think it's time for Congress to vote to demonstrate that the American people are united, and committed, to this fight.

My fellow Americans, these are the steps that we can take together to defeat the terrorist threat. Let me now say a word about what we should not do.

We should not be drawn once more into a long and costly ground war in Iraq or Syria. That's what groups like ISIL want. They know they can't defeat us on the battlefield. ISIL fighters were part of the insurgency that we faced in Iraq. But they also know that if we occupy foreign lands, they can maintain insurgencies for years, killing thousands of our troops, draining our resources, and using our presence to draw new recruits.

The strategy that we are using now – airstrikes, Special Forces, and working with local forces who are fighting to regain control of their own country – that is how we'll achieve a more sustainable victory. And it won't require us sending a new generation of Americans overseas to fight and die for another decade on foreign soil.

Here's what else we cannot do. We cannot turn against one another by letting this fight be defined as a war between America and Islam. That, too, is what groups like ISIL want. ISIL does not speak for Islam. They are thugs and killers, part of a cult of death, and they account for a tiny fraction of more than a billion Muslims around the world – including millions of patriotic Muslim Americans who reject their hateful ideology. Moreover, the vast majority of terrorist victims around the world are Muslim. If we're to succeed in defeating terrorism we must enlist Muslim communities as some of our strongest allies, rather than push them away through suspicion and hate.

That does not mean denying the fact that an extremist ideology has spread within some Muslim communities. This is a real problem that Muslims must confront, without excuse. Muslim leaders here and around the globe have to continue working with us to decisively and unequivocally reject the hateful ideology that groups like ISIL and al Qaeda promote; to speak out against not just acts of violence, but also those interpretations of Islam that are incompatible with the values of religious tolerance, mutual respect, and human dignity.

But just as it is the responsibility of Muslims around the world to root out misguided ideas that lead to radicalization, it is the responsibility of all Americans – of every faith – to reject discrimination. It is our responsibility to reject religious tests on who we admit into this country. It's our responsibility to reject proposals that Muslim Americans should somehow be treated differently. Because when we travel down that road, we lose. That kind of divisiveness, that betrayal of our values plays into the hands of groups like ISIL. Muslim Americans are our friends and our neighbors, our co-workers, our sports heroes – and, yes, they are our men and women in uniform who are willing to die in defense of our country. We have to remember that.

My fellow Americans, I am confident we will succeed in this mission because we are on the right side of history. We were founded upon a belief in human dignity – that no matter who you are, or where you come from, or what you look like, or what religion you practice, you are equal in the eyes of God and equal in the eyes of the law.

Even in this political season, even as we properly debate what steps I and future Presidents must take to keep our country safe, let's make sure we never forget what makes us exceptional. Let's not forget that freedom is more powerful than fear; that we have always met challenges – whether war or depression, natural disasters or terrorist attacks – by coming together around our common ideals as one nation, as one people. So long as we stay true to that tradition, I have no doubt America will prevail.

Thank you. God bless you, and may God bless the United States of America.

❧ 25 ❧

REMARKS AT A NATURALIZATION CEREMONY, WASHINGTON, D.C.

DEC. 15, 2015

Well, good morning, everybody. Thank you Deputy Secretary Mayorkas, Judge Roberts, and Director Rodriguez. Thank you to our Archivist, David Ferriero, and everyone at the National Archives for hosting us here today in this spectacular setting.

And to my fellow Americans, our newest citizens – I'm so excited. You are men and women from more than 25 countries, from Brazil to Uganda, from Iraq to the Philippines. You may come from teeming cities or rural villages. You don't look alike. You don't worship the same way. But here, surrounded by the very documents whose values bind us together as one people, you've raised your hand and sworn a sacred oath. I'm proud to be among the first to greet you as "my fellow Americans."

What a remarkable journey all of you have made. And as of today, your story is forever woven into the larger story of this nation. In the brief time that we have together, I want to share that story with you. Because even as you've put in the work required to become a citizen, you still have a demanding and rewarding task ahead of you – and that is the hard work of active citizenship. You have rights and you have responsibilities. And now you have to help us write the next great chapter in America's story.

Just about every nation in the world, to some extent, admits immigrants. But there's something unique about America. We don't simply welcome new immigrants, we don't simply welcome new arrivals – we are born of immigrants. That is who we are. Immigration is our origin story. And for more than two centuries, it's remained at the core of our national character; it's our oldest tradition. It's who we are. It's part of what makes us exceptional.

After all, unless your family is Native American, one of the first Americans, our families – all of our families – come from someplace else. The first refugees were the Pilgrims themselves – fleeing religious persecution, crossing the stormy Atlantic to reach a new world where they might live and pray freely. Eight signers of the Decla-

ration of Independence were immigrants. And in those first decades after independence, English, German, and Scottish immigrants came over, huddled on creaky
ships, seeking what Thomas Paine called "asylum for the persecuted lovers of civil
and religious liberty..."

Down through the decades, Irish Catholics fleeing hunger, Italians fleeing poverty
filled up our cities, rolled up their sleeves, built America. Chinese laborers jammed in
steerage under the decks of steamships, making their way to California to build the
Central Pacific Railroad that would transform the West – and our nation. Wave after
wave of men, women, and children

– from the Middle East and the Mediterranean, from Asia and Africa – poured
into Ellis Island, or Angel Island, their trunks bursting with their most cherished
possessions – maybe a photograph of the family they left behind, a family Bible, or a
Torah, or a Koran. A bag in one hand, maybe a child in the other, standing for hours
in long lines. New York and cities across America were transformed into a sort of
global fashion show. You had Dutch lace caps and the North African fezzes, stodgy
tweed suits and colorful Caribbean dresses.

And perhaps, like some of you, these new arrivals might have had some moments
of doubt, wondering if they had made a mistake in leaving everything and everyone
they ever knew behind. So life in America was not always easy. It wasn't always easy
for new immigrants. Certainly it wasn't easy for those of African heritage who had
not come here voluntarily, and yet in their own way were immigrants themselves.
There was discrimination and hardship and poverty. But, like you, they no doubt
found inspiration in all those who had come before them. And they were able to
muster faith that, here in America, they might build a better life and give their children something more.

Just as so many have come here in search of a dream, others sought shelter from
nightmares. Survivors of the Holocaust. Soviet Refuseniks. Refugees from Vietnam,
Laos, Cambodia. Iraqis and Afghans fleeing war. Mexicans, Cubans, Iranians
leaving behind deadly revolutions. Central American teenagers running from gang
violence. The Lost Boys of Sudan escaping civil war. They're people like Fulbert
Florent Akoula from the Republic of Congo, who was granted asylum when his
family was threatened by political violence. And today, Fulbert is here, a proud
American.

We can never say it often or loudly enough: Immigrants and refugees revitalize
and renew America. Immigrants like you are more likely to start your own business.
Many of the Fortune 500 companies in this country were founded by immigrants or
their children. Many of the tech startups in Silicon Valley have at least one immigrant
founder.

Immigrants are the teachers who inspire our children, and they're the doctors
who keep us healthy. They're the engineers who design our skylines, and the artists
and the entertainers who touch our hearts. Immigrants are soldiers, sailors, airmen,
Marines, Coast Guardsmen who protect us, often risking their lives for an America
that isn't even their own yet. As an Iraqi, Muhanned Ibrahim Al Naib was the target
of death threats for working with American forces. He stood by his American
comrades, and came to the U.S. as a refugee. And today, we stand by him. And we

are proud to welcome Muhanned as a citizen of the country that he already helped to defend.

We celebrate this history, this heritage, as an immigrant nation. And we are strong enough to acknowledge, as painful as it may be, that we haven't always lived up to our own ideals. We haven't always lived up to these documents.

From the start, Africans were brought here in chains against their will, and then toiled under the whip. They also built America. A century ago, New York City shops displayed those signs, "No Irish Need Apply." Catholics were targeted, their loyalty questioned – so much so that as recently as the 1950s and '60s, when JFK had to run, he had to convince people that his allegiance wasn't primarily to the Pope.

Chinese immigrants faced persecution and vicious stereotypes, and were, for a time, even banned from entering America. During World War II, German and Italian residents were detained, and in one of the darkest chapters in our history, Japanese immigrants and even Japanese American citizens were forced from their homes and imprisoned in camps. We succumbed to fear. We betrayed not only our fellow Americans, but our deepest values. We betrayed these documents. It's happened before.

And the biggest irony of course was – is that those who betrayed these values were themselves the children of immigrants. How quickly we forget. One generation passes, two generation passes, and suddenly we don't remember where we came from. And we suggest that somehow there is "us" and there is "them," not remembering we used to be "them."

On days like today, we need to resolve never to repeat mistakes like that again. We must resolve to always speak out against hatred and bigotry in all of its forms – whether taunts against the child of an immigrant farmworker or threats against a Muslim shopkeeper. We are Americans. Standing up for each other is what the values enshrined in the documents in this room compels us to do — especially when it's hard. Especially when it's not convenient. That's when it counts. That's when it matters – not when things are easy, but when things are hard.

The truth is, being an American is hard. Being part of a democratic government is hard. Being a citizen is hard. It is a challenge. It's supposed to be. There's no respite from our ideals. All of us are called to live up to our expectations for ourselves – not just when it's convenient, but when it's inconvenient. When it's tough. When we're afraid. The tension throughout our history between welcoming or rejecting the stranger, it's about more than just immigration. It's about the meaning of America, what kind of country do we want to be. It's about the capacity of each generation to honor the creed as old as our founding: "E Pluribus Unum" – that out of many, we are one.

Scripture tells us, "For we are strangers before you, and sojourners, as were all our fathers." "We are strangers before you." In the Mexican immigrant today, we see the Catholic immigrant of a century ago. In the Syrian seeking refuge today, we should see the Jewish refugee of World War II. In these new Americans, we see our own American stories – our parents, our grandparents, our aunts, our uncles, our cousins who packed up what they could and scraped together what they had. And their paperwork wasn't always in order. And they set out for a place that was more than just a piece of land, but an idea.

America: A place where we can be a part of something bigger. A place where we can contribute our talents and fulfill our ambitions and secure new opportunity for ourselves and for others. A place where we can retain pride in our heritage, but where we recognize that we have a common creed, a loyalty to these documents, a loyalty to our democracy; where we can criticize our government, but understand that we love it; where we agree to live together even when we don't agree with each other; where we work through the democratic process, and not through violence or sectarianism to resolve disputes; where we live side by side as neighbors; and where our children know themselves to be a part of this nation, no longer strangers, but the bedrock of this nation, the essence of this nation.

And that's why today is not the final step in your journey. More than 60 years ago, at a ceremony like this one, Senator John F. Kennedy said, "No form of government requires more of its citizens than does the American democracy." Our system of self-government depends on ordinary citizens doing the hard, frustrating but always essential work of citizenship – of being informed. Of understanding that the government isn't some distant thing, but is you. Of speaking out when something is not right. Of helping fellow citizens when they need a hand. Of coming together to shape our country's course.

And that work gives purpose to every generation. It belongs to me. It belongs to the judge. It belongs to you. It belongs to you, all of us, as citizens. To follow our laws, yes, but also to engage with your communities and to speak up for what you believe in. And to vote – to not only exercise the rights that are now yours, but to stand up for the rights of others.

Birtukan Gudeya is here from Ethiopia. She said, "The joy of being an American is the joy of freedom and opportunity. We have been handed a work in progress, one that can evolve for the good of all Americans." I couldn't have said it better.

That is what makes America great – not just the words on these founding documents, as precious and valuable as they are, but the progress that they've inspired. If you ever wonder whether America is big enough to hold multitudes, strong enough to withstand the forces of change, brave enough to live up to our ideals even in times of trial, then look to the generations of ordinary citizens who have proven again and again that we are worthy of that.

That's our great inheritance – what ordinary people have done to build this country and make these words live. And it's our generation's task to follow their example in this journey – to keep building an America where no matter who we are or what we look like, or who we love or what we believe, we can make of our lives what we will.

You will not and should not forget your history and your past. That adds to the richness of American life. But you are now American. You've got obligations as citizens. And I'm absolutely confident you will meet them. You'll set a good example for all of us, because you know how precious this thing is. It's not something to take for granted. It's something to cherish and to fight for.

Thank you. May god bless you. May god bless the United States of America.

❦ 26 ❦

2016 STATE OF THE UNION ADDRESS
JANUARY 12, 2016

Thank you. Mr. Speaker, Mr. Vice President, Members of Congress, my fellow Americans: Tonight marks the eighth year that I've come here to report on the State of the Union. And for this final one, I'm going to try to make it a little shorter. I know some of you are antsy to get back to Iowa. [Laughter] I've been there. I'll be shaking hands afterwards if you want some tips. [Laughter]

Now, I understand that because it's an election season, expectations for what we will achieve this year are low. But, Mr. Speaker, I appreciate the constructive approach that you and other leaders took at the end of last year to pass a budget and make tax cuts permanent for working families. So I hope we can work together this year on some bipartisan priorities like criminal justice reform and helping people who are battling prescription drug abuse and heroin abuse. So, who knows, we might surprise the cynics again.

But tonight I want to go easy on the traditional list of proposals for the year ahead. Don't worry, I've got plenty–[laughter]–from helping students learn to write computer code to personalizing medical treatments for patients. And I will keep pushing for progress on the work that I believe still needs to be done: fixing a broken immigration system, protecting our kids from gun violence, equal pay for equal work, paid leave, raising the minimum wage. All these things still matter to hard-working families. They're still the right thing to do. And I won't let up until they get done.

But for my final address to this Chamber, I don't want to just talk about next year. I want to focus on the next 5 years, the next 10 years, and beyond. I want to focus on our future.

We live in a time of extraordinary change, change that's reshaping the way we live, the way we work, our planet, our place in the world. It's change that promises amazing medical breakthroughs, but also economic disruptions that strain working families. It promises this education for girls in the most remote villages, but also connects terrorists plotting an ocean away. It's change that can broaden opportunity or widen inequality. And whether we like it or not, the pace of this change will only accelerate.

America has been through big changes before: wars and depression, the influx of new immigrants, workers fighting for a fair deal, movements to expand civil rights. Each time, there have been those who told us to fear the future; who claimed we could slam the brakes on change; who promised to restore past glory if we just got some group or idea that was threatening America under control. And each time, we overcame those fears. We did not, in the words of Lincoln, adhere to the "dogmas of the quiet past." Instead, we thought anew and acted anew. We made change work for us, always extending America's promise outward, to the next frontier, to more people. And because we did, because we saw opportunity with a–where others saw peril, we emerged stronger and better than before.

What was true then can be true now. Our unique strengths as a nation– our optimism and work ethic, our spirit of discovery, our diversity, our commitment to rule of law–these things give us everything we need to ensure prosperity and security for generations to come.

In fact, it's in that spirit that we have made progress these past 7 years. That's how we recovered from the worst economic crisis in generations. That's how we reformed our health care system and reinvented our energy sector. That's how we delivered more care and benefits to our troops coming home and our veterans. That's how we secured the freedom in every State to marry the person we love.

But such progress is not inevitable. It's the result of choices we make together. And we face such choices right now. Will we respond to the changes of our time with fear, turning inward as a nation, turning against each other as a people? Or will we face the future with confidence in who we are, in what we stand for, in the incredible things that we can do together?

So let's talk about the future and four big questions that I believe we as a country have to answer, regardless of who the next President is or who controls the next Congress. First, how do we give everyone a fair shot at opportunity and security in this new economy? Second, how do we make technology work for us and not against us, especially when it comes to solving urgent challenges like climate change? Third, how do we keep America safe and lead the world without becoming its policeman? And finally, how can we make our politics reflect what's best in us and not what's worst?

Let me start with the economy and a basic fact: The United States of America right now has the strongest, most durable economy in the world. We're in the middle of the longest streak of private sector job creation in history. More than 14 million new jobs, the strongest 2 years of job growth since the 1990s, an unemployment rate cut in half. Our auto industry just had its best year ever. That's just part of a manufacturing surge that's created nearly 900,000 new jobs in the past 6 years. And we've done all this while cutting our deficits by almost three-quarters.

Anyone claiming that America's economy is in decline is peddling fiction. Now, what is true–and the reason that a lot of Americans feel anxious–is that the economy has been changing in profound ways, changes that started long before the great recession hit, changes that have not let up.

Today, technology doesn't just replace jobs on the assembly line, but any job where work can be automated. Companies in a global economy can locate anywhere, and they face tougher competition. As a result, workers have less leverage for a raise. Companies have less loyalty to their communities. And more and more wealth and income is concentrated at the very top.

All these trends have squeezed workers, even when they have jobs, even when the economy is growing. It's made it harder for a hard-working family to pull itself out of poverty, harder for young people to start their careers, tougher for workers to retire when they want to. And although none of these trends are unique to America, they do offend our uniquely American belief that everybody who works hard should get a fair shot.

For the past 7 years, our goal has been a growing economy that also works better for everybody. We've made progress, but we need to make more. And despite all the political arguments that we've had these past few years, there are actually some areas where Americans broadly agree.

We agree that real opportunity requires every American to get the education and training they need to land a good-paying job. The bipartisan reform of No Child Left Behind was an important start, and together, we've increased early childhood education, lifted high school graduation rates to new highs, boosted graduates in fields like engineering. In the coming years, we should build on that progress, by providing pre-K for all and offering every student the hands-on computer science and math classes that make them job-ready on day one. We should recruit and support more great teachers for our kids.

And we have to make college affordable for every American. No hard- working student should be stuck in the red. We've already reduced student loan payments by— to 10 percent of a borrower's income. And that's good. But now we've actually got to cut the cost of college. Providing 2 years of community college at no cost for every responsible student is one of the best ways to do that, and I'm going to keep fighting to get that started this year. It's the right thing to do.

But a great education isn't all we need in this new economy. We also need benefits and protections that provide a basic measure of security. It's not too much of a stretch to say that some of the only people in America who are going to work the same job, in the same place, with a health and retirement package for 30 years are sitting in this Chamber. [Laughter] For everyone else, especially folks in their forties and fifties, saving for retirement or bouncing back from job loss has gotten a lot tougher. Americans understand that at some point in their careers, in this new economy, they may have to retool, they may have to retrain. But they shouldn't lose what they've already worked so hard to build in the process.

That's why Social Security and Medicare are more important than ever. We shouldn't weaken them, we should strengthen them. And for Americans short of retirement, basic benefits should be just as mobile as everything else is today. That, by the way, is what the Affordable Care Act is all about. It's about filling the gaps in employer-based care so that when you lose a job or you go back to school or you strike out and launch that new business, you'll still have coverage. Nearly 18 million people have gained coverage so far. And in the process, health care inflation has slowed. And our businesses have created jobs every single month since it became law.

Now, I'm guessing we won't agree on health care anytime soon, but– [laughter]–a little applause back there. [Laughter] Just a guess. But there should be other ways parties can work together to improve economic security. Say a hard-working American loses his job. We shouldn't just make sure that he can get unemployment insurance, we should make sure that program encourages him to retrain for a business that's ready to hire him. If that new job doesn't pay as much, there should be a system of wage insurance in place so that he can still pay his bills. And even if he's going from job to job, he should still be able to save for retirement and take his savings with him. That's the way we make the new economy work better for everybody.

I also know Speaker Ryan has talked about his interest in tackling poverty. America is about giving everybody willing to work a chance, a hand up. And I'd welcome a serious discussion about strategies we can all support, like expanding tax cuts for low-income workers who don't have children.

But there are some areas where–we just have to be honest–it has been difficult to find agreement over the last 7 years. And a lot of them fall under the category of what role the Government should play in making sure the system's not rigged in favor of the wealthiest and biggest corporations. And it's an honest disagreement, and the American people have a choice to make.

I believe a thriving private sector is the lifeblood of our economy. I think there are outdated regulations that need to be changed. There is redtape that needs to be cut. [Applause] There you go! Yes! See? But after years now of record corporate profits, working families won't get more opportunity or bigger paychecks just by letting big banks or big oil or hedge funds make their own rules at everybody else's expense. Middle class families are not going to feel more secure because we allowed attacks on collective bargaining to go unanswered. Food stamp recipients did not cause the financial crisis; recklessness on Wall Street did. Immigrants aren't the principal reason wages haven't gone up; those decisions are made in the boardrooms that all too often put quarterly earnings over long-term returns. It's sure not the average family watching tonight that avoids paying taxes through offshore accounts. [Laughter]

The point is, I believe that in this new economy, workers and startups and small businesses need more of a voice, not less. The rules should work for them. And I'm not alone in this. This year, I plan to lift up the many businesses who have figured out that doing right by their workers or their customers or their communities ends up being good for their shareholders. And I want to spread those best practices across America. That's part of a brighter future.

In fact, it turns, out many of our best corporate citizens are also our most creative. And this brings me to the second big question we as a country have to answer: How do we reignite that spirit of innovation to meet our biggest challenges?

Sixty years ago, when the Russians beat us into space, we didn't deny Sputnik was up there. [Laughter] We didn't argue about the science or shrink our research and development budget. We built a space program almost overnight. And 12 years later, we were walking on the Moon.

Now, that spirit of discovery is in our DNA. America is Thomas Edison and the Wright Brothers and George Washington Carver. America is Grace Hopper and Katherine Johnson and Sally Ride. America is every immigrant and entrepreneur from Boston to Austin to Silicon Valley, racing to shape a better future. That's who we are.

And over the past 7 years, we've nurtured that spirit. We've protected an open Internet and taken bold new steps to get more students and low- income Americans online. We've launched next-generation manufacturing hubs and online tools that give an entrepreneur everything he or she needs to start a business in a single day. But we can do so much more.

Last year, Vice President Biden said that with a new moonshot, America can cure cancer. Last month, he worked with this Congress to give scientists at the National Institutes of Health the strongest resources that they've had in over a decade. Well–so tonight I'm announcing a new national effort to get it done. And because he's gone to the mat for all of us on so many issues over the past 40 years, I'm putting Joe in charge of mission control. For the loved ones we've all lost, for the families that we can still save, let's make America the country that cures cancer once and for all. What do you say, Joe? Let's make it happen.

Now, medical research is critical. We need the same level of commitment when it comes to developing clean energy sources. Look, if anybody still wants to dispute the science around climate change, have at it. [Laughter] You will be pretty lonely, because you'll be debating our military, most of America's business leaders, the majority of the American people, almost the entire scientific community, and 200 nations around the world who agree it's a problem and intend to solve it. But even if the planet wasn't at stake, even if 2014 wasn't the warmest year on record–until 2015 turned out to be even hotter–why would we want to pass up the chance for American businesses to produce and sell the energy of the future? Listen, 7 years ago, we made the single biggest investment in clean energy in our history. Here are the results. In fields from Iowa to Texas, wind power is now cheaper than dirtier, conventional power. On rooftops from Arizona to New York, solar is saving Americans tens of millions of dollars a year on their energy bills and employs more Americans than coal in jobs that pay better than average. We're taking steps to give homeowners the freedom to generate and store their own energy, something, by the way, that environmentalists and Tea Partiers have teamed up to support. And meanwhile, we've cut our imports of foreign oil by nearly 60 percent and cut carbon pollution more than any other country on Earth. Gas under 2 bucks a gallon ain't bad either. [Laughter]

Now we've got to accelerate the transition away from old, dirtier energy sources. Rather than subsidize the past, we should invest in the future, especially in communities that rely on fossil fuels. We do them no favor when we don't show them where the trends are going. And that's why I'm going to push to change the way we manage our oil and coal resources so that they better reflect the costs they impose on taxpayers and our planet. And that way, we put money back into those communities and put tens of thousands of Americans to work building a 21st-century transportation system.

Now, none of this is going to happen overnight. And yes, there are plenty of entrenched interests who want to protect the status quo. But the jobs we'll create, the money we'll save, the planet we'll preserve– that is the kind of future our kids and our grandkids deserve. And it's within our grasp.

Now, climate change is just one of many issues where our security is linked to the rest of the world. And that's why the third big question that we have to answer together is how to keep America safe and strong without either isolating ourselves or trying to nation-build everywhere there's a problem.

Now, I told you earlier all the talk of America's economic decline is political hot air. Well, so is all the rhetoric you hear about our enemies getting stronger and America getting weaker. Let me tell you something: The United States of America is the most powerful nation on Earth. Period. [Applause] Period. It's not even close. [Applause] It's not even close. It's not even close. We spend more on our military than the next eight nations combined. Our troops are the finest fighting force in the history of the world. [Applause] All right. No nation attacks us directly, or our allies, because they know that's the path to ruin. Surveys show our standing around the world is higher than when I was elected to this office, and when it comes to every important international issue, people of the world do not look to Beijing or Moscow to lead. They call us. So I think it's useful to level set here, because when we don't, we don't make good decisions.

Now, as someone who begins every day with an intelligence briefing, I know this is a dangerous time. But that's not primarily because of some looming superpower out there, and it's certainly not because of diminished American strength. In today's world, we're threatened less by evil empires and more by failing states.

The Middle East is going through a transformation that will play out for a generation, rooted in conflicts that date back millennia. Economic headwinds are blowing in from a Chinese economy that is in significant transition. Even as their economy severely contracts, Russia is pouring resources in to prop up Ukraine and Syria, client states that they saw slipping away from their orbit. And the international system we built after World War II is now struggling to keep pace with this new reality. It's up to us, the United States of America, to help remake that system. And to do that well, it means that we've got to set priorities. Priority number one is protecting the American people and going after terrorist networks. Both Al Qaida and now ISIL pose a direct threat to our people, because in today's world, even a handful of terrorists who place no value on human life, including their own, can do a lot of damage. They use the Internet to poison the minds of individuals inside our country. Their actions undermine and destabilize our allies. We have to take them out.

But as we focus on destroying ISIL, over-the-top claims that this is world war III just play into their hands. Masses of fighters on the back of pickup trucks, twisted souls plotting in apartments or garages, they pose an enormous danger to civilians; they have to be stopped. But they do not threaten our national existence. That is the story ISIL wants to tell. That's the kind of propaganda they use to recruit. We don't need to build them up to show that we're serious, and we sure don't need to push away vital allies in this fight by echoing the lie that ISIL is somehow representative of one of the world's largest religions. We just need to call them what they are: killers and fanatics who have to be rooted out, hunted down, and destroyed.

And that's exactly what we're doing. For more than a year, America has led a coalition of more than 60 countries to cut off ISIL's financing, disrupt their plots, stop the flow of terrorist fighters, and stamp out their vicious ideology. With nearly 10,000 airstrikes, we're taking out their leadership, their oil, their training camps, their weapons. We're training, arming, and supporting forces who are steadily reclaiming territory in Iraq and Syria.

If this Congress is serious about winning this war and wants to send a message to our troops and the world, authorize the use of military force against ISIL. Take a vote. [Applause] Take a vote. But the American people should know that with or without congressional action, ISIL will learn the same lessons as terrorists before them. If you doubt America's commitment–or mine–to see that justice is done, just ask Usama bin Laden. Ask the leader of Al Qaida in Yemen, who was taken out last year, or the perpetrator of the Benghazi attacks, who sits in a prison cell. When you come after Americans, we go after you. And it may take time, but we have long memories, and our reach has no limits.

Our foreign policy has to be focused on the threat from ISIL and Al Qaida, but it can't stop there. For even without ISIL, even without Al Qaida, instability will continue for decades in many parts of the world: in the Middle East, in Afghanistan and parts of Pakistan, in parts of Central America, in Africa and Asia. Some of these places may become safe havens for new terrorist networks. Others will just fall victim to ethnic conflict or famine, feeding the next wave of refugees. The world will look to us to help solve these problems, and our answer needs to be more than tough talk or calls to carpet-bomb civilians. That may work as a TV sound bite, but it doesn't pass muster on the world stage.

We also can't try to take over and rebuild every country that falls into crisis, even if it's done with the best of intentions. That's not leadership; that's a recipe for quagmire, spilling American blood and treasure that ultimately will weaken us. It's the lesson of Vietnam; it's the lesson of Iraq. And we should have learned it by now.

Now, fortunately there is a smarter approach: a patient and disciplined strategy that uses every element of our national power. It says America will always act, alone if necessary, to protect our people and our allies, but on issues of global concern, we will mobilize the world to work with us and make sure other countries pull their own weight. That's our approach to conflicts like Syria, where we're partnering with local forces and leading international efforts to help that broken society pursue a lasting peace. That's why we built a global coalition, with sanctions and principled diplomacy, to prevent a nuclear-armed Iran. And as we speak, Iran has rolled back its nuclear program, shipped out its uranium stockpile, and the world has avoided another war.

That's how we stopped the spread of Ebola in West Africa. Our military, our doctors, our development workers–they were heroic; they set up the platform that then allowed other countries to join in behind us and stamp out that epidemic. Hundreds of thousands, maybe a couple million, lives were saved.

That's how we forged a Trans-Pacific Partnership to open markets and protect workers and the environment and advance American leadership in Asia. It cuts 18,000 taxes on products made in America, which will then support more good jobs here in America. With TPP, China does not set the rules in that region, we do. You want to show our strength in this new century? Approve this agreement. Give us the tools to enforce it. It's the right thing to do.

Let me give you another example. Fifty years of isolating Cuba had failed to promote democracy. It set us back in Latin America. That's why we restored diplomatic relations, opened the door to travel and commerce, positioned ourselves to improve the lives of the Cuban people. So if you want to consolidate our leadership and credibility in the hemisphere, recognize that the cold war is over. Lift the embargo.

The point is, American leadership in the 21st century is not a choice between ignoring the rest of the world—except when we kill terrorists— or occupying and rebuilding whatever society is unraveling. Leadership means a wise application of military power and rallying the world behind causes that are right. It means seeing our foreign assistance as a part of our national security, not something separate, not charity.

When we lead nearly 200 nations to the most ambitious agreement in history to fight climate change, yes, that helps vulnerable countries, but it also protects our kids. When we help Ukraine defend its democracy or Colombia resolve a decades-long war, that strengthens the international order we depend on. When we help African countries feed their people and care for the sick, it's the right thing to do, and it prevents the next pandemic from reaching our shores. Right now we're on track to end the scourge of HIV/AIDS. That's within our grasp. And we have the chance to accomplish the same thing with malaria, something I'll be pushing this Congress to fund this year.

That's American strength. That's American leadership. And that kind of leadership depends on the power of our example. That's why I will keep working to shut down the prison at Guantanamo. It is expensive, it is unnecessary, and it only serves as a recruitment brochure for our enemies. There's a better way.

And that's why we need to reject any politics—any politics—that targets people because of race or religion. Let me just say this. This is not a matter of political correctness, this is a matter of understanding just what it is that makes us strong. The world respects us not just for our arsenal, it respects us for our diversity and our openness and the way we respect every faith.

His Holiness Pope Francis told this body from the very spot that I'm standing on tonight that "to imitate the hatred and violence of tyrants and murderers is the best way to take their place." When politicians insult Muslims, whether abroad or our fellow citizens, when a mosque is vandalized or a kid is called names, that doesn't make us safer. That's not telling it what—telling it like it is. It's just wrong. It diminishes us in the eyes of the world. It makes it harder to achieve our goals. It betrays who we are as a country. "We the People." Our Constitution begins with those three simple words, words we've come to recognize mean all the people, not just some; words that insist we rise and fall together, that that's how we might perfect our

Union. And that brings me to the fourth and maybe most important thing that I want to say tonight.

The future we want–all of us want–opportunity and security for our families, a rising standard of living, a sustainable, peaceful planet for our kids–all that is within our reach. But it will only happen if we work together. It will only happen if we can have rational, constructive debates. It will only happen if we fix our politics.

A better politics doesn't mean we have to agree on everything. This is a big country: different regions, different attitudes, different interests. That's one of our strengths too. Our Founders distributed power between States and branches of government and expected us to argue, just as they did, fiercely, over the size and shape of government, over commerce and foreign relations, over the meaning of liberty and the imperatives of security.

But democracy does require basic bonds of trust between its citizens. It doesn't work if we think the people who disagree with us are all motivated by malice. It doesn't work if we think that our political opponents are unpatriotic or trying to weaken America. Democracy grinds to a halt without a willingness to compromise or when even basic facts are contested or when we listen only to those who agree with us. Our public life withers when only the most extreme voices get all the attention. And most of all, democracy breaks down when the average person feels their voice doesn't matter, that the system is rigged in favor of the rich or the powerful or some special interest.

Too many Americans feel that way right now. It's one of the few regrets of my Presidency: that the rancor and suspicion between the parties has gotten worse instead of better. I have no doubt, a President with the gifts of Lincoln or Roosevelt might have better bridged the divide, and I guarantee, I'll keep trying to be better so long as I hold this office.

But, my fellow Americans, this cannot be my task–or any President's– alone. There are a whole lot of folks in this Chamber, good people, who would like to see more cooperation, would like to see a more elevated debate in Washington, but feel trapped by the imperatives of getting elected, by the noise coming out of your base. I know; you've told me. It's the worst kept secret in Washington. And a lot of you aren't enjoying being trapped in that kind of rancor.

But that means if we want a better politics–and I'm addressing the American people now–if we want a better politics, it's not enough just to change a Congressman or change a Senator or even change a President. We have to change the system to reflect our better selves.

I think we've got to end the practice of drawing our congressional districts so that politicians can pick their voters and not the other way around. Let a bipartisan group do it.

I believe we've got to reduce the influence of money in our politics so that a handful of families or hidden interests can't bankroll our elections. And if our existing approach to campaign finance reform can't pass muster in the courts, we need to work together to find a real solution. Because it's a problem. And most of you don't like raising money. [Laughter] I know. I've done it.

We've got to make it easier to vote, not harder. We need to modernize it for the way we live now. This is America: We want to make it easier for people to participate. And over the course of this year, I intend to travel the country to push for reforms that do just that. But I can't do these things on my own. Changes in our political process—in not just who gets elected, but how they get elected—that will only happen when the American people demand it. It depends on you. That's what's meant by a government of, by, and for the people.

What I'm suggesting is hard. It's a lot easier to be cynical; to accept that change is not possible and politics is hopeless and the problem is, all the folks who are elected don't care; and to believe that our voices and our actions don't matter. But if we give up now, then we forsake a better future. Those with money and power will gain greater control over the decisions that could send a young soldier to war or allow another economic disaster or roll back the equal rights and voting rights that generations of Americans have fought, even died, to secure. And then, as frustration grows, there will be voices urging us to fall back into our respective tribes, to scapegoat fellow citizens who don't look like us or pray like us or vote like we do or share the same background.

We can't afford to go down that path. It won't deliver the economy we want. It will not produce the security we want. But most of all, it contradicts everything that makes us the envy of the world.

So, my fellow Americans, whatever you may believe, whether you prefer one party or no party, whether you supported my agenda or fought as hard as you could against it, our collective futures depends on your willingness to uphold your duties as a citizen. To vote. To speak out. To stand up for others, especially the weak, especially the vulnerable, knowing that each of us is only here because somebody, somewhere, stood up for us. We need every American to stay active in our public life—and not just during election time—so that our public life reflects the goodness and the decency that I see in the American people every single day.

It is not easy. Our brand of democracy is hard. But I can promise that a little over a year from now, when I no longer hold this office, I will be right there with you as a citizen, inspired by those voices of fairness and vision, of grit and good humor and kindness, that have helped America travel so far. Voices that help us see ourselves not, first and foremost, as Black or White or Asian or Latino, not as gay or straight, immigrant or native born, not Democrat or Republican, but as Americans first, bound by a common creed. Voices Dr. King believed would have the final word: voices of "unarmed truth and unconditional love."

And they're out there, those voices. They don't get a lot of attention; they don't seek a lot of fanfare; but they're busy doing the work this country needs doing. I see them everywhere I travel in this incredible country of ours. I see you, the American people. And in your daily acts of citizenship, I see our future unfolding.

I see it in the worker on the assembly line who clocked extra shifts to keep his company open and the boss who pays him higher wages instead of laying him off. I see it in the dreamer who stays up late at night to finish her science project and the teacher who comes in early, maybe with some extra supplies that she bought because she knows that that young girl might someday cure a disease.

I see it in the American who served his time, made bad mistakes as a child, but now is dreaming of starting over. And I see it in the business owner who gives him that second chance. The protester determined to prove that justice matters and the young cop walking the beat, treating everybody with respect, doing the brave, quiet work of keeping us safe.

I see it in the soldier who gives almost everything to save his brothers, the nurse who tends to him till he can run a marathon, the community that lines up to cheer him on. It's the son who finds the courage to come out as who he is and the father whose love for that son overrides everything he's been taught.

I see it in the elderly woman who will wait in line to cast her vote as long as she has to, the new citizen who casts his vote for the first time, the volunteers at the polls who believe every vote should count. Because each of them, in different ways, know how much that precious right is worth.

That's the America I know. That's the country we love: clear eyed, big hearted, undaunted by challenge. Optimistic that unarmed truth and unconditional love will have the final word. That's what makes me so hopeful about our future. I believe in change because I believe in you, the American people. And that's why I stand here as confident as I have ever been that the state of our Union is strong.

Thank you. God bless you. God bless the United States of America. Thank you.

27

REMARKS AT A VISIT OF THE 2015 NBA CHAMPION GOLDEN STATE WARRIORS

FEBRUARY 4, 2016

W elcome to the White House, everybody. Give it up for the NBA Champion Golden State Warriors! Everybody please have a seat. Now, let me begin by saying I was hoping that Riley Curry would be here today – to share the podium with me, but I guess I'm going to have to get media training some other day. (Laughter.)

The East Room is not as loud as the "Roaracle," but Dub Nation is well represented. We've got some members of my Cabinet and Congress in the house who are big fans, and I don't just mean Harrison Barnes, who apparently they call "The Senator." (Laughter.) He's from Iowa, so maybe he's got some politics in his blood. But we've got one of the biggest Golden State Warrior fans around, our Leader in the House of Representatives, Democratic Leader Nancy Pelosi. We've got Republican Leader Kevin McCarthy is here, so this is bipartisan. We have Mayor Schaaf is here. So we're glad you're here to celebrate the best in the Bay.

I also want to recognize Warriors Executive Board member and NBA legend, one of the greatest of all time, the logo, Jerry West. As well as owner Joe Lacob, and General Manager Bob Myers. Give them a big round of applause.

Now, it is rare to be in the presence of guys from the greatest team in NBA history. So we're pretty lucky today, because we've got one of those players in the house – Steve Kerr from the 1995-'96 Chicago Bulls! (Laughter and applause.) It's good to see you back. (Laughter.)

Now, for those of you who don't know, the Warriors started this season without Coach Kerr, who was recovering from back surgery. So Luke Walton stepped up and led the team to a ridiculous 39-4 record. Unfortunately, the NBA won't let Luke count those wins as his own. (Laughter.) Which, man, that doesn't seem fair. (Laughter.) You defied the cynics, you accomplished big things, you racked up a great record, and you don't get enough credit. (Laughter and applause.) I can't imagine how that feels. (Laughter.)

Now, let's face it, the Warriors are in the midst of a pretty special two-year run. Folks are saying that they are "revolutionizing" basketball. They are so good that they seem to be just breaking the game itself. And I don't play anymore, but I still know a little bit about basketball, and this really is one of the best that we've ever seen. Great shooting, great passing, a small-ball "nuclear lineup" – it's almost not fair. And they play not just well, but they play well together. They play as a team the way basketball is supposed to be played. And it's beautiful to watch when they're working on all cylinders.

Now, let's face it, "beautiful" was not how folks described the Warriors for many years. (Laughter.) I may be one of the few who are old enough to remember the last time they were good, back in the middle of the '70s, I was – the last time they won a championship – I was 10 years old. (Laughter.) So the franchise, it had some good teams and some great players, but it had been struggling. One college player forgot that there was even a team in Oakland – that was Klay Thompson, by the way. (Laughter.)

But a few years ago, Joe Lacob took over, pointed to that 1975 championship banner and said, "That's a very lonely flag. We need another one." And last year they got it – 67 wins, 16 straight at one point. That used to seem like a lot until this year – (laughter) – where they started off 24-0. Ended last season with their first title in 40 years.

And obviously, a big part of that was league MVP, Steph Curry. Steph is a pretty good shooter. (Laughter.)

For those of you who watched the game against the Wizards last night, he was – to use slang – he was "clowning." (Laughter.) He was all jumping up and down. (Laughter and applause.) Just settle down. By the way, for the record, I heard during this summer, after our golf game, that Steph was using the excuse of Secret Service being intimidating for why he lost the match. That is not the case. (Laughter.) But he will have another opportunity. Obviously, watching Steph play is incredible. And for anybody who enjoys basketball, it is just a lot of fun.

But it's not just Steph. There's the other "Splash Brother," Klay, who dropped 37 points in a quarter, and whose jump shot is actually a little prettier. (Laughter.) I'm just saying. There were Barnes dunks, Bogut blocks, Draymond Green showing us "heart over height" every single night. Draymond is also known to add a few more words that I cannot repeat. (Laughter.) Then you've got a couple of unselfish All-Stars in their own right that were coming off the bench – Andre Iguodala and David Lee. And a bench that was so good that an opposing coach complained, "they've got two starting lineups."

In the Finals, Golden State faced Cleveland and a guy named LeBron. Down two games to one, Coach Kerr had the guts to shake up the lineup – and it worked. Andre came off the bench, played great D, took home the Finals MVP. And it was a perfect example of the kind of team this is – everybody doing their part, everybody ready to step up at any moment. Unselfish play. Folks looking out for each other.

And it's the same kind of selflessness that the Warriors show in their community, as well. They've led the way for the NBA's commitment to our My Brother's Keeper initiative, promoting mentoring in the Bay Area and nationwide. I know they met with some students in the White House mentor program earlier today. This team is also supporting the city's Oakland Promise effort to help more kids make it through college. You've had players take a stand against gun violence. They've worked with Michelle's Let's Move initiative. They've dressed up as Santa to deliver Christmas presents to those in need. And the first time I met Steph was because he had partnered with the U.N. Foundation to donate three anti-malarial mosquito nets for every three-pointer he makes. So last night, that's 33 nets. (Laughter.) So keep shooting, Steph. Not that he needs any encouragement, obviously. (Laughter.)

The point is, this is a great basketball team, but it's a great organization, it's a great culture. And these are outstanding young men. And some of them I've met before. Steph I've gotten to know a little better. They're just – they're the kind of people you want representing a city, representing the NBA, and the kind of people that you want our kids to be rooting for.

So they have a lot to be proud of. Good luck for the rest of this season. Maybe you'll break that Bulls record. But as Coach Kerr pointed out, he wins either way. Either way, he's got the record. (Laughter and applause.)

So thanks, everybody. Congratulations.

28

ADDRESS TO THE CUBAN PEOPLE, HAVANA, CUBA

MARCH 22, 2016

Thank you. Muchas gracias. Thank you so much. Thank you very much. President Castro, the people of Cuba, thank you so much for the warm welcome that I have received, that my family have received, and that our delegation has received. It is an extraordinary honor to be here today.

Before I begin, please indulge me. I want to comment on the terrorist attacks that have taken place in Brussels. The thoughts and the prayers of the American people are with the people of Belgium. We stand in solidarity with them in condemning these outrageous attacks against innocent people. We will do whatever is necessary to support our friend and ally, Belgium, in bringing to justice those who are responsible. And this is yet another reminder that the world must unite, we must be together, regardless of nationality, or race, or faith, in fighting against the scourge of terrorism. We can – and will – defeat those who threaten the safety and security of people all around the world.

To the government and the people of Cuba, I want to thank you for the kindness that you've shown to me and Michelle, Malia, Sasha, my mother-in-law, Marian.

"Cultivo una rosa blanca." In his most famous poem, Jose Marti made this offering of friendship and peace to both his friend and his enemy. Today, as the President of the United States of America, I offer the Cuban people el saludo de paz.

Havana is only 90 miles from Florida, but to get here we had to travel a great distance – over barriers of history and ideology; barriers of pain and separation. The blue waters beneath Air Force One once carried American battleships to this island – to liberate, but also to exert control over Cuba. Those waters also carried generations of Cuban revolutionaries to the United States, where they built support for their cause. And that short distance has been crossed by hundreds of thousands of Cuban exiles – on planes and makeshift rafts – who came to America in pursuit of freedom and opportunity, sometimes leaving behind everything they owned and every person that they loved.

Like so many people in both of our countries, my lifetime has spanned a time of isolation between us. The Cuban Revolution took place the same year that my father came to the United States from Kenya. The Bay of Pigs took place the year that I was born. The next year, the entire world held its breath, watching our two countries, as humanity came as close as we ever have to the horror of nuclear war. As the decades rolled by, our governments settled into a seemingly endless confrontation, fighting battles through proxies. In a world that remade itself time and again, one constant was the conflict between the United States and Cuba.

I have come here to bury the last remnant of the Cold War in the Americas. I have come here to extend the hand of friendship to the Cuban people.

I want to be clear: The differences between our governments over these many years are real and they are important. I'm sure President Castro would say the same thing – I know, because I've heard him address those differences at length. But before I discuss those issues, we also need to recognize how much we share. Because in many ways, the United States and Cuba are like two brothers who've been estranged for many years, even as we share the same blood.

We both live in a new world, colonized by Europeans. Cuba, like the United States, was built in part by slaves brought here from Africa. Like the United States, the Cuban people can trace their heritage to both slaves and slave-owners. We've welcomed both immigrants who came a great distance to start new lives in the Americas.

Over the years, our cultures have blended together. Dr. Carlos Finlay's work in Cuba paved the way for generations of doctors, including Walter Reed, who drew on Dr. Finlay's work to help combat Yellow Fever. Just as Marti wrote some of his most famous words in New York, Ernest Hemingway made a home in Cuba, and found inspiration in the waters of these shores. We share a national past-time – La Pelota – and later today our players will compete on the same Havana field that Jackie Robinson played on before he made his Major League debut. And it's said that our greatest boxer, Muhammad Ali, once paid tribute to a Cuban that he could never fight – saying that he would only be able to reach a draw with the great Cuban, Teofilo Stevenson.

So even as our governments became adversaries, our people continued to share these common passions, particularly as so many Cubans came to America. In Miami or Havana, you can find places to dance the Cha-Cha-Cha or the Salsa, and eat ropa vieja. People in both of our countries have sung along with Celia Cruz or Gloria Estefan, and now listen to reggaeton or Pitbull. (Laughter.) Millions of our people share a common religion – a faith that I paid tribute to at the Shrine of our Lady of Charity in Miami, a peace that Cubans find in La Cachita.

For all of our differences, the Cuban and American people share common values in their own lives. A sense of patriotism and a sense of pride – a lot of pride. A profound love of family. A passion for our children, a commitment to their education. And that's why I believe our grandchildren will look back on this period of isolation as an aberration, as just one chapter in a longer story of family and of friendship.

But we cannot, and should not, ignore the very real differences that we have – about how we organize our governments, our economies, and our societies. Cuba has a one-party system; the United States is a multi-party democracy. Cuba has a socialist economic model; the United States is an open market. Cuba has emphasized the role and rights of the state; the United States is founded upon the rights of the individual.

Despite these differences, on December 17th 2014, President Castro and I announced that the United States and Cuba would begin a process to normalize relations between our countries. Since then, we have established diplomatic relations and opened embassies. We've begun initiatives to cooperate on health and agriculture, education and law enforcement. We've reached agreements to restore direct flights and mail service. We've expanded commercial ties, and increased the capacity of Americans to travel and do business in Cuba.

And these changes have been welcomed, even though there are still opponents to these policies. But still, many people on both sides of this debate have asked: Why now? Why now?

There is one simple answer: What the United States was doing was not working. We have to have the courage to acknowledge that truth. A policy of isolation designed for the Cold War made little sense in the 21st century. The embargo was only hurting the Cuban people instead of helping them. And I've always believed in what Martin Luther King, Jr. called "the fierce urgency of now" – we should not fear change, we should embrace it.

That leads me to a bigger and more important reason for these changes: Creo en el pueblo Cubano. I believe in the Cuban people. This is not just a policy of normalizing relations with the Cuban government. The United States of America is normalizing relations with the Cuban people.

And today, I want to share with you my vision of what our future can be. I want the Cuban people – especially the young people – to understand why I believe that you should look to the future with hope; not the false promise which insists that things are better than they really are, or the blind optimism that says all your problems can go away tomorrow. Hope that is rooted in the future that you can choose and that you can shape, and that you can build for your country.

I'm hopeful because I believe that the Cuban people are as innovative as any people in the world.

In a global economy, powered by ideas and information, a country's greatest asset is its people. In the United States, we have a clear monument to what the Cuban people can build: it's called Miami. Here in Havana, we see that same talent in cuentapropistas, cooperatives and old cars that still run. El Cubano inventa del aire.

Cuba has an extraordinary resource – a system of education which values every boy and every girl. And in recent years, the Cuban government has begun to open up to the world, and to open up more space for that talent to thrive. In just a few years, we've seen how cuentapropistas can succeed while sustaining a distinctly Cuban spirit. Being self-employed is not about becoming more like America, it's about being yourself.

Look at Sandra Lidice Aldama, who chose to start a small business. Cubans, she said, can "innovate and adapt without losing our identity...our secret is in not copying or imitating but simply being ourselves."

Look at Papito Valladeres, a barber, whose success allowed him to improve conditions in his neighborhood. "I realize I'm not going to solve all of the world's problems," he said. "But if I can solve problems in the little piece of the world where I live, it can ripple across Havana."

That's where hope begins – with the ability to earn your own living, and to build something you can be proud of. That's why our policies focus on supporting Cubans, instead of hurting them. That's why we got rid of limits on remittances – so ordinary Cubans have more resources. That's why we're encouraging travel – which will build bridges between our people, and bring more revenue to those Cuban small businesses. That's why we've opened up space for commerce and exchanges – so that Americans and Cubans can work together to find cures for diseases, and create jobs, and open the door to more opportunity for the Cuban people.

As President of the United States, I've called on our Congress to lift the embargo. It is an outdated burden on the Cuban people. It's a burden on the Americans who want to work and do business or invest here in Cuba. It's time to lift the embargo. But even if we lifted the embargo tomorrow, Cubans would not realize their potential without continued change here in Cuba. It should be easier to open a business here in Cuba. A worker should be able to get a job directly with companies who invest here in Cuba. Two currencies shouldn't separate the type of salaries that Cubans can earn. The Internet should be available across the island, so that Cubans can connect to the wider world – and to one of the greatest engines of growth in human history.

There's no limitation from the United States on the ability of Cuba to take these steps. It's up to you. And I can tell you as a friend that sustainable prosperity in the 21st century depends upon education, health care, and environmental protection. But it also depends on the free and open exchange of ideas. If you can't access information online, if you cannot be exposed to different points of view, you will not reach your full potential. And over time, the youth will lose hope.

I know these issues are sensitive, especially coming from an American President. Before 1959, some Americans saw Cuba as something to exploit, ignored poverty, enabled corruption. And since 1959, we've been shadow-boxers in this battle of geopolitics and personalities. I know the history, but I refuse to be trapped by it.

I've made it clear that the United States has neither the capacity, nor the intention to impose change on Cuba. What changes come will depend upon the Cuban people. We will not impose our political or economic system on you. We recognize that every country, every people, must chart its own course and shape its own model. But having removed the shadow of history from our relationship, I must speak honestly about the things that I believe – the things that we, as Americans, believe. As Marti said, "Liberty is the right of every man to be honest, to think and to speak without hypocrisy."

So let me tell you what I believe. I can't force you to agree, but you should know what I think. I believe that every person should be equal under the law. Every child deserves the dignity that comes with education, and health care and food on the table and a roof over their heads. I believe citizens should be free to speak their mind without fear – to organize, and to criticize their government, and to protest peacefully, and that the rule of law should not include arbitrary detentions of people who exercise those rights. I believe that every person should have the freedom to practice their faith peacefully and publicly. And, yes, I believe voters should be able to choose their governments in free and democratic elections.

Not everybody agrees with me on this. Not everybody agrees with the American people on this. But I believe those human rights are universal. I believe they are the rights of the American people, the Cuban people, and people around the world.

Now, there's no secret that our governments disagree on many of these issues. I've had frank conversations with President Castro. For many years, he has pointed out the flaws in the American system – economic inequality; the death penalty; racial discrimination; wars abroad. That's just a sample. He has a much longer list. (Laughter.) But here's what the Cuban people need to understand: I welcome this open debate and dialogue. It's good. It's healthy. I'm not afraid of it.

We do have too much money in American politics. But, in America, it's still possible for somebody like me – a child who was raised by a single mom, a child of mixed race who did not have a lot of money – to pursue and achieve the highest office in the land. That's what's possible in America.

We do have challenges with racial bias – in our communities, in our criminal justice system, in our society – the legacy of slavery and segregation. But the fact that we have open debates within America's own democracy is what allows us to get better. In 1959, the year that my father moved to America, it was illegal for him to marry my mother, who was white, in many American states. When I first started school, we were still struggling to desegregate schools across the American South. But people organized; they protested; they debated these issues; they challenged government officials. And because of those protests, and because of those debates, and because of popular mobilization, I'm able to stand here today as an African-American and as President of the United States. That was because of the freedoms that were afforded in the United States that we were able to bring about change.

I'm not saying this is easy. There's still enormous problems in our society. But democracy is the way that we solve them. That's how we got health care for more of our people. That's how we made enormous gains in women's rights and gay rights. That's how we address the inequality that concentrates so much wealth at the top of our society. Because workers can organize and ordinary people have a voice, American democracy has given our people the opportunity to pursue their dreams and enjoy a high standard of living.

Now, there are still some tough fights. It isn't always pretty, the process of democracy. It's often frustrating. You can see that in the election going on back home. But just stop and consider this fact about the American campaign that's taking place right now. You had two Cuban Americans in the Republican Party, running against the legacy of a black man who is President, while arguing that they're the best person to beat the Democratic nominee who will either be a woman or a Democratic Socialist. (Laughter and applause.) Who would have believed that back in 1959? That's a measure of our progress as a democracy.

So here's my message to the Cuban government and the Cuban people: The ideals that are the starting point for every revolution – America's revolution, Cuba's revolution, the liberation movements around the world – those ideals find their truest expression, I believe, in democracy. Not because American democracy is perfect, but precisely because we're not. And we – like every country – need the space that democracy gives us to change. It gives individuals the capacity to be catalysts to think in new ways, and to reimagine how our society should be, and to make them better.

There's already an evolution taking place inside of Cuba, a generational change. Many suggested that I come here and ask the people of Cuba to tear something down – but I'm appealing to the young people of Cuba who will lift something up, build something new. El futuro de Cuba tiene que estar en las manos del pueblo Cubano.

And to President Castro – who I appreciate being here today – I want you to know, I believe my visit here demonstrates you do not need to fear a threat from the United States. And given your commitment to Cuba's sovereignty and self-determination, I am also confident that you need not fear the different voices of the Cuban people – and their capacity to speak, and assemble, and vote for their leaders. In fact, I'm hopeful for the future because I trust that the Cuban people will make the right decisions.

And as you do, I'm also confident that Cuba can continue to play an important role in the hemisphere and around the globe – and my hope is, is that you can do so as a partner with the United States.

We've played very different roles in the world. But no one should deny the service that thousands of Cuban doctors have delivered for the poor and suffering. Last year, American health care workers – and the U.S. military – worked side-by-side with Cubans to save lives and stamp out Ebola in West Africa. I believe that we should continue that kind of cooperation in other countries.

We've been on the different side of so many conflicts in the Americas. But today, Americans and Cubans are sitting together at the negotiating table, and we are helping the Colombian people resolve a civil war that's dragged on for decades. That kind of cooperation is good for everybody. It gives everyone in this hemisphere hope.

We took different journeys to our support for the people of South Africa in ending apartheid. But President Castro and I could both be there in Johannesburg to pay tribute to the legacy of the great Nelson Mandela. And in examining his life and his words, I'm sure we both realize we have more work to do to promote equality in our own countries – to reduce discrimination based on race in our own countries. And in Cuba, we want our engagement to help lift up the Cubans who are of African descent – who've proven that there's nothing they cannot achieve when given the chance.

We've been a part of different blocs of nations in the hemisphere, and we will continue to have profound differences about how to promote peace, security, opportunity, and human rights. But as we normalize our relations, I believe it can help foster a greater sense of unity in the Americas – todos somos Americanos.

From the beginning of my time in office, I've urged the people of the Americas to leave behind the ideological battles of the past. We are in a new era. I know that many of the issues that I've talked about lack the drama of the past. And I know that part of Cuba's identity is its pride in being a small island nation that could stand up for its rights, and shake the world. But I also know that Cuba will always stand out because of the talent, hard work, and pride of the Cuban people. That's your strength. Cuba doesn't have to be defined by being against the United States, any more than the United States should be defined by being against Cuba. I'm hopeful for the future because of the reconciliation that's taking place among the Cuban people.

I know that for some Cubans on the island, there may be a sense that those who left somehow supported the old order in Cuba. I'm sure there's a narrative that lingers here which suggests that Cuban exiles ignored the problems of pre-Revolutionary Cuba, and rejected the struggle to build a new future. But I can tell you today that so many Cuban exiles carry a memory of painful – and sometimes violent – separation. They love Cuba. A part of them still considers this their true home. That's why their passion is so strong. That's why their heartache is so great. And for the Cuban American community that I've come to know and respect, this is not just about politics. This is about family – the memory of a home that was lost; the desire to rebuild a broken bond; the hope for a better future the hope for return and reconciliation.

For all of the politics, people are people, and Cubans are Cubans. And I've come here – I've traveled this distance – on a bridge that was built by Cubans on both sides of the Florida Straits. I first got to know the talent and passion of the Cuban people in America. And I know how they have suffered more than the pain of exile – they also know what it's like to be an outsider, and to struggle, and to work harder to make sure their children can reach higher in America.

So the reconciliation of the Cuban people – the children and grandchildren of revolution, and the children and grandchildren of exile – that is fundamental to Cuba's future.

You see it in Gloria Gonzalez, who traveled here in 2013 for the first time after 61 years of separation, and was met by her sister, Llorca. "You recognized me, but I didn't recognize you," Gloria said after she embraced her sibling. Imagine that, after 61 years.

You see it in Melinda Lopez, who came to her family's old home. And as she was walking the streets, an elderly woman recognized her as her mother's daughter, and began to cry. She took her into her home and showed her a pile of photos that included Melinda's baby picture, which her mother had sent 50 years ago. Melinda later said, "So many of us are now getting so much back."

You see it in Cristian Miguel Soler, a young man who became the first of his family to travel here after 50 years. And meeting relatives for the first time, he said, "I realized that family is family no matter the distance between us."

Sometimes the most important changes start in small places. The tides of history can leave people in conflict and exile and poverty. It takes time for those circumstances to change. But the recognition of a common humanity, the reconciliation of people bound by blood and a belief in one another – that's where progress begins. Understanding, and listening, and forgiveness. And if the Cuban people face the future together, it will be more likely that the young people of today will be able to live with dignity and achieve their dreams right here in Cuba.

The history of the United States and Cuba encompass revolution and conflict;

struggle and sacrifice; retribution and, now, reconciliation. It is time, now, for us to leave the past behind. It is time for us to look forward to the future together – un future de esperanza. And it won't be easy, and there will be setbacks. It will take time. But my time here in Cuba renews my hope and my confidence in what the Cuban people will do. We can make this journey as friends, and as neighbors, and as family – together. Si se puede. Muchas gracias.

29

REMARKS ON EQUAL PAY DAY AT THE BELMONT-PAUL WOMEN'S EQUALITY NATIONAL MUSEUM

APRIL 12, 2016

Thank you very much, everybody. Thank you. Thank you. Everybody, please, have a seat. Have a seat.

Well, hello, everybody. Thank you to Chitra for the introduction. It should be noted that today is Equal Pay Day, which means a woman has to work about this far into 2016 just to earn what a man earned in 2015. And what better place to commemorate this day than here at this house, where some of our country's most important history took place, and where this history needs to inform the work that remains to be done.

I want to thank some of the leaders who've worked to keep the house standing. We've got members of Congress like Senator Barbara Mikulski, who's fought to preserve this site for years and has been the longest-serving woman in the United States Senate. We are so proud of her. Our Secretary of the Interior, Sally Jewell, and her team, as we celebrate the 100th birthday of the National Park Service this year.

One of our greatest athletes of all time, one of the earliest advocates for equal pay for professional female athletes, and a heroine of mine when I was still young and fancied myself a tennis player – (laughter) – Billie Jean King is in the house. And the National Woman's Party Board of Directors, Page Harrington, and the Executive Director of the House and the Museum. Over the years, Page and her staff have built a community and cared for this house, repairing every cracked pipe and patching every leaked roof. We are grateful for their stewardship. I know it was not easy.

Equal pay for equal work should be a fundamental principle of our economy. It's the idea that whether you're a high school teacher, a business executive, or a professional soccer player or tennis player, your work should be equally valued and rewarded, whether you are a man or a woman.

It's a simple ideal. It's a simple principle. It's one that our Leader of the Democratic Caucus in the House, Nancy Pelosi, has been fighting for, for years. But it's one where we still fall short. Today, the typical woman who works full-time earns 79 cents for every dollar that a typical man makes. And the gap is even wider for women of color. The typical black woman makes only 60 cents, a Latino woman 55 cents for every dollar that a white man earns. Now, if we truly value fairness, then America should be a level playing field where everyone who works hard gets a chance to succeed. And that's good for America, because we don't want some of our best players on the sidelines.

That's why the first bill that I signed as President was the Lilly Ledbetter Fair Pay Act. Earlier this year, on the anniversary of that day, the Equal Employment Opportunity Commission and the Department of Labor acted to begin collecting annual data on pay by gender, race, and ethnicity. And this action will strengthen the enforcement of equal pay laws that are already on the books, and help employers address pay gaps on their own.

And to build on these efforts, Congress needs to pass the Paycheck Fairness Act to put sensible rules in place and make sure – and make sure that employees who discuss their salaries don't face retaliation by their employers.

But I'm not here just to say we should close the wage gap. I'm here to say we will close the wage gap. And if you don't believe me, then – if you don't believe that we're going to close our wage gap, you need to come visit this house, because this house has a story to tell.

This is the story of the National Women's Party, whose members fought to have their voices heard. These women first organized in 1912, with little money but big hopes for equality for women all around the world. They wanted an equal say over their children, over their property, their earnings, their inheritance; equal rights to their citizenship and a say in their government; equal opportunities in schools, in universities, workplaces, public service, and, yes, equal pay for equal work. And they understood that the power of their voice in our democracy was the first step in achieving these broader goals.

Their leader, Alice Paul, was a brilliant community organizer and political strategist, and she recruited women and men from across the country to join their cause. And they began picketing seven days a week in front of the White House to demand their right to vote. They were mocked. They were derided. They were arrested. They were beaten. There were force-feedings during hunger strikes. And through all this, women, young and old, kept marching for suffrage, kept protesting for suffrage.

And in 1920, they won that right. We ratified the 19th Amendment. But the suffragists didn't stop there. They moved into this historic house and they continued their work. From these rooms, steps away from the Capitol, they drafted speeches and letters and legislation. They pushed Congress and fought for the passage of the Equal Rights Amendment. They advocated for the inclusion of women in the U.N. Charter and the 1964 Civil Rights Act. They campaigned for women who were running for Congress.

This house became a hotbed of activism, a centerpiece for the struggle for equality, a monument to fight not just for women's equality, but ultimately, for equality for everybody. Because one of the things we've learned is, is that the effort to make sure that everybody is treated fairly is connected.

And so, today, I'm very proud to designate it as America's newest national monument – the Belmont-Paul Women's Equality National Monument, right here in Washington, D.C.

We do this to help tell the story of these suffragists. In these rooms, they pursued ideals which shouldn't be relegated to the archives of history, shouldn't be behind glass cases, because the story of their fighting is our story. I want young girls and boys to come here, 10, 20, 100 years from now, to know that women fought for equality, it was not just given to them. I want them to come here and be astonished that there was ever a time when women could not vote. I want them to be astonished that there was ever a time when women earned less than men for doing the same work. I want them to be astonished that there was ever a time when women were vastly outnumbered in the boardroom or in Congress, that there was ever a time when a woman had never sat in the Oval Office.

I don't know how long it will take to get there, but I know we're getting closer to that day, because of the work of generations of active, committed citizens. One of the interesting things, as I was just looking through some of the rooms – there was Susan B. Anthony's desk. You had Elizabeth Cady Stanton's chair. And you realize that those early suffragists had proceeded Alice Paul by a generation. They had passed away by the time that the vote was finally granted to women. And it makes you realize – and I say this to young people all the time – that this is not a sprint, this is a marathon. It's not the actions of one person, one individual, but it is a collective effort, where each generation has its own duty, its own responsibility, its own role to fulfill in advancing the cause of our democracy.

That's why we're getting closer, because I know there's a whole new generation of women and men who believe so deeply that we've got to close these gaps. I have faith because what this house shows us is that the story of America is a story of progress. And it will continue to be a story of progress as long as people are willing to keep pushing and keep organizing, and, yes, keep voting for people committed to this cause and to full equality for every American.

And so I'm hoping that a young generation will come here and draw inspiration from the efforts of people who came before them. After women won the right to vote, Alice Paul, who lived most of her life in this very house, said, "It is incredible to me that any woman should consider the right for full equality won. It has just begun." And that's the thing about America – we are never finished. We are a constant work in progress. And our future belongs to every free woman and man who takes up the hard work of citizenship, to win full equality and shape our own destiny.

That is the story that this house tells. It is now a national monument that young people will be inspired by for years to come. It would not have happened without the extraordinary efforts of many of the people in this room – not only their active support of this house and preserving it, but also the outstanding example that they are setting, that you are setting.

I'm very proud of you. Congratulations. Thank you very much, everybody.

30

SPEECH AT THE HIROSHIMA PEACE MEMORIAL

MAY 27, 2016

Seventy-one years ago, on a bright, cloudless morning, death fell from the sky and the world was changed. A flash of light and a wall of fire destroyed a city and demonstrated that mankind possessed the means to destroy itself.

Why do we come to this place, to Hiroshima? We come to ponder a terrible force unleashed in a not so distant past. We come to mourn the dead, including over 100,000 in Japanese men, women and children; thousands of Koreans; a dozen Americans held prisoner. Their souls speak to us. They ask us to look inward, to take stock of who we are and what we might become.

It is not the fact of war that sets Hiroshima apart. Artifacts tell us that violent conflict appeared with the very first man. Our early ancestors, having learned to make blades from flint and spears from wood, used these tools not just for hunting, but against their own kind. On every continent, the history of civilization is filled with war, whether driven by scarcity of grain or hunger for gold; compelled by nationalist fervor or religious zeal. Empires have risen and fallen. Peoples have been subjugated and liberated. And at each juncture, innocents have suffered, a countless toll, their names forgotten by time.

The World War that reached its brutal end in Hiroshima and Nagasaki was fought among the wealthiest and most powerful of nations. Their civilizations had given the world great cities and magnificent art. Their thinkers had advanced ideas of justice and harmony and truth. And yet, the war grew out of the same base instinct for domination or conquest that had caused conflicts among the simplest tribes; an old pattern amplified by new capabilities and without new constraints. In the span of a few years, some 60 million people would die – men, women, children no different than us, shot, beaten, marched, bombed, jailed, starved, gassed to death.

There are many sites around the world that chronicle this war – memorials that tell stories of courage and heroism; graves and empty camps that echo of unspeakable depravity. Yet in the image of a mushroom cloud that rose into these skies, we are most starkly reminded of humanity's core contradiction; how the very spark that marks us as a species – our thoughts, our imagination, our language, our tool-making, our ability to set ourselves apart from nature and bend it to our will – those very things also give us the capacity for unmatched destruction.

How often does material advancement or social innovation blind us to this truth. How easily we learn to justify violence in the name of some higher cause. Every great religion promises a pathway to love and peace and righteousness, and yet no religion has been spared from believers who have claimed their faith as a license to kill. Nations arise, telling a story that binds people together in sacrifice and cooperation, allowing for remarkable feats, but those same stories have so often been used to oppress and dehumanize those who are different.

Science allows us to communicate across the seas and fly above the clouds; to cure disease and understand the cosmos. But those same discoveries can be turned into ever-more efficient killing machines.

The wars of the modern age teach this truth. Hiroshima teaches this truth. Techno-logical progress without an equivalent progress in human institutions can doom us. The scientific revolution that led to the splitting of an atom requires a moral revolu-tion, as well.

That is why we come to this place. We stand here, in the middle of this city, and force ourselves to imagine the moment the bomb fell. We force ourselves to feel the dread of children confused by what they see. We listen to a silent cry. We remember all the innocents killed across the arc of that terrible war, and the wars that came before, and the wars that would follow.

Mere words cannot give voice to such suffering, but we have a shared responsi-bility to look directly into the eye of history and ask what we must do differently to curb such suffering again. Someday the voices of the hibakusha will no longer be with us to bear witness. But the memory of the morning of August 6th, 1945 must never fade. That memory allows us to fight complacency. It fuels our moral imagina-tion. It allows us to change.

And since that fateful day, we have made choices that give us hope. The United States and Japan forged not only an alliance, but a friendship that has won far more for our people than we could ever claim through war. The nations of Europe built a Union that replaced battlefields with bonds of commerce and democracy. Oppressed peoples and nations won liberation. An international community established institu-tions and treaties that worked to avoid war and aspire to restrict and roll back, and ultimately eliminate the existence of nuclear weapons.

Still, every act of aggression between nations; every act of terror and corruption and cruelty and oppression that we see around the world shows our work is never done. We may not be able to eliminate man's capacity to do evil, so nations — and the alliances that we've formed — must possess the means to defend ourselves. But among those nations like my own that hold nuclear stockpiles, we must have the courage to escape the logic of fear, and pursue a world without them.

We may not realize this goal in my lifetime. But persistent effort can roll back the possibility of catastrophe. We can chart a course that leads to the destruction of these stockpiles. We can stop the spread to new nations, and secure deadly materials from fanatics.

And yet that is not enough. For we see around the world today how even the crudest rifles and barrel bombs can serve up violence on a terrible scale. We must change our mindset about war itself — to prevent conflict through diplomacy, and strive to end conflicts after they've begun; to see our growing interdependence as a cause for peaceful cooperation and not violent competition; to define our nations not by our capacity to destroy, but by what we build.

And perhaps above all, we must reimagine our connection to one another as members of one human race. For this, too, is what makes our species unique. We're not bound by genetic code to repeat the mistakes of the past. We can learn. We can choose. We can tell our children a different story — one that describes a common humanity; one that makes war less likely and cruelty less easily accepted.

We see these stories in the hibakusha — the woman who forgave a pilot who flew the plane that dropped the atomic bomb, because she recognized that what she really hated was war itself; the man who sought out families of Americans killed here, because he believed their loss was equal to his own.

My own nation's story began with simple words: All men are created equal, and endowed by our Creator with certain unalienable rights, including life, liberty and the pursuit of happiness. Realizing that ideal has never been easy, even within our own borders, even among our own citizens.

But staying true to that story is worth the effort. It is an ideal to be strived for; an ideal that extends across continents, and across oceans. The irreducible worth of every person, the insistence that every life is precious; the radical and necessary notion that we are part of a single human family — that is the story that we all must tell.

That is why we come to Hiroshima. So that we might think of people we love – the first smile from our children in the morning; the gentle touch from a spouse over the kitchen table; the comforting embrace of a parent — we can think of those things and know that those same precious moments took place here seventy-one years ago. Those who died — they are like us. Ordinary people understand this, I think. They do not want more war. They would rather that the wonders of science be focused on improving life, and not eliminating it.

When the choices made by nations, when the choices made by leaders reflect this simple wisdom, then the lesson of Hiroshima is done.

The world was forever changed here. But today, the children of this city will go through their day in peace. What a precious thing that is. It is worth protecting, and then extending to every child. That is the future we can choose — a future in which Hiroshima and Nagasaki are known not as the dawn of atomic warfare, but as the start of our own moral awakening.

31

2016 MEMORIAL DAY ADDRESS AT ARLINGTON CEMETERY

MAY 30, 2016

Secretary Carter, General Dunford, Mr. Hallinan, Major General Becker, members of our Armed Forces, veterans, and most of all, our Gold Star families: I'm honored to be with you once again as we pay our respects, as Americans, to those who gave their lives for us all.

Here, at Arlington, the deafening sounds of combat have given way to the silence of these sacred hills. The chaos and confusion of battle has yielded to perfect, precise rows of peace. The Americans who rest here, and their families – the best of us, those from whom we asked everything – ask of us today only one thing in return: that we remember them.

If you look closely at the white markers that grace these hills, one thing you'll notice is that so many of the years – dates of birth and dates of death – are so close together. They belong to young Americans; those who never lived to be honored as veterans for their service – men who battled their own brothers in Civil War, those who fought as a band of brothers an ocean away, men and women who redefine heroism for a new generation. There are generals buried beside privates they led. Americans known as "Dad" or "Mom." Some only known to God. As Mr. Hallinan, a Marine who then watched over these grounds has said, "everyone here is someone's hero."

Those who rest beneath this silence – not only here at Arlington, but at veterans' cemeteries across our country and around the world, and all who still remain missing – they didn't speak the loudest about their patriotism. They let their actions do that. Whether they stood up in times of war, signed up in times of peace, or were called up by a draft board, they embodied the best of America.

As Commander-in-Chief, I have no greater responsibility than leading our men and women in uniform; I have no more solemn obligation sending them into harm's way. I think about this every time I approve an operation as President. Every time, as a husband and father, that I sign a condolence letter. Every time Michelle and I sit at the bedside of a wounded warrior or grieve and hug members of a Gold Star Family.

Less than one percent of our nation wears the uniform, and so few Americans sees this patriotism with their own eyes or knows someone who exemplifies it. But every day, there are American families who pray for the sound of a familiar voice when the phone rings. For the sound of a loved one's letter or email arriving. More than one million times in our history, it didn't come. And instead, a car pulled up to the house. And there was a knock on the front door. And the sounds of Taps floated through a cemetery's trees.

For us, the living – those of us who still have a voice – it is our responsibility, our obligation, to fill that silence with our love and our support and our gratitude – and not just with our words, but with our actions. For truly remembering, and truly honoring these fallen Americans means being there for their parents, and their spouses, and their children – like the boys and girls here today, wearing red shirts and bearing photos of the fallen. Your moms and dads would be so proud of you. And we are, too.

Truly remembering means that after our fallen heroes gave everything to get their battle buddies home, we have to make sure our veterans get everything that they have earned, from good health care to a good job. And we have to do better; our work is never done. We have to be there not only when we need them, but when they need us.

Thirty days before he would be laid to rest a short walk from here, President Kennedy told us that a nation reveals itself not only by the people it produces, but by those it remembers. Not everyone will serve. Not everyone will visit this national sanctuary. But we remember our best in every corner of our country from which they came. We remember them by teaching our children at schools with fallen heroes' names, like Dorie Miller Elementary in San Antonio. Or being good neighbors in communities named after great generals, like McPherson, Kansas. Or when we walk down 1st Sgt. Bobby Mendez Way in Brooklyn, or drive across the Hoover Dam on a bridge that bears Pat Tillman's name.

We reveal ourselves in our words and deeds, but also by the simple act of listening. My fellow Americans, today and every day, listen to the stories these Gold Star families and veterans have to tell. Ask about who he or she was, why they volunteered. Hear from those who loved them about what their smile looked like, and their laugh sounded like, and the dreams they had for their lives.

Since we gathered here one year ago, more than 20 brave Americans have given their lives for the security of our people in Afghanistan. We pray for them all, and for their families. In Iraq, in our fight against ISIL, three Americans have given their lives in combat on our behalf. And today, I ask you to remember their stories, as well.

Charles Keating, IV – Charlie, or Chuck, or "C-4" – was born into a family of veterans, All-American athletes and Olympians – even a Gold Medalist. So, naturally, Charlie, and the love of his life, Brooke, celebrated their anniversary on the Fourth of July. She called him the "huge goofball" everybody wanted to be friends with – the adventurer who surfed and spearfished and planned to sail around the world.

When the Twin Towers fell, he was in high school, and he decided to enlist –

joined the SEALs because, he told his friends, it was the hardest thing to do. He deployed to Afghanistan and three times to Iraq, earning a Bronze Star for valor. Earlier this month, while assisting local forces in Iraq who had come under attack, he gave his life.

A few days later, one of his platoon mates sent Charlie's parents a letter from Iraq. "Please tell everyone Chuck saved a lot of lives today," it said. He left us, "with that big signature smile on his handsome face, as always. Chuck was full of aloha, but was also a ferocious warrior." Today, we honor Chief Special Warfare Officer Charles Keating IV.

Louis Cardin was the sixth of seven children, a Californian with an infectious wit who always had a joke at the ready to help someone get through a tough time. When his siblings ran around the house as kids, his mom, Pat, would yell after them: "Watch that baby's safety margin!" Today, she realizes that what she was really doing was raising a Marine. As a teenager, he proudly signed up. Louie graduated high school on a Friday. Three days later, on Monday morning, the Marines came to pick him up. That was 10 years ago. One morning this March, a Marine knocked on his mother's door again. On his fifth tour, at a fire base in Iraq, Louie gave his life while protecting the Marines under his command.

Putting others before himself was what Louie did best. He chose to live in the barracks with his buddies even when he could have taken a house off base. He volunteered to babysit for friends who needed a date night. He'd just earned a promotion to mentor his fellow Marines. When they brought Louie home, hundreds of strangers lined freeway overpasses and the streets of Southern California to salute him. And today, we salute Staff Sergeant Louis Cardin.

Joshua Wheeler's sister says he was "exactly what was right about this world. He came from nothing and he really made something of himself." As a kid, Josh was the one who made sure his brother and four half-sisters were dressed and fed and off to school. When there wasn't food in the cupboard, he grabbed his hunting rifle and came back with a deer for dinner. When his country needed him, he enlisted in the Army at age 19.

He deployed to Iraq and Afghanistan – 14 times; earned 11 Bronze Stars, four for valor. Last October, as ISIL terrorists prepared to execute 70 hostages, Josh and his fellow Special Ops went in and rescued them. Every single one walked free. "We were already dead," one of the hostages said, "then God sent us a force from the sky." That force was the U.S. Army, including Josh Wheeler.

Josh was the doting dad who wrote notes to his kids in the stacks of books he read. Flying home last summer to be with his wife, Ashley, who was about to give birth, he scribbled one note in the novel he was reading, just to tell his unborn son he was on his way. Ashley Wheeler is with us here today, holding their 10-month-old son, David. Ashley says Josh's memory makes her think about how can she be a better citizen. And she hopes it's what other people think about, too. Today, this husband and father rests here, in Arlington, in Section 60. And as Americans, we resolve to be better – better people, better citizens, because of Master Sergeant Joshua Wheeler.

A nation reveals itself not only by the people it produces, but by those it remembers. We do so not just by hoisting a flag, but by lifting up our neighbors. Not just by pausing in silence, but by practicing in our own lives the ideals of opportunity and liberty and equality that they fought for. We can serve others, and contribute to the causes they believed in, and above all, keep their stories alive so that one day, when he grows up and thinks of his dad, an American like David Wheeler can tell them, as well, the stories of the lives that others gave for all of us.

We are so proud of them. We are so grateful for their sacrifice. We are so thankful to those families of the fallen. May God bless our fallen and their families. May He bless all of you. And may He forever bless these United States of America.

32

FAREWELL ADDRESS, CHICAGO, ILLINOIS

SEPT. 24, 2016

H ello, Chicago! It's good to be home! Thank you, everybody. Thank you. Thank you so much. Thank you. All right, everybody sit down. We're on live TV here. I've got to move. You can tell that I'm a lame duck because nobody is following instructions. Everybody have a seat.

My fellow Americans – Michelle and I have been so touched by all the well wishes that we've received over the past few weeks. But tonight, it's my turn to say thanks. Whether we have seen eye-to-eye or rarely agreed at all, my conversations with you, the American people, in living rooms and in schools, at farms, on factory floors, at diners and on distant military outposts –– those conversations are what have kept me honest, and kept me inspired, and kept me going. And every day, I have learned from you. You made me a better President, and you made me a better man.

So I first came to Chicago when I was in my early 20s. And I was still trying to figure out who I was, still searching for a purpose in my life. And it was a neighborhood not far from here where I began working with church groups in the shadows of closed steel mills. It was on these streets where I witnessed the power of faith, and the quiet dignity of working people in the face of struggle and loss.

[…] This is where I learned that change only happens when ordinary people get involved and they get engaged, and they come together to demand it.

After eight years as your President, I still believe that. And it's not just my belief. It's the beating heart of our American idea –– our bold experiment in self-government. It's the conviction that we are all created equal, endowed by our Creator with certain unalienable rights, among them life, liberty, and the pursuit of happiness. It's the insistence that these rights, while self-evident, have never been self-executing; that We, the People, through the instrument of our democracy, can form a more perfect union.

What a radical idea. A great gift that our Founders gave to us: The freedom to chase our individual dreams through our sweat and toil and imagination, and the imperative to strive together, as well, to achieve a common good, a greater good.

For 240 years, our nation's call to citizenship has given work and purpose to each new generation. It's what led patriots to choose republic over tyranny, pioneers to trek west, slaves to brave that makeshift railroad to freedom. It's what pulled immigrants and refugees across oceans and the Rio Grande. It's what pushed women to reach for the ballot. It's what powered workers to organize. It's why GIs gave their lives at Omaha Beach and Iwo Jima, Iraq and Afghanistan. And why men and women from Selma to Stonewall were prepared to give theirs, as well.

So that's what we mean when we say America is exceptional – not that our nation has been flawless from the start, but that we have shown the capacity to change and make life better for those who follow. Yes, our progress has been uneven. The work of democracy has always been hard. It's always been contentious. Sometimes it's been bloody. For every two steps forward, it often feels we take one step back. But the long sweep of America has been defined by forward motion, a constant widening of our founding creed to embrace all and not just some.

If I had told you eight years ago that America would reverse a great recession, reboot our auto industry, and unleash the longest stretch of job creation in our history – if I had told you that we would open up a new chapter with the Cuban people, shut down Iran's nuclear weapons program without firing a shot, take out the mastermind of 9/11 – if I had told you that we would win marriage equality, and secure the right to health insurance for another 20 million of our fellow citizens — if I had told you all that, you might have said our sights were set a little too high. But that's what we did. That's what you did.

You were the change. You answered people's hopes, and because of you, by almost every measure, America is a better, stronger place than it was when we started.

In 10 days, the world will witness a hallmark of our democracy [...] the peaceful transfer of power from one freely elected President to the next. I committed to President-elect Trump that my administration would ensure the smoothest possible transition, just as President Bush did for me. Because it's up to all of us to make sure our government can help us meet the many challenges we still face.

We have what we need to do so. We have everything we need to meet those challenges. After all, we remain the wealthiest, most powerful, and most respected nation on Earth. Our youth, our drive, our diversity and openness, our boundless capacity for risk and reinvention means that the future should be ours. But that potential will only be realized if our democracy works. Only if our politics better reflects the decency of our people. Only if all of us, regardless of party affiliation or particular interests, help restore the sense of common purpose that we so badly need right now.

That's what I want to focus on tonight: The state of our democracy. Understand, democracy does not require uniformity. Our founders argued. They quarreled. Eventually they compromised. They expected us to do the same. But they knew that democracy does require a basic sense of solidarity — the idea that for all our outward differences, we're all in this together; that we rise or fall as one.

There have been moments throughout our history that threatens that solidarity. And the beginning of this century has been one of those times. A shrinking world, growing inequality; demographic change and the specter of terrorism -- these forces haven't just tested our security and our prosperity, but are testing our democracy, as well. And how we meet these challenges to our democracy will determine our ability to educate our kids, and create good jobs, and protect our homeland. In other words, it will determine our future.

To begin with, our democracy won't work without a sense that everyone has economic opportunity. And the good news is that today the economy is growing again. Wages, incomes, home values, and retirement accounts are all rising again. Poverty is falling again. The wealthy are paying a fairer share of taxes even as the stock market shatters records. The unemployment rate is near a 10-year low. The uninsured rate has never, ever been lower. Health care costs are rising at the slowest rate in 50 years. And I've said and I mean it – if anyone can put together a plan that is demonstrably better than the improvements we've made to our health care system and that covers as many people at less cost, I will publicly support it.

Because that, after all, is why we serve. Not to score points or take credit, but to make people's lives better.

But for all the real progress that we've made, we know it's not enough. Our economy doesn't work as well or grow as fast when a few prosper at the expense of a growing middle class and ladders for folks who want to get into the middle class. That's the economic argument. But stark inequality is also corrosive to our democratic ideal. While the top one percent has amassed a bigger share of wealth and income, too many families, in inner cities and in rural counties, have been left behind – the laid-off factory worker; the waitress or health care worker who's just barely getting by and struggling to pay the bills – convinced that the game is fixed against them, that their government only serves the interests of the powerful – that's a recipe for more cynicism and polarization in our politics.

But there are no quick fixes to this long-term trend. I agree, our trade should be fair and not just free. But the next wave of economic dislocations won't come from overseas. It will come from the relentless pace of automation that makes a lot of good, middle-class jobs obsolete.

And so we're going to have to forge a new social compact to guarantee all our kids the education they need – to give workers the power to unionize for better wages; to update the social safety net to reflect the way we live now, and make more reforms to the tax code so corporations and individuals who reap the most from this new economy don't avoid their obligations to the country that's made their very success possible.

We can argue about how to best achieve these goals. But we can't be complacent about the goals themselves. For if we don't create opportunity for all people, the disaffection and division that has stalled our progress will only sharpen in years to come.

There's a second threat to our democracy – and this one is as old as our nation itself. After my election, there was talk of a post-racial America. And such a vision, however well-intended, was never realistic. Race remains a potent and often divisive force in our society. Now, I've lived long enough to know that race relations are better than they were 10, or 20, or 30 years ago, no matter what some folks say. You can see it not just in statistics, you see it in the attitudes of young Americans across the political spectrum.

But we're not where we need to be. And all of us have more work to do. If every economic issue is framed as a struggle between a hardworking white middle class and an undeserving minority, then workers of all shades are going to be left fighting for scraps while the wealthy withdraw further into their private enclaves. If we're unwilling to invest in the children of immigrants, just because they don't look like us, we will diminish the prospects of our own children – because those brown kids will represent a larger and larger share of America's workforce. And we have shown that our economy doesn't have to be a zero-sum game. Last year, incomes rose for all races, all age groups, for men and for women.

So if we're going to be serious about race going forward, we need to uphold laws against discrimination – in hiring, and in housing, and in education, and in the criminal justice system. That is what our Constitution and our highest ideals require.

But laws alone won't be enough. Hearts must change. It won't change overnight. Social attitudes oftentimes take generations to change. But if our democracy is to work in this increasingly diverse nation, then each one of us need to try to heed the advice of a great character in American fiction – Atticus Finch – who said "You never really understand a person until you consider things from his point of view...until you climb into his skin and walk around in it."

For blacks and other minority groups, it means tying our own very real struggles for justice to the challenges that a lot of people in this country face – not only the refugee, or the immigrant, or the rural poor, or the transgender American, but also the middle-aged white guy who, from the outside, may seem like he's got advantages, but has seen his world upended by economic and cultural and technological change. We have to pay attention, and listen.

For white Americans, it means acknowledging that the effects of slavery and Jim Crow didn't suddenly vanish in the '60s – that when minority groups voice discontent, they're not just engaging in reverse racism or practicing political correctness. When they wage peaceful protest, they're not demanding special treatment but the equal treatment that our Founders promised.

For native-born Americans, it means reminding ourselves that the stereotypes about immigrants today were said, almost word for word, about the Irish, and Italians, and Poles – who it was said we're going to destroy the fundamental character of America. And as it turned out, America wasn't weakened by the presence of these newcomers; these newcomers embraced this nation's creed, and this nation was strengthened.

So regardless of the station that we occupy, we all have to try harder. We all have to start with the premise that each of our fellow citizens loves this country just as much as we do; that they value hard work and family just like we do; that their children are just as curious and hopeful and worthy of love as our own.

And that's not easy to do. For too many of us, it's become safer to retreat into our own bubbles, whether in our neighborhoods or on college campuses, or places of worship, or especially our social media feeds, surrounded by people who look like us and share the same political outlook and never challenge our assumptions. The rise of naked partisanship, and increasing economic and regional stratification, the splintering of our media into a channel for every taste – all this makes this great sorting seem natural, even inevitable. And increasingly, we become so secure in our bubbles that we start accepting only information, whether it's true or not, that fits our opinions, instead of basing our opinions on the evidence that is out there.

And this trend represents a third threat to our democracy. But politics is a battle of ideas. That's how our democracy was designed. In the course of a healthy debate, we prioritize different goals, and the different means of reaching them. But without some common baseline of facts, without a willingness to admit new information, and concede that your opponent might be making a fair point, and that science and reason matter – then we're going to keep talking past each other, and we'll make common ground and compromise impossible.

And isn't that part of what so often makes politics dispiriting? How can elected officials rage about deficits when we propose to spend money on preschool for kids, but not when we're cutting taxes for corporations? How do we excuse ethical lapses in our own party, but pounce when the other party does the same thing? It's not just dishonest, this selective sorting of the facts; it's self-defeating. Because, as my mother used to tell me, reality has a way of catching up with you.

Take the challenge of climate change. In just eight years, we've halved our dependence on foreign oil; we've doubled our renewable energy; we've led the world to an agreement that has the promise to save this planet. But without bolder action, our children won't have time to debate the existence of climate change. They'll be busy dealing with its effects: more environmental disasters, more economic disruptions, waves of climate refugees seeking sanctuary.

Now, we can and should argue about the best approach to solve the problem. But to simply deny the problem not only betrays future generations, it betrays the essential spirit of this country – the essential spirit of innovation and practical problem-solving that guided our Founders.

It is that spirit, born of the Enlightenment, that made us an economic powerhouse – the spirit that took flight at Kitty Hawk and Cape Canaveral; the spirit that cures disease and put a computer in every pocket.

It's that spirit – a faith in reason, and enterprise, and the primacy of right over might – that allowed us to resist the lure of fascism and tyranny during the Great Depression; that allowed us to build a post-World War II order with other democracies, an order based not just on military power or national affiliations but built on principles – the rule of law, human rights, freedom of religion, and speech, and assembly, and an independent press.

That order is now being challenged – first by violent fanatics who claim to speak for Islam; more recently by autocrats in foreign capitals who see free markets and open democracies and and civil society itself as a threat to their power. The peril each poses to our democracy is more far-reaching than a car bomb or a missile. It represents the fear of change; the fear of people who look or speak or pray differently; a contempt for the rule of law that holds leaders accountable; an intolerance of dissent and free thought; a belief that the sword or the gun or the bomb or the propaganda machine is the ultimate arbiter of what's true and what's right.

Because of the extraordinary courage of our men and women in uniform, because of our intelligence officers, and law enforcement, and diplomats who support our troops – no foreign terrorist organization has successfully planned and executed an attack on our homeland these past eight years. And although Boston and Orlando and San Bernardino and Fort Hood remind us of how dangerous radicalization can be, our law enforcement agencies are more effective and vigilant than ever. We have taken out tens of thousands of terrorists – including bin Laden. The global coalition we're leading against ISIL has taken out their leaders, and taken away about half their territory. ISIL will be destroyed, and no one who threatens America will ever be safe.

And to all who serve or have served, it has been the honor of my lifetime to be your Commander-in-Chief. And we all owe you a deep debt of gratitude.

But protecting our way of life, that's not just the job of our military. Democracy can buckle when we give in to fear. So, just as we, as citizens, must remain vigilant against external aggression, we must guard against a weakening of the values that make us who we are.

And that's why, for the past eight years, I've worked to put the fight against terrorism on a firmer legal footing. That's why we've ended torture, worked to close Gitmo, reformed our laws governing surveillance to protect privacy and civil liberties. That's why I reject discrimination against Muslim Americans, who are just as patriotic as we are.

That's why we cannot withdraw from big global fights – to expand democracy, and human rights, and women's rights, and LGBT rights. No matter how imperfect our efforts, no matter how expedient ignoring such values may seem, that's part of defending America. For the fight against extremism and intolerance and sectarianism and chauvinism are of a piece with the fight against authoritarianism and nationalist aggression. If the scope of freedom and respect for the rule of law shrinks around the world, the likelihood of war within and between nations increases, and our own freedoms will eventually be threatened.

So let's be vigilant, but not afraid. ISIL will try to kill innocent people. But they cannot defeat America unless we betray our Constitution and our principles in the fight. Rivals like Russia or China cannot match our influence around the world – unless we give up what we stand for – and turn ourselves into just another big country that bullies smaller neighbors.

Which brings me to my final point: Our democracy is threatened whenever we take it for granted. All of us, regardless of party, should be throwing ourselves into the task of rebuilding our democratic institutions. When voting rates in America are some of the lowest among advanced democracies, we should be making it easier, not harder, to vote. When trust in our institutions is low, we should reduce the corrosive influence of money in our politics, and insist on the principles of transparency and ethics in public service. When Congress is dysfunctional, we should draw our congressional districts to encourage politicians to cater to common sense and not rigid extremes.

But remember, none of this happens on its own. All of this depends on our participation; on each of us accepting the responsibility of citizenship, regardless of which way the pendulum of power happens to be swinging.

Our Constitution is a remarkable, beautiful gift. But it's really just a piece of parchment. It has no power on its own. We, the people, give it power. We, the people, give it meaning. With our participation, and with the choices that we make, and the alliances that we forge. Whether or not we stand up for our freedoms. Whether or not we respect and enforce the rule of law. That's up to us. America is no fragile thing. But the gains of our long journey to freedom are not assured.

In his own farewell address, George Washington wrote that self-government is the underpinning of our safety, prosperity, and liberty, but "from different causes and from different quarters much pains will be taken...to weaken in your minds the conviction of this truth." And so we have to preserve this truth with "jealous anxiety;" that we should reject "the first dawning of every attempt to alienate any portion of our country from the rest or to enfeeble the sacred ties" that make us one.

America, we weaken those ties when we allow our political dialogue to become so corrosive that people of good character aren't even willing to enter into public service; so coarse with rancor that Americans with whom we disagree are seen not just as misguided but as malevolent. We weaken those ties when we define some of us as more American than others; when we write off the whole system as inevitably corrupt, and when we sit back and blame the leaders we elect without examining our own role in electing them.

It falls to each of us to be those those anxious, jealous guardians of our democracy; to embrace the joyous task we've been given to continually try to improve this great nation of ours. Because for all our outward differences, we, in fact, all share the same proud title, the most important office in a democracy: Citizen. Citizen.

So, you see, that's what our democracy demands. It needs you. Not just when there's an election, not just when your own narrow interest is at stake, but over the full span of a lifetime. If you're tired of arguing with strangers on the Internet, try talking with one of them in real life. If something needs fixing, then lace up your shoes and do some organizing. If you're disappointed by your elected officials, grab a clipboard, get some signatures, and run for office yourself. Show up. Dive in. Stay at it.

Sometimes you'll win. Sometimes you'll lose. Presuming a reservoir of goodness in other people, that can be a risk, and there will be times when the process will disappoint you. But for those of us fortunate enough to have been a part of this work, and to see it up close, let me tell you, it can energize and inspire. And more often than not, your faith in America – and in Americans – will be confirmed.

Mine sure has been. Over the course of these eight years, I've seen the hopeful faces of young graduates and our newest military officers. I have mourned with grieving families searching for answers, and found grace in a Charleston church. I've seen our scientists help a paralyzed man regain his sense of touch. I've seen wounded warriors who at points were given up for dead walk again. I've seen our doctors and volunteers rebuild after earthquakes and stop pandemics in their tracks. I've seen the youngest of children remind us through their actions and through their generosity of our obligations to care for refugees, or work for peace, and, above all, to look out for each other.

So that faith that I placed all those years ago, not far from here, in the power of ordinary Americans to bring about change – that faith has been rewarded in ways I could not have possibly imagined. And I hope your faith has, too. Some of you here tonight or watching at home, you were there with us in 2004, in 2008, 2012 – maybe you still can't believe we pulled this whole thing off. Let me tell you, you're not the only ones.

Michelle – Michelle LaVaughn Robinson, girl of the South Side – for the past 25 years, you have not only been my wife and mother of my children, you have been my best friend. You took on a role you didn't ask for and you made it your own, with grace and with grit and with style and good humor. You made the White House a place that belongs to everybody. And the new generation sets its sights higher because it has you as a role model. So you have made me proud. And you have made the country proud.

Malia and Sasha, under the strangest of circumstances, you have become two amazing young women. You are smart and you are beautiful, but more importantly, you are kind and you are thoughtful and you are full of passion. You wore the burden of years in the spotlight so easily. Of all that I've done in my life, I am most proud to be your dad.

To Joe Biden – the scrappy kid from Scranton who became Delaware's favorite son – you were the first decision I made as a nominee, and it was the best. Not just because you have been a great Vice President, but because in the bargain, I gained a brother. And we love you and Jill like family, and your friendship has been one of the great joys of our lives.

To my remarkable staff: For eight years – and for some of you, a whole lot more – I have drawn from your energy, and every day I tried to reflect back what you displayed – heart, and character, and idealism. I've watched you grow up, get married, have kids, start incredible new journeys of your own. Even when times got tough and frustrating, you never let Washington get the better of you. You guarded against cynicism. And the only thing that makes me prouder than all the good that we've done is the thought of all the amazing things that you're going to achieve from here.

And to all of you out there – every organizer who moved to an unfamiliar town, every kind family who welcomed them in, every volunteer who knocked on doors, every young person who cast a ballot for the first time, every American who lived and breathed the hard work of change – you are the best supporters and organizers anybody could ever hope for, and I will be forever grateful. Because you did change the world. You did.

And that's why I leave this stage tonight even more optimistic about this country than when we started. Because I know our work has not only helped so many Americans, it has inspired so many Americans – especially so many young people out there – to believe that you can make a difference – to hitch your wagon to something bigger than yourselves.

Let me tell you, this generation coming up – unselfish, altruistic, creative, patriotic

– I've seen you in every corner of the country. You believe in a fair, and just, and inclusive America. You know that constant change has been America's hallmark; that it's not something to fear but something to embrace. You are willing to carry this hard work of democracy forward. You'll soon outnumber all of us, and I believe as a result the future is in good hands.

My fellow Americans, it has been the honor of my life to serve you. I won't stop. In fact, I will be right there with you, as a citizen, for all my remaining days. But for now, whether you are young or whether you're young at heart, I do have one final ask of you as your President – the same thing I asked when you took a chance on me eight years ago. I'm asking you to believe. Not in my ability to bring about change – but in yours.

I am asking you to hold fast to that faith written into our founding documents; that idea whispered by slaves and abolitionists; that spirit sung by immigrants and homesteaders and those who marched for justice; that creed reaffirmed by those who planted flags from foreign battlefields to the surface of the moon; a creed at the core of every American whose story is not yet written: Yes, we can.

Yes, we did. Yes, we can.

Thank you. God bless you. May God continue to bless the United States of America.

Made in the USA
Middletown, DE
28 November 2020